T0193482

GRAVEL
and
GRIT

GRAVEL
and
GRIT

A White Boyhood in the Segregated South

A Memoir by

AL PRICE

Library of Congress Control Number: 2020908848
ISBN: Hardcover   978-1-9845-7769-6
                   Softcover   978-1-9845-7768-9
                   eBook   978-1-9845-7767-2

Rev. date: 08/19/2020

To order additional copies of this book, contact:
Xlibris
844-714-8691
www.Xlibris.com
Orders@Xlibris.com
808872

Dedication

To the memory of
My father and mother,
Alvin Theo and Sara Christine Price;
My grandfather and grandmother Helm
Eldon Philip and Ethel Langham Helm;
My grandfather and grandmother Price
Pleades Lee and Sarah Beatrice "Mom Bea" Price

Maybe being a Southern writer has always been more than stereotypes of ceiling fans and panting dogs in dirt yards. Maybe being a Southern writer is only a matter of loving a damaged and damaging place, of loving its flawed and beautiful people, so much that you have to stay there, observing and recording and believing, against all odds, that one day it will finally live up to the promise of its own good heart.

—Margaret Renkl, "What Is a Southern Writer, Anyway?" *New York Times*, July 9, 2018

CONTENTS

ACKNOWLEDGMENTS

By far the most enjoyable part of getting this book written was the opportunity to sit down and hear the stories of so many others who lived during the days of my childhood. Their thoughts and memories were freely shared. I could see how cathartic it was for them to relive those years however sad or joyful with someone who was actually interested. The sun has now gone down in the west for some of these willing souls. For others on this list, fast falls the eventide, and the darkness deepens. I hope they all know that their testimonies and oral contributions will now live forever.

Here is a list of those I recall who shared their materials, time, heart, and soul: Joanne Mooney, Janie Armstrong, Harold Hughes, Gerald Fly, Eleanor Ann Boyle, Margaret Jean Ross, Mike Worsham, Birbon Brooks, Johnnie Roland, Lizzie Earle, Danny Forsyth, Dr. Joseph Atkins, Lucille Hines, Lillie Pearl Bland, Mac Haywood, Patty Lou Johnson Armstrong, Henry Carrier, Jack Gurner, Tom Cox, Betty Doria, J. E. Blankenship, Larry Kent, John Wayne Purdy, Neal Crocker, Dave and Emma Hovey, Bill Clark, Lillie Beth Porter, Sarah Williams, Louise White, and Bill Price.

I must mention the proofers and editors who helped make this publication possible: Chris Pepple of Memphis, a professional proofer and author, my first reader who graciously and meticulously reviewed the extended manuscript. Mary Dunbar, a local writer for the *Chester County Independent*, also read the text. Peggy Jeanes of Jackson, Mississippi, the founding editor of *Mississippi History Now*, the online publication of the Mississippi Historical Society, suggested valuable direction with my formatting and content. Francis Flaherty, a former editor of the *New York Times*, was patient with me as a novice writer needing basic insight and motivated me by commending the good. I am most grateful because he saw that somewhere within the vast number of pages originally submitted was something of genuine substance. Last, Rickey Pittman, an experienced and professional proofer and editor, who helped whip this memoir into tiptop shape line by line. His contributions were invaluable, including, like Francis Flaherty, reminding me that this story was worth telling.

INTRODUCTION

In William Faulkner's novel *Absalom, Absalom!* (1936), one of his characters raises a question about the South and whether Southerners even have the right to exist. The Canadian Shreve McCannon asks his Mississippi friend Quentin Compson, "Tell about the South. What's it like there? What do they do there? Why do they live there? Why do they live at all?"

It is not surprising that the South is the most written about region of our country. The stories are usually of a romanticized life or a people demonized.

Margaret Mitchell's novel about the Old South, *Gone with the Wind* (1930), has been the most influential work creating an idyllic image of Deep South culture. Supposedly, there was a time when Southerners' lives consisted mainly of barbecues and elegant balls, where belles were unapproachable, and where leisurely gentlemen lived mainly off inherited wealth and seldom worked. Gentlemen had to show a well-defined honor in all their dealings, while women had to follow the moral imperative not to show cleavage until after 3:00 p.m. White plantation owners and their families, along with their slaves, were all happy with their ascribed social status or "place" in Southern life. The stereotypes in the novel and movie became a part of our belief and value system, many of which are nostalgically admired and coveted to this day.

The idealization of the Old South continued in *The Birth of a Nation* (1915) and the subsequent film. Col. Ben Cameron and family are Southerners whose mission was to restore its former glory by organizing the vigilante Ku Klux Klan to take power away from evil blacks and carpetbaggers. In the film, the Klan is the cultural savior that is finally ushered into the pearly gates of heaven. Much of the resurgence of the Klan in the 1910s, 1920s, and 1930s was related to this racist imagery.

Romanticizing the rural South was most prominently portrayed by the "Vanderbilt Agrarians," a group of "unreconstructed" white apologists who defended segregation and the prevailing racial morés of the time in *I'll Take My Stand* (1930). Even though they glorified rural life in the South, the twelve authors had little to no experience in actual farming.

A plethora of novelists in more recent times present the same longing imagery of an idealized yesteryear. One example is Paul Yarbrough in *Mississippi Cotton* (2011). Even though the story is set in 1951 in the Mississippi Delta, the author asserts in the prologue that after "Central African Negroes were transported to the New World, their agrarian masters moved in and developed their world." So the South rescued these slaves, becoming their savior like parents to dependent children to civilize them as if they had no culture in Africa. Yarbrough also suggests that every Southerner should have in his library three books—*Gone with the Wind*, *I'll Take My Stand*, and the *Bible*. Such sentiments are commonly found in the neo-Confederacy ideology today.

The opposition view tended to demonize the South and its people in the extreme. Pre-Civil War writers who stoked the fires of hatred against the South as a region included William Lloyd Garrison, John Greenleaf Whittier, James Russell Lowell, and Ralph Waldo Emerson. They were called radical abolitionists, who often fictionalized the people of the South by claiming that hatred of slavery was synonymous with hatred of all who lived in these slaveholding states. Garrison, in particular, stated Southerners were "thieves and adulterers . . . who trample law and order beneath their feet; . . . ruffians who insult, pollute, and lacerate helpless women; and . . . conspirators against the lives and liberties of New England citizens."

No novel evoked as much negative emotion against the South as did Harriet Beecher Stowe's pre-Civil War novel *Uncle Tom's Cabin.* Her focus was on the harsh master–slave relationship in the old plantation system and the cruel mistreatment of slaves. Her characters were as stereotyped as the impressions left of all non-slaveholding citizens. There is no doubt, however, that her novel raised consciousness over the inhuman aspects of the institution of slavery.

In the 1970s, Canadian singer Neil Young had this line in his song "Southern Man": "I heard screaming, bullwhips cracking, how long, how long?" This overgeneralization was countered with defensive lyrics by Lynyrd Skynyrd in their song "Sweet Home Alabama" (where the skies are so blue): "I heard Mr. Young sing about her. Well, I heard ol' Neil put her down. I hope Neil Young will remember. Southern man don't need him around anyhow."

Other approaches reflect various related perspectives. Fred Hobson's *Tell about the South: The Southern Rage to Explain* (1983) divides the literature about the South into two categories: First, in the "school of remembrance," he includes such writers as Edmund Ruffin, William Alexander Percy, and Donald Davidson. Second, in the "school of shame and guilt," he places Howard Odum, W. J. Cash, and Lillian Smith.

My memoir as a white kid growing up in the era of Jim Crow presents another view often overlooked. How did my own early cultural socialization into the dominant expectations of exclusion and intolerance in the rural South affect my life? This endeavor shows the gradual reconstruction of my values as a white person who eventually was transformed into someone with respect and acceptance of people from different backgrounds. I am not the only Southerner who has followed that path, but in my view, this was my greatest accomplishment as a human being.

So the truth is that we are like all humanity; we have our devil side and our angel side, our gravel and grit. Our unique overwrought conscience has made us struggle fiercely with these two forces. Eventually, we work out some sort of compromise between the two, and the result is who we really are, but even then, we're not always sure. Consequently, you can find many different character types all along this continuum.

There is a time in our lives when we become nostalgic about our growing-up years and the experiences and memories of childhood. We start asking questions and wondering about our early years. Far too late in life, I began my journey back to rural Central Mississippi, where my family lived on a gravel road between Oakland and Coffeeville, once the land of the Choctaw and Chickasaw Indians. Large farming operations abounded, and black people made up close to half of the population. Both black and white families sharecropped and mainly lived in poverty, living year to year.

Significant events in the civil rights movement occurred nearby: the murder of Emmett Till in 1955; the violence that ensued when James Meredith attempted to enroll at the University of Mississippi in 1962; the Civil Rights March Against Fear from Memphis to Jackson in 1966, during which James Meredith was shot; numerous other local incidences of injustice that did not make national news; and the remarkable efforts by a generation of African American parents who risked everything to ensure equal educational opportunities.

On my visits, I discovered feelings long since pushed aside and relived the joys, the serious times, and the injustices. For as long as I have lived, the years and the places of my childhood have most shaped my sense of identity, a product of a culture that taught me both gravel (the coarse, shameful, and unflattering side) and grit (the determined will to survive, provide, and endure).

Grit can also refer to an indomitable spirit and courage. That is what my parents and grandparents had when I was growing up. They struggled against great odds and possessed enormous survival skills.

This memoir, covering the Great Depression years as described by my parents through the first twenty-five years of my life, relies heavily on personal recollection as sometimes looking through a glass darkly handed down generation after generation. They include memories of eyewitnesses, interviews, credible documents, and the literature of the era. I have sought creative ways to present stories of real events by real people. I have reimagined scenes in an effort to express the real emotions of those who lived them, including my own.

I will start with the economic conditions and deprivations experienced by so many Americans during the Great Depression. For my parents and grandparents to survive this period, they had to rely on grit and many other personal qualities of work while doing without and welcoming changes in political and economic policies. Entwined around all these issues were the twin towers of Southern culture—race and religion—that overshadowed almost every aspect of daily life.

My parents and grandparents were not alone in that community with their daily struggles. African Americans experienced a double whammy. Not only did they not have much opportunity for economic mobility, but they also had to face the harsh realities of racism and discrimination exerted on many fronts. Their endurance and survival are even more remarkable. The stress and strain they placed on the status quo left many of them assaulted, jailed, lynched, and killed. Eventually, the civil rights movement led to transformational change.

My story of growing up in rural and small-town Mississippi is different in the sense that it is framed within a cultural context, occasionally amusing, humorous, informative, poetic, compelling, and even heinous. My training in a variety of disciplines adds flavor from a sociological, psychological, religious, historical, regional, and philosophical perspective. Yes, there is some social commentary woven into the stories. While it might be true that others have made the same observations in the past, I have made them within my own experience.

Readers are taken on the inside of their lives in the small communities where I grew up on that rural road in Yalobusha County, Mississippi. William Faulkner once said, "I discovered that my own little postage stamp of native soil was worth writing about and that I would never live long enough to exhaust it." I know that I could never fully capture the drama and realities of that time on my little postage stamp of earth. And I know that my memories are but selections of a much larger experience. The fragments I do recall have helped me understand better the evolution of the development and reformulation (in some cases) of my own values as I moved from one chapter in my life to another.

This is a chronicle about staying alive, persevering, coping, and succeeding that coexisted with another side of our humanity. In an age today of "hooking up" and "hanging out," the lives of my parents and grandparents may sound very strange, backward, or primitive. Theirs was an age of self-sufficiency, fierce independence, and grit, though they often wondered if there was a future and a hope for them and their posterity and whether someday they might actually own a little piece of God's good earth. African Americans' concerns were even more basic: whether they would ever have equal civil and human rights under the law.

My grandparents, born in the late 1800s, were yeoman farmers on the share. Strong women worked side by side with their husbands and begot sons and daughters who would save the world from tyranny. Here, in this world of sunshine and toil, these common people, both black and white, endured, survived, and prevailed. It was also here that some white citizens made one last bloody, fatal gasp to preserve the cultural curse of Jim Crow. Black Americans left a legacy of fighting for their country both overseas and at home. For many white Southerners, the spiritual paradox swung emotions back and forth and as unpredictable as the wind. Most of these folks from the "greatest generation" have now gone the way of all the earth. Their lives reflected both the coarse gravel along with remarkable grit. In the end, they made the world a little better with more rights, freedom, and inclusion, all for their children. Soon, their stories will be lost in the faded visions of our memories. Symbols of their lives will only be found in picture albums, some personal belongings, and grave monuments. This account may not be your story, but it is my story.

I

~~~

LICKING OLD MAN DEPRESSION (1932–1941)

Now a severe famine struck the land . . .
And there was no relief from the terrible famine
throughout the land.
—Genesis 26:1; 43:1 (NLT)

As FAR BACK as I can remember, sitting at the dinner table, Mother and Dad would sometimes silently stare into space, not eating or wanting to talk about it unless there was a word or an event that triggered a memory. Once, Dad mentioned that he would go out to the old smokehouse and sift through the dirt on the ground, trying to find a handful of salt with which to season the food. He said that he had seen the time when he would have walked a mile for one nail. As far as the East is from the West is how far removed they wanted to be from those times. I heard much about that period in school and in the conversations of adults. I could tell that it must have been a really hard time because it definitely left psychological and physical scars on my parents who survived. I did not live through the Great Depression, but my parents made me think that I did.

At the beginning of the 1930s, profound hopelessness and despair set in. The future was bleak even for those who thought there was a future. The economic conditions were far worse for those living and working the small farms in rural areas in the South. Even when they could produce a crop, they received very little compensation. They were forgotten, out of sight and out of mind. They seldom went to town and then only when there was a way. Most of the emergency relief efforts were set up in cities and towns, ignoring the rural areas altogether. That is where my folks lived, both on my father's and mother's side of the family. They were not visible from the main roads and in dilapidated frame houses on a dirt trail with a spring or well for their water source.

Restlessness and anger began to appear despite feeling that surely the government would do something rather than let people starve to death. Desperate citizens were on the verge of revolt. They waited and waited and endured because they found a strength they didn't know they had. Their survival was a marvel of American history. They continued to try to find some work every day. Occasionally, someone came by the house, asking for something to eat. People spared what they could, knowing that "but for the grace of God, go I." Parents worried. Families anguished. Everyone did without. They wearied as they had to "go savin'." They appeared much older than they were. The hoary head and my grandfather have always gone together.

NOT ONE CHILD TO SPARE

What hurt parents the most in the "just getting by" category from Reconstruction, the Gilded Age, the Great Depression until the economic boom following WWII was the knowledge that they were trying so hard to make a suitable living for their family, but it seemed they just could "never get ahead." Most of the time, they were just busted flat. Above all, they wanted their children to have life better than they were having. It was all about survival by the day and the future of the children. It pained parents not to be able to provide their children with some of the material things other children had. They often wondered how the children felt about going without.

There was one unspoken fear that rose above every other fear. Parents had heard about some wealthy family in town who came to know one of the children in the rural areas and befriended him or her. The child was invited into their home, and sometimes the family bought the child something the parents could not afford. Eventually, the family asked the child if they would like to come and live with them. They made promises of nice clothes, travel, and a formal education in some large university. Then the moment came when the child, with prompting from the town family, asked their parents if he or she could go and live with the other family. The heart of many a father and mother just sank to its lowest level at that point. Occasionally, you heard that some had actually allowed their child to go after the promise of some form of compensation. But for most families, this was an appalling and despicable thing to do.

There were times when a family could sense that another family was working on their child with the intent of taking him or her away. I knew of a family who visited the people attempting to seduce their child and announced to them, "Our son or daughter is not for sale," and then demanded that they quit their efforts.

Of course, some of those families wanting to have and to raise someone else's child had benevolent intentions. They reasoned that they could give them so much more and that it would be a relief on the child's real parents. There were examples of these families raising someone else's child, and the result worked out for all concerned.

And of course, there were some poor families that just didn't try very hard to provide for their children. In addition, the children were not shown real love, given much time, or reassured of their safety. Some experienced nutritional, medical, and emotional neglect and physical and sexual abuse. At that time, these were not primary issues that social service groups were addressing. In fact, the small welfare departments that did exist were more concerned about other things such as seeing it as their job to see how few people they could help. In these situations, some well-meaning family would attempt to rescue a child from such a home environment. It would be difficult, however, because some of these families viewed their children as a possession to be used for monetary gain.

Those who ended up with another family sometimes enjoyed the benefit of all those promised things, including the college education. I know of one case where the adopted son was sent to law school, and he became a successful attorney. But in most of these cases, a mother and father were heartbroken over their loss but felt helpless to do anything about it. Most families, however, would do anything to keep their children. They worked their fingers to the bone for them and sacrificed things for themselves that the child might have a decent life.

Years after I was grown, I came across an old book, published in 1878, titled *Mother, Home and Heaven*, containing a series of short stories and poems, arranged by Theo Cuyler. One of those poems is titled "Not One Child to Spare," written by Ethel L. Beers.

The poem contains this introduction: "A father and mother in straitened circumstances, with seven children, were offered by a wealthy, but childless neighbor, a comfortable provision, on condition that they would give him one of their children. This moving poem tells the result."

"Which shall it be? Which shall it be?"
I looked at John—John looked at me,
(Dear, patient John, who loves me yet,
As well as though my locks were jet),
And when I found that I must speak,
My voice seemed strangely low and weak;
"Tell me again what Robert said!"
And then I listening bent my head.
"This is his letter:—'I will give
A house and land while you shall live,
If, in return, from out of your seven,
One child to me for aye is given.'"
I looked at John's old garments worn,
I thought of all that John had borne
Of poverty, and work, and care,
Which I, though willing, could not share;
I thought of seven mouths to feed,
Of seven little children's need,
And then of this.—"Come, John," said I,
"We'll choose among them as they lie
Asleep;" so, walking hand in hand,
Dear John and I surveyed our band—
First to the cradle lightly stepped,
Where Lillian the baby slept.

A glory 'gainst the pillow white;
Softly the father stooped to lay
His rough hand down in loving way,
When dream or whisper made her stir,
And huskily he said: "Not her, not her."
We stopped beside the trundle-bed,
And one long ray of lamplight shed
Athwart the boyish faces there,
In sleep so pitiful and fair;
I saw on Jamie's rough, red cheek,
A tear undried. Ere John could speak,
"He's but a baby, too," said I,
And kissed him as we hurried by.
Pale patient Robbie's angel face
Still in his sleep bore suffering's trace.
"No, for a thousand crowns, not him,"
He whispered, while our eyes were dim.
Poor Dick! Bad Dick! Our wayward son,
Turbulent, reckless, idle one—
Could he be spared? "Nay, He who gave
Bid us befriend him to his grave;
Only a mother's heart can be
Patient enough for such as he;
And so," said John "I would not dare
To send him from her bedside prayer."
Then stole we softly up above
And knelt by Mary, child of love.
"Perhaps for her 'twoud better be,"
I said to John, quite silently,
He lifted up a curl that lay

Across her cheek in willful way,
And shook his head, "Nay, love, not thee,"
The while my heart beat audibly.
Only one more, our eldest lad,
Trusty and truthful, good and glad—
So like his father. "No, John, no—
I cannot, will not, let him go."
And so we wrote, in courteous way,
We could not drive one child away;
And afterward toil lighter seemed,
Thinking of that of which we dreamed.
Happy in truth that not one face
Was missed from its accustomed place;
Thankful to work for all the seven,
Trusting the rest to One in heaven!

KEEPING A DEATHBED REQUEST

Prior to the Great Depression, families drew inspiration from the stories handed down through the generations of manly valor, courage in the face of danger, overcoming, and surviving. Certain values about keeping your word were held up as indicators of a person's character and reputation. Of special importance was keeping a deathbed request by a loved one. Our story involved my grandfather, one of his brothers, and the death of their father during the Spanish flu in 1918.

Eldon Helm's parents were Moses Herschel and Betty Phillips Helm, who were married in Morgantown, Kentucky, in 1874. The couple hoped that maybe one of their children would be able to care for them in their later years. Granddaddy and Grandmother were the least able to care for his parents, not owning any land themselves. Since life expectancy at birth was only around forty-eight at the turn of the century, someone in their forties was considered old. Moses Herschel died during one of the harshest and coldest winters in history. But before he died, he made one last deathbed request. You see, he had not lived in Mississippi long enough to get attached to its land and people. When he stood at death's door at age seventy, he gathered the family around and got Granddaddy to promise that he would bury him in the Starbuck Cemetery in Perry County, Tennessee. Moses Herschel convinced himself that he could rest in peace only if he returned to Tennessee. Granddaddy agreed he would take him there for burial, not knowing what lay ahead.

The winter of 1918 had temperatures below freezing for weeks at a time. Granddaddy was in a dilemma, but one thing for certain: If you promised something to a loved one on his or her deathbed, you were morally, spiritually, and culturally obligated, lest you lose all credibility and respect as a human being. There was never any question of whether, just how could it be done. Uncle Earl Helm, one of Granddaddy's brothers and a well-traveled New Orleans racehorse gambler, was the obvious one to help him get Moses Herschel to the promised cemetery so their father could finally rest in peace.

When they planned the several-hundred-mile journey, they first went through the stage of cussing the promise.

"Why in hell did you make this promise?"

"Well, dammit, I didn't know he would die during the worst winter of our lifetime." They went back and forth for a while, before realizing that they best be making their plans. They gathered all the money and food they could find and put his casket on a freight train heading north into Tennessee. Eventually, they rented a wagon and team of mules to take them to the ferry at Perryville on the banks of the Tennessee River. After cussing all that distance, they finally reached the river, only to discover that it had been frozen completely over for a week with no thawing in sight. (The Alvin C. York Bridge that now spans the river was not built until 1930.)

Granddaddy and Uncle Earl cussed some more.

The river was frozen so hard one could actually walk across provided you could keep from sliding on the ice. At this point, they would finish the task come hell or high water (in this case, frozen). They started their dangerous trek pushing the casket over the frozen river, when they learned something remarkable. It seemed that the report of these two sons bringing their deceased father hundreds of miles to carry out a deathbed request had spread. Everyone along the countryside was talking about this noble deed and demonstration of love. These two determined men were not too sure about it being all that noble, but it was a pleasant surprise to have such adulation from people they didn't know.

A crowd gathered on the Perry County side of the river to welcome them and provide for their needs. They had built a big fire by which they could warm themselves, and the women brought plenty of hot food and drink. Finally, it appeared they were going to get Moses Herschel in the ground at his beloved Starbuck Cemetery. Local men helped dig the grave in the cold, cold earth and participated in a solemn burial ceremony. Afterward, these two men of grit and character returned to Mississippi with only momentary profane outbursts of regret when they were nearly frozen stiff.

This real story has several parallels in American novels. Larry McMurtry, author of *Lonesome Dove* (1985), tells of Texas Ranger Woodrow Call making a deathbed promise to his fellow ranger, Augustus "Gus" McCray. Gus wanted to be buried on the banks of a river near Lonesome Dove because of his romantic memories of the spot. Woodrow brought Gus all the way from Montana to South Texas to bury his friend, a journey that created quite a news story.

In the novel *As I Lay Dying* (1930) by William Faulkner, a poor rural family struggles to get their wife and mother, Addie Bundren, back to her hometown of Jefferson, Mississippi, for burial, which was her stated wish before dying. Their odyssey also includes almost losing her coffin while crossing a river.

According to those who told the story about Granddaddy and Uncle Earl, they pulled Grandma Betty (as we called her) aside and said, "The first chance you get, go up to the Coffeeville Cemetery and be picking you out a burial plot."

She lived in Mississippi long enough to want to be buried beneath its fertile soil. She died in December 1949, thirty-one years later, while living with Uncle Rue Helm. I remember her funeral and burial in the Coffeeville City Cemetery.

MY FATHER JOINS ROOSEVELT'S TREE ARMY

At the height of the Great Depression, when it appeared all hope was lost for my father, like the rising sun on the eastern horizon, a presidential candidate promised a "new deal" for Americans. He seemed to be aware of the plight of the working class and the country itself. Franklin Delano Roosevelt was elected president and became the transformational leader demanded by a broken nation.

When Dad was in high school at Oakland in 1930, he wondered what his life would be like. As a fifteen-year-old, he had ambition and spent many hours thinking about a way to improve his future. Oakland had a regional high school with on-campus dormitories for those from other places who wished to graduate with a diploma. Most towns didn't offer high school.

He observed that football provided one avenue to increase his life chances and earn a college scholarship. He thought he was doing well at first, but often, he didn't have a way home after practice and had to walk close to five miles. Dad never had been really healthy, and he missed some school and practices. He was born with a vision problem called lazy eye. At age six, he had surgery in Oxford, but it was a failure. For the rest of his life, he was blind in his left eye, but he never complained. A few years later, he developed appendicitis and had to have surgery, which put him behind in his schoolwork. The problems with catching up in school, football, and his health began to mount. At that time, students had to buy their own textbooks. His family didn't even have enough for daily needs and certainly not enough to buy all five children textbooks for school. So like so many other young people at the time, he quit school in the ninth grade and left his football and college dream behind.

Not graduating would hurt my father and my mother for their entire lives. Being able to pay for schoolbooks and eventually graduating from high school during this era was only for a privileged few. Discouragement, despair, and disappointment dogged my father all his life. Being blind in one eye closed avenues for betterment one by one, so he went home to help his beloved mother on the little farm. They attempted cotton crops, but in the South, the money hardly paid for expenses. Given the times in the early 1930s, hope was all but lost for Alvin Theo Price, my father. To him, lashing seas leaped everywhere about him. He always felt like Jacob of old when he said, "All things are against me." The invaders were always lurking nearby, twisting his soul. There seemed always to be some unknown waves rolling against him or a hiding rock on a treacherous shoal.

It was 1935, when one of Roosevelt's New Deal programs came to Yalobusha County, Mississippi. The word spread about this opportunity among the jobless young farm boys and among those who lost their businesses or the few jobs that had been available. Suddenly, there was a small crack in the door of opportunity.

Upon taking office as president, FDR immediately began a massive revitalization of the nation's economy, which was in shambles. He created many programs designed to put the country's young men back to work. Roosevelt spurned the idea of a dole. He felt that he could preserve the pride of American workers in their own ability to work and earn a living. Self-respect would be maintained, so his programs concentrated on creating jobs.

The Roosevelt presidency was famous for several acclaimed accomplishments early on. The Emergency Conservation Work Act, better known as the Civilian Conservation Corps (CCC), was probably the most successful. Drawing upon his own convictions about preserving the land through reforestation and the need to preserve a generation of jobless and often hungry young men, he decided that he could save both. The CCC boys became known as Roosevelt's Tree Army, and from 1933 to 1942, they planted three billion trees to renew the decimated forests and land. This was especially needed in those states devastated by the Dust Bowl. From his inauguration on March 4, 1933, to the induction of the first CCC enrollee, only thirty-seven days had elapsed.

My father filled out his application for the CCC camp on July 8, 1935, when he was nineteen years old. The eligibility requirements included being a U.S. citizen, unemployed, unmarried, and between the ages of eighteen and twenty-six. Enlistment was for a duration of six months, though most of the men reenlisted.

The boys who had been approved for the camp were to meet in Grenada, Mississippi, on August 22, 1935. A total of 175 eager young men were put on a special train for a ride up to Coffeeville, where they were met and welcomed at the train station by 300 Coffeeville residents. Company 3496 was officially organized that same day. The company's strength was increased the very next day by the arrival of 30 men from Senatobia. By the end of the month, the authorized limit had been reached, and the men were now ready to get to work.

They began immediately helping cooperating farmers in the area to control erosion and rebuild the soil. By far their largest project was the establishment of a one-hundred-acre nursery. They grew hardwood trees of almost every variety. They were shipped to government projects throughout the South. The Coffeeville camp was chosen for this project because of its history of hard work and reliability. In recognition of these qualities, Company 3496 was awarded the banner for "Best Company-District D, CCC, 4th quarter, 1935." These men could brag about this honor for the rest of their lives. They didn't, though, because these men had too many bad memories of that entire era. And in later years, it seemed that some people didn't want to recognize the worth of what they did. Some people even made fun of these work projects by saying such things as "the WPA stood for 'we piddle around.'" But down deep, the boys knew they had made a huge difference in soil conservation and had helped their country and their families. The positive effects of what the boys did for the land remain to this day.

CCC records reveal that more than 70 percent of the boys joining all across the country were malnourished and poorly clothed. My father entered at 5 feet 10 inches tall but only weighed 126 pounds—skin and bones as we would say. These conditions soon changed with the availability of health care, dental care, toiletries, uniforms, three square meals a day, a hard day's work, and a decent place to sleep. In return, they were paid a dollar a day for their work. The CCC boys received $5 at the end of the month, and $25 was sent to their mothers back home. The family could take that money and buy desperately needed shoes, clothes, groceries, and other necessities. The boys' $5 also had a lot of spending power when they went to town on weekends. For most of these boys, this was more money than they ever had at one time. Their spending revitalized the local economies. Records indicated no reported revolts or strikes. One newsletter reminded the boys why they were there: "This is a training station we're going to leave morally and physically fit to lick 'Old Man Depression.'"

The camps provided numerous recreational activities, including a baseball team, tumbling, and a boxing team. And they could even attend night school to further their education, including vocational training. Records indicated that more than 90 percent of all enrollees participated in some area of the educational program. Throughout the years of the CCC, more than forty thousand boys were taught how to read and write. Most of all, they had a profound sense of pride in knowing that they were working on a job, completing constructive projects for the country, being paid for their work, and helping the family survive back home.

There were all-black CCC camps with over two hundred thousand enrolled. Even though they were segregated, they received equal pay and housing. Roosevelt wanted them to develop the same personal pride as the other camps. Blacks were promoted to be education directors in the 143 segregated locations. Many whites didn't believe that blacks wanted to work; the record indicates otherwise. They worked hard and gained the respect of some white people.

With $5 in hand, the boys could go downtown for some recreation. Young unmarried women in the area flocked to town to see these strong, ruddy, well-dressed, and healthy young men. Many met their wife-to-be during this time. My mother and one of her sisters, Stella Ruth, wandered over to Coffeeville on Saturday nights to check out the social scene. It was there that they met their husbands. At first, Stella Ruth went out with my dad, and Mother went out with J. D. Tribble from Oakland. They then switched partners and ended up marrying.

On one weekend visit home, my father finally was able to go to town in Oakland with a little jingle in his pockets. His favorite fruit was bananas. Previously, he might have enough money to buy one banana. He loved bananas and swore that one day he would have enough money to buy all he could eat at one time. After joining the CCC, and having his $5 to spend, he started buying one banana after another that day to see how many he could devour. He said he ate six before he could eat no more. A lifelong dream was fulfilled. We may think today that was an insignificant matter. Sometimes small pleasures like that make a huge difference in the way one views himself and his future.

Once, my dad and I were driving along on Highway 7, and he said, "You see all those pine trees? I helped to plant those." He spoke with a degree of pride that earlier in his life, he had done something valuable that would last a long time. Regretfully now, I wish I had asked him more about that critical time in his life.

To this very day, what those young boys did left an observable mark along the countryside. These young boys improved millions of acres of federal and state lands and parks, building new roads, erecting telephone lines, planting trees, building fire towers, protecting the natural habitats of wildlife, creating drainage systems, and building campgrounds, picnic shelters, swimming pools, and restrooms. By 1942, nearly every state could point to some permanent projects left by the CCC.

Eventually, additional funding for the CCC camps ceased in 1942 because of opposition to the program and because it was felt that the war effort should receive all the attention of the government. It should not be disputed, however, that the CCC was one of the most successful New Deal programs of the Great Depression. I would argue that it was one of the most successful public works efforts in our history. Most of all, it left an army of well-built, confident, and trained young men. Afterward, they were preferred in hiring because employers believed that those boys in the CCC knew what a full day's work meant and could carry out orders in a disciplined way. By its end, more than three million men served in the CCC.

THE FIRESIDE CHATS

During his efforts to revive the nation's workforce and its economic stability, and during the challenges of a world war, Roosevelt sought to reassure the people directly. My parents told me how neighbors gathered at a house where there was a radio to hear the president speak about current issues. Afterward, they said, "Well, it seems the president understands the problem and what needs to be done. Yeah, he laid it on the line, all right. Just hope he can get Congress to go along. He really has a heavy load to bear, but he seemed to be saying that it could be done, and I believe him."

Those intimate radio chats from Roosevelt gave citizens hope and inspiration during two of the most turbulent decades of our history.

From 1933 to 1944, the president gave thirty of these talks that were broadcast over the radio right into the homes of the American people. They were called fireside chats because the setting was informal, and he used the language of everyday people. Humorist Will Rogers wrote after the president had discussed the banking crisis, "He made everyone understand it, even the bankers." He gave listeners updates on progress, dispelled rumors, and even asked for their help.

Looking back, much of this success was because of the fact that Roosevelt could inspire a depressed people beset by the notion that they would always be poor. No, they would go to work, get paid for that honorable work, and be trained and educated in a land now flowing with milk and honey. Amazingly, this grand idea was set into motion in less than three months. FDR saved the country from a revolt and turned hopelessness into hope for the future. The wealthy scoffed at such an effort, calling it socialism and communism. They predicted gambling and drunkenness and a poor use of our tax dollars. Those jobless boys didn't see it that way, and neither did Roosevelt. He loved to visit the camps and sit with the boys and talk. He once famously said, "The test of our progress is not whether we add more to the abundance of those who have much; it is whether we provide enough for those who have too little."

For some high-browed elites, I suppose it is hard to relate to boys who could get a toothbrush, a daily bath, some new clothes, and a little money ($1 a day) for the first time in their lives. Many of the boys had never possessed two pairs of shoes before. Reveille meant getting up for roll call, making the bed, and cleaning up. At breakfast, there was plenty of nutritious food. By 7:30 a.m., they were on a truck going to work. Lunch was brought to the fields. By 4:00 p.m., they were back at the barracks for rest and recreation and a hot meal at 6:00 p.m. They could see in themselves a healthier body that was gaining good, solid weight. Newsreels showed these men saying, "All I ever wanted was just a chance."

These were the pioneers of the green movement. When you travel a mountain road, visit a state or national park, hike a trail, or ski on a mountain slope, realize that the CCC boys probably built it. In the 1920s and 1930s, big timber companies had stripped much of the land, creating floods that washed away fertile soil. These soldiers of the CCC effectively stopped the raping of the land. These were some of the first environmentalists and reflected the goal of another great president, Theodore Roosevelt.

Pictures and articles about the various camps were published in the *Annual of District D, Fourth Corps Area* in 1936. This district covered Mississippi and parts of Alabama. After finding one of these annuals, it was easy to spot my father since he was the only one wearing glasses. All the boys looked like they were in great physical shape and looked dapper in their uniforms with ties. They were now trained in various skills and ready to compete in the job market. They were ready to marry and start a family. Many of these well-trained men went on to volunteer for World War II or to be drafted into the armed forces.

In reviewing my father's discharge papers, I saw some commendable remarks by his superiors. He was honorably discharged on September 30, 1936, after a little more than a year in the CCC camp. Discipline in the camps had been maintained by the fear of a dishonorable discharge. His performance was deemed satisfactory. Under remarks, it is stated that he had "no authorized or unauthorized absences, no appointments or demotions, no incapacitations due to own conduct, no indebtedness." I wish he had known that his son looked at these commendations and was proud of his record.

Actually, what these boys did was biblical and spiritual in nature. God gave humankind dominion over his "good earth," to keep and to tend to its needs. The world's oldest profession was gardener, whose responsibility was to tend the land diligently. As people who have been blessed with the fruits of this wonderful planet, it is clear that we are to be good stewards of this possession. God never intended that we pollute and abuse his world in the name of greed and profit on behalf of environmental corruption. Roosevelt wanted to conserve this land and the future of those young men at the same time. But left unabated, unchecked, and unregulated, our selfishness and greed will someday cause nature to react against us because of these sins against the good earth.

THE TALK

My mother was the eldest of eight children born to Eldon and Ethel Helm of Coffeeville, Mississippi, whose economic background was similar to my father's. Five of Mother's siblings were girls, and it became her assigned task to carry out the wishes of my grandmother. Mother took her job quite seriously and authoritatively, which was always resented by the other children. The unintended consequence was that Mother became quite skilled in the traits of mothering, healing, reprimanding, giving orders, and consoling, all of which, I suppose, prepared her for her own later role as mother.

My grandfather always pursued the hope that the next year would yield a more productive crop and thus increase his ability to purchase some better things for his family. I've heard several of the Helm sisters refer to a time in late fall when Granddaddy conducted his annual talk to the family. Knowing that the time was coming up, they began to speculate what would be said that year. Each family member had his or her own wishes as to something special they hoped the family could afford after the crops had been harvested. Most expected the same speech they heard the year before. The talk went something like this:

> Well, after we didn't do so well last year, we thought this year might be different, and we would have a bumper crop. I know that each of you had something in mind that you wanted to buy. After settling up, it looks like we can buy each one a new pair of shoes. You remember not enough rain/too much rain/too hot and dry/not enough seed/not enough help/plow broke/mule died/boll weevils. The landlord wants to go up on the rent, but I talked him out of it by promising to take him some fresh vegetables and watermelons when we go to town. Maybe next year, we'll do better.

The children knew the speech quite well by then and mouthed the words they knew were coming. The boys left embittered. Some of the girls cried; others felt consoled and encouraged. One of the younger girls would lay her head in Grandmother's lap. My mother stood as the doyenne in the group. Each went to his or her private spot and silently reflected on their future but always with hope.

Even in the midst of their deprivation, they didn't consider how they were blessing the lives of many others. One day Grandmother said, "I can't see any smoke coming out of Aunt Jenny's house. We better check on her." Aunt Jenny was an elderly black lady, not only infirm but also nearly blind, who lived with her irresponsible son. In 1939, she could remember the end of the Civil War.

It was a cold winter day, and she said to my granddaddy, "If you could just build me a fire." Her son had not come home that night. "I don't know where my wandering boy was last night. I can get up and make me something to eat." Aunt Jenny was always so grateful for what her neighbors did and somewhat ashamed that her son didn't always take care of her. Granddaddy built her a warm fire, and Grandmother took her some food. Finally, the son came in from a night of carousing. Granddaddy didn't hesitate to tell him what he needed to hear: "Tom, if you don't pay more attention to your mother, one of these days, she will burn up in this house."

When black neighbors had someone on their deathbed, white neighbors sat with the family at night. There was an unspoken empathy that grew out of the realization that everybody had suffering and trials. In some communities (and this varied from family to family), white families that hurt or harmed a black family were not highly regarded. This was before the raised racial consciousness of the 1950s and early 1960s that enforced segregation in nearly all its forms.

Along with all the economic issues came health problems and questions about how to receive adequate treatment. Many of the families had to rely on home remedies. The plight of older people was especially difficult. Pneumonia, the most dreaded illness, was the leading cause of death in the United States at this time. One-third of all the people contracting it died. Families and neighbors banded together, seeking to provide whatever care they could. This was before the widespread introduction of antibiotic drugs and before Social Security and Medicare. The sickness came to be called the old man's friend because the sufferer often slipped peacefully away in their sleep. This gave a dignified end to a period of considerable suffering.

—◀○▶—

HOW GRANDDADDY'S HEMORRHOIDS SAVED A CROP

John L. and Thomas Eldon, mother's two younger brothers, were often described as "real rounders" when they were young, meaning there was not much they wouldn't try at one time or another. There were three types: just your regular rounder, a real rounder, and a hellish rounder.

They were still at home during the 1930s and helping Granddad on his small farm west of Oakland, where he was renting and raising a small crop to "put food on the table." But the CCC camp opportunity was too enticing for them to turn away. Thomas was sent out to California to fight forest fires, build fire trails, and construct mountain roads that are used today. John L. was sent to Virginia to help with some special project. One's skill sometimes dictated in what part of the country he served.

Poor old Granddad was virtually left to raise his crop alone. While the six daughters, including my mother, did what they could, he felt he desperately needed the help of John L., who was now assigned to a local unit. He wrote to the CCC administrative office and asked if they could spare John L. two days a week to come back home and help him on the farm, especially since he had developed a serious health problem. CCC officials decided to send some medical personnel to Granddaddy's house to inspect his need and to verify his health problems. They were instructed to bring back evidence. "Well, Mr. Helm, you have shown us the crop you are attempting to raise. One of the pictures we got is of your five-year-old daughter planting some sweet potatoes. We took enough pictures that validate your crop claim. Now what about your health problem?"

Granddad told them he was suffering from a really bad case of hemorrhoids that would not shrink. The official stated that he needed more evidence than just his verbal assurance.

Granddaddy said, "Well, I suppose then you want to see them."

He was more than a little irritated at this point that they wouldn't take his word for it. So he lowered his pants and said, "Okay, come on in a little closer so you can take a real good look at them. And while you are down there, why don't you take that camera you brought and take some real close-up pictures of them too? Then you'll have your evidence to show your commanding officer."

The government men did not say anything much but actually did take the pictures and took their evidence back with them. Someone at the head office was quite impressed, or should I say appalled, by such pictures and approved John L. coming home two days a week to help Granddaddy raise that crop. I must admit that I have received much perverted pleasure out of visualizing that commanding officer looking at Granddaddy's hemorrhoids. The family heard that the officer told the CCC officials that he did not need to see any more evidence. I wonder how many times hemorrhoids have saved a crop.

MOM BEA AND PLEA

The year was 1932 in Oakland, Mississippi, and my father's family was barely surviving out on Rural Route 1. There was Mom Bea, the mother of five children, three boys and two girls (one four-month-old daughter had died), and who had been widowed four years earlier. Pleades Lee "Plea" Price, my grandfather, had been crippled by a falling tree some years earlier and died in 1928. With no money for adequate treatment, he was bedridden for several years and unable to provide a living for his family. That hurt him deeply every day, and he anguished and cried until his death. Not being able to work and make a living was the biggest blow to a person's feeling of self-worth and sense of dignity in that community.

In those days, there were very few public jobs in Oakland and especially so for women. So Mom Bea held the family together the best she could. They would grow nearly all their food off the land, get milk from several milk cows, and kill hogs for meat in the smokehouse. They would sew many of their clothes and patch the ones with tears or holes. The children would ask the neighbors for odd jobs to make a little money. But really there was never enough of anything. Their condition worsened by the year, and like much of the rest of the country in the depth of the Great Depression, they began to lose hope that their life would ever be any better.

In February 1901, Mattie Lou was born to the young expectant couple. She must have been a "beautiful baby" as infants were so often described. Plea and Mom Bea decided who she favored, counted her fingers and toes, and smiled a lot. Maybe they stayed up at night watching her breathe when she had a cold. Mom Bea sang to her, talked to her about her future, and played with her on the big bed. They were proud parents to hold her up and claim her as their very own. Then in June, only four months later, she breathed her last breath and died. Sudden death happened often to aged men and children small during that time.

What sadness must have pervaded the souls of this couple! Questions, no doubt, flooded their mourning minds. What did we do wrong? Was it our fault? Why would God take such a beautiful baby? Will we ever survive? Will we have other children? Mattie Lou was buried in the Sayle Cemetery not far from their home. No doubt they walked over there and wept at her gravesite many times.

When a precious baby dies, the parents think that others don't really understand what a fine baby she actually was. I remember a wall memory plaque in Mom Bea's house, but I never really read what was on it. Many years later, when my aunt Alice McAllister died, the cousins were dividing up some of her belongings. She had inherited the wall plaque from Mom Bea. I took it home and decided that this little girl would not be forgotten, not in my lifetime. The plaque hangs in the hallway by other family pictures.

The memorial depicts a white dove with a ribbon in its mouth, and on the ribbon are the words "Gone but not forgotten." Below it is an hourglass with only a small portion of sand missing from the top part. At the base, it reads, "In Loving Remembrance, Our Dear Babe, Mattie Lou Price, Died June 28, 1901, Age 4 months, 14 days." Inscribed is this poem:

> Sleep on in thy beauty,
> Thou sweet angel child,
> By sorrow unblighted,
> By sin undefiled.
> Like the dove to the ark,
> Thou hast flown to thy rest,
> From the wild sea of strife,
> To the home of the blest.

CARING FOR "LITTLE WILLIE"

Growing up, I always noticed how much the Willie Tribble family respected Mom Bea, who was a Tribble before she married into the

Price family. My mother's sister, Stella Ruth, married J. D. Tribble, and his father was Willie Tribble, a younger brother of Mom Bea.

Now this might be a bit confusing because J. D. Tribble is my great-uncle on my father's side and my uncle on my mother's side. J. D. is my father's uncle on his mother's side and a brother-in-law on my mother's side. In the rural South, such family combinations are fairly common. As far as I can ascertain, though, I don't think any cousins married other cousins at least in their early years.

Many years later, I found out why the Tribbles thought highly of my Mom Bea. Willie came from a large family, and when he was quite small, his mother died. His father married a woman who had several children as well. The new wife decided they could not care for that many children. They made the decision that they would have to give one of the children away for someone else to raise. They settled on little Willie as the one they would give away. Mom Bea was one of those older sisters in that same family. When she heard that her father and stepmother were going to give little Willie away, she was horrified at losing her little brother in this fashion. Mom Bea was living on her own, and she determined that one way or another, Willie would stay in the family. She went to the house, fetched little Willie and all his belongings (she actually hid him), and took him to where she lived to raise him until he could care for himself. And this she did!

Not only did Mom Bea's own children rise up to call her blessed, but Willie and his children did also. What a remarkable story of love and caring! I wish I had known this story while Mom Bea lived. You know, I want to hear that story again when the Lord comes to reward the faithful.

◄O►

FRUGALITY DEFINED AS "GO SAVIN'"

Plea and Mom Bea would go on to have three sons and two daughters. Alvin Theo, my father, was the youngest, born in 1915, and married Christine Helm in 1939. Mom Bea always spoke with so much pride about her children. Those children absolutely adored their mother all her life. With very little after her husband died in 1928, she held them all together till they were grown. After the children left home, they showered her with nice gifts they were unable to give her when they were much younger.

Though quiet, unassuming, and a gentle little lady, Mom Bea was the family's stronghold in those early days and source of encouragement. She had this saying that I know those children grew tired of hearing: "We're just going to have to 'go savin'." They all knew what that meant. It just seemed, though, that it was a continuous necessity. I am sure they wondered if there might ever be a time when they wouldn't have to go savin' and could have at least a little extra money, better clothes, better food, and a vision for a better life. There was a saying at the time, "Use it up, wear it out, and make it do or do without."

My father said that all the children promised one another that when they grew up and had jobs of their own, they would repay their dear mother for all the sacrifices she made for them. I remember well on Sunday afternoons when all her children and their children gathered at her house, they brought nice gifts, not just for her birthday or Christmas but at other times as well. Mom Bea was always so humble about it. She would say, "That is so nice, maybe too nice for me to wear. I'll put it in the dresser drawer and save it for just the right time." When she died, she still had those gifts in her drawer. Personally, I think it was scars from the Great Depression that left her feeling there might come a similar time when she would need this more, but right now, she had to save it.

That value of having to be so frugal was ingrained into my father at an early age. It demonstrated itself throughout his life. As a result, he saved everything he thought he might be able to use someday. He always built a storage shed to keep all his collected belongings everyplace we lived.

Today the idea of trying to live one's life without spending money is unfathomable. How could anyone ever survive very long without having some money to spend? Yes, in the 1930s, many had to live that way. A family might have had some small amount of money from selling eggs, chickens, or ax handles or sewing, ironing, and washing for people. Occasionally, a neighbor might have some work for you to do. A little money could be made by picking cotton for those with larger farming operations. But usually, that money had to be used for absolute necessities, such as saving the farm and the family.

SOLVING COMPLEX ECONOMIC THEORY ON THE FRONT PORCH

I often heard it said that front-porch philosophy was some of the best. Some adult men were talking as they lounged on the front porch where we lived, including my grandfather Helm, an uncle, and my father. They said something like this:

> It seems to me that the way to get this country back on its feet is to provide opportunity for the working people. Because when they have money, they spend it

on things that help these small businesses. They buy clothes, cars, furniture, build houses, things like that. In turn, that creates a greater demand for products and for jobs. Everybody prospers and the benefits rise to others. Little Buddy (that's what I was called growing up), it's like a teapot on the stove full of water. When it gets hot enough, the steam rises into the air. You see wealth and prosperity rises when the working people have money to spend, and that is how others get rich, and everybody has a little piece of the pie.

"STAY ALL NIGHT, STAY A LITTLE LONGER"

To escape the worries of the time, folks still found time to enjoy themselves. One of the common activities was to gather at someone's house, or even in an empty house, and make music, dance, and court. My aunt Janie Florence told me about an evening when several groups of boys and girls got together at the Old Robinson Place, which was vacant at the time. It stood on a hill and was pretty much isolated off the main road. Group dating was common, and the Helm sisters were good at it since there were so many of them.

These events required someone to make the music, a lantern for light, and someone to provide a few refreshments. People got there any way they could. During one of those nights, a storm came up, and it rained so much the bottomland below the house flooded. The truth was that the revelers relished the thought that they just might have to stay there all night. Seemed that Granddaddy had gone over to the party—I suppose to check up on his girls. He decided that he best get on back home, stating that he could get out because he had ridden a mule over there. In the midst of the excitement and laughter, the group decided to stay and dance all night.

When I heard this tale, I couldn't help but think of that old Bob Wills song of that time:

> Stay all night, stay a little longer;
> Dance all night, dance a little longer.
> Pull off your coat, throw it in the corner;
> Don't see why you can't stay a little longer.

PLOWBOY FRIENDS

My father frequently spoke of the boys he knew growing up on the Hunt Place, McKnight Place, Coulter Place, Arnold Place, Frost Place, and the Richard Place. Most of these boys had the same kind of life—lived on either a one-mule or two-horse farm, grew their own food, killed hogs, and hunted for meat, but the happier times were swimming in creek holes or in stealing watermelons. They always said the melons tasted better when they were stolen, but their ethical rule was to get only what you could eat. Usually, someone picked a guitar on the front porch for added pleasure. Going to town was a rarity because of a lack of transportation. These boys served as a buffer for one another to lighten the load.

For a little extra fun, my father and his friends built a cabin in the woods made out of poles. On Saturday nights, they brought food from the kitchens, built a fire, and cooked. A coal-oil lantern provided the light. Afterward, the two Pannell brothers picked and sang the popular songs of the day. Occasionally, someone had some moonshine whiskey to drink. After many years passed, they said they didn't remember about the whiskey. When pressed, they also admitted that no women were ever denied access to their party.

My aunts shared with me how the women primped for such remote social occasions before they could afford store-bought cosmetics. Flowers pinned on clothes or hair could do wonders. Flour on a rag rubbed on the face gave it a little color or covered unsightly spots. The black soot off the burned end of a match was used for eye shadow. Those with light complexion pinched their faces in certain places for a redder cheek. After all, that is what Scarlett O'Hara did. What amazing creativity!

Two brothers who lived nearby, Ray and Harold Hughes, were Dad's best friends and often did a lot of work together and also engaged in a lot of pleasure and mischief. Once, while hunting, Ray was snakebit, and my father cut the place open and sucked out the poison. Ray finally got to a doctor and recovered, crediting Dad with saving his life. These boys went on to join the CCC camps and, like so many other Mississippi boys, ended up in Oregon, Washington, and California building roads. Their greatest joy, however, was simply getting to town on Saturdays, when they could catch a ride.

FEAR GAVE WAY TO HOPE

And thus ended a decade that would forever be remembered as the Great Depression. They had to be frugal and be good stewards of all their few possessions. Before 1932, the assumption of government was that the way to feed the chickens was to feed the cattle first. The historical accounts say that the Depression lasted about ten years, from 1929 to 1939. A historian was asked whether there had ever been anything like it before. The answer was that yes, and it was called the Dark Ages, and it lasted four hundred years. The hymns had lyrics to remind blacks and poor whites that all their trials were worth it because someday they would supposedly understand it farther along in the by and by. They found comfort in the words "tempted and tried we're oft made to wonder, why it should by thus all the day long." What is it that gives people a sense of self-worth? For most people, it is the knowledge that they have a job, are doing something constructive in society, and are providing for their family. These Americans wanted to work, had worked all their lives, and had strong backs and willing hands. When your job is lost and you cannot find another, you begin to develop self-doubt. You may begin to wonder, "Maybe God is trying me for something better. Maybe God is punishing me for some sin." The thoughts and questions were many, but endurance was the overriding aspiration. Some economists believed the Great Depression was evidence that dehumanized capitalism was a dangerous ideology. Several countries changed their political structures. A worldwide recession set in, causing massive levels of poverty, hunger, and unemployment. The people of Germany were especially vulnerable to exploitation. Loans to Germany dried up, their industrial production slumped, and millions were unemployed. Nazi party leaders were able to persuade the people to choose fascism, and their leader became Adolf Hitler. And the next decade saw the United States engaged in a war against tyrants and despots, affecting the life of every American family, including my own. Could it be that if there had been other economic policies in play from 1929 to 1933, the Great Depression might have been avoided as well as a world war and the Holocaust?

My parents survived that dreadful decade with a strong physical and emotional fiber developed from a special kind of grit, which prepared them for other challenging times that lay ahead.

II

BIRTH AND WAR

There is a time for everything, a season for every
activity under heaven . . .
A time to give birth . . . a time for war and a time
for peace.
—Ecclesiastes 3:1, 2, 8 (NLT)

MOTHER AND DAD met soon after his discharge from the CCC
camp in Coffeeville, where boys were made into men of strength
with the strong will to believe they could do some things well in life.
These boys were attractive physical specimens admired by women
who frequently placed themselves in the social life of Coffeeville on
weekends, where they met these fine-looking prospects for marriage.
My mother and father were married in 1939, and I was born on April
11, 1941, Route 1, Oakland, Mississippi.

Actually, 1941 was an eventful year in other ways. First, FDR was the greatest transformational president of the United States that we ever had. But signs of impending war were everywhere. The Japanese bombed Pearl Harbor on December 7, "a day that will live in infamy," Roosevelt said. We declared war on Japan, and Roosevelt named the "four freedoms" for Americans: freedom of speech, freedom of worship, freedom from want, and freedom from fear. Bob Hope made his first radio broadcast from a military base with the theme song "Thanks for the Memories."

A number of firsts were attributed to the year. The first network TV commercial was aired. The Chicago Cubs were the first Major League Baseball team to play an organ at games. The first FM radio started in Nashville, Tennessee. Cheerios were sold for the first time, and penicillin treatment became available to help treat infection.

In the entertainment realm, some of the top tunes were "Deep in the Heart of Texas" and "Chattanooga Choo Choo." The best movies included *How Green Was My Valley*, *Citizen Kane*, and *The Maltese Falcon*. Jimmy Stewart was the best actor, and Ginger Rogers was the best actress.

"YOU ARE MY SUNSHINE"

My parents lived on what was called the Old Robinson Place, at the back of the Hunt Place, out in the country from Oakland. Since it was a log house, I thought, *Now if I ever wanted to enter politics, I could claim an Abraham Lincoln kind of upbringing.* Used to, these houses and any land that might go with it were named after some previous owner. The house was located about a mile off the main road, where it could not be seen by anyone just passing by.

In earlier days, houses were built near a spring for a source of needed water if no well had been dug. The house design was usually the same, with a front porch, one or two rooms on the left side, and two rooms on the right side, with at least one fireplace in one of the front rooms and a flue in the kitchen for a wood cookstove. Sometimes there was a hallway from the front of the house to the back called a dogtrot. A back porch was a luxury. In the backyard was a woodpile for the stove and wood for the fireplace, a washpot for washing clothes, and a clothesline. Not all houses had an outhouse. Occasionally, some folks had a chicken coop containing roosting poles and with hens' nests for laying eggs. Some of the places might have had an old leaning barn for hay and the cattle.

A small amount of land came with the place, but Dad couldn't farm much of it because he didn't have the necessary farming equipment. We had a vegetable garden, an important source for most of our food throughout the year. My father was hired to work with a highway crew, but to catch a ride to work, he had to walk several miles one way. Mother was left at the house, with no neighbors in sight, all day to complete the domestic chores.

For some reason, Daddy was able to get Old Dr. Donaldson to come deliver me. Maybe they felt that their firstborn deserved to be delivered by a real doctor; I really don't know. He had to come a far piece out in the country. Usually, the doctors parked their cars out on the main road rather than try to drive down a cow path, trail, or a field road. From what I was always told, my home birth was normal. But I still think of what all could have happened because on occasion, there were complications when neither the mother nor the child survived. In a home birth, nothing could equal the magnificence of new life surrounded by loved ones contrasted with a birth in an institution amid strangers. At least that's the way I explain it.

My relatives have told me about how delighted Mother and Daddy were to have their bundle of joy in the world. My parents attempted the best they could to make sure I had opportunities they never had. They sent this announcement to the *Coffeeville Courier*: "Mr. and Mrs. Alvin Price, Oakland, Rt. 1, are rejoicing over a fine boy born the 11th. His name is Alvin Helm Price." There was now a new incentive to work even harder. I am sure they envisioned a brighter future for me than what they had. There must have been times when the future looked hopeless, making only enough money to get by. But this generation always thought there would be a better day just around the corner, and you would often hear a person say, "You just never know what another day may bring." They knew of their own willingness to work hard, to persevere, and to "go savin'."

Mother told me about her happiest moments when she gave me a bath in a wash pan, put clean clothes on me, and laid me in the middle of a fresh bed. She fanned me for a while and then made me laugh. It was hard to hold me in one arm and carry a bucketload of water in the other up a steep hill. She never left me alone. If anything, I was probably overprotected all the years I was home. My mother collected sayings about babies: "Of all the joys that lighten suffering earth, what joy is welcomed like a newborn child?" (Caroline Norton). And she found this one by Larry Barretto: "Babies are bits of stardust blown from the hand of God."

She sang to me a popular song of the time titled "You Are My Sunshine," made famous by Jimmy Davis, former governor of Louisiana.

> You are my sunshine, my only sunshine
> You make me happy when skies are gray.
> You'll never know dear how much I love you

Please don't take my sunshine away
The other night dear as I lay sleeping
I dreamed I held you by my side
But when I woke dear, I was mistaken
So I hung my head and I cried

Once, I was cranky and couldn't be satisfied. My parents tried everything to make me happy, and nothing worked. Finally, I said, "Sing shun shine." And I suppose that worked.

Another old song Mother sang to me as a baby became a big hit by Fats Domino later titled "My Blue Heaven." The lyrics were by George Whiting in 1927, and many artists have recorded the song.

When whippoorwill call
And evenin' is nigh
I'll hurry to my blue heaven
Just Molly and me
Just Molly and me
And the baby makes three
Be happy in my blue heaven

Soon after I was born, my grandparents—Joanne, Mary Elizabeth, and Thomas Eldon—moved into the house. The loft seemed the best place for Thomas to have a bed away from all the women and noise. On Saturday night, beds were taken down, furniture moved around so that there was room to court, make music, and dance. Thomas helped Dad do a little farming, and it was there one day while hoeing cotton that Thomas received his induction papers to go and fight in World War II.

◄O►

OAKLAND'S LEGENDARY MIDWIVES

Babies were delivered by either Old Dr. Donaldson from Oakland or by a midwife who lived in the community, some of whom had been trained by the doctor. In the African American areas around Oakland, the names of Lizar Winters, Patty Kimble, Celia Davis, and Rachel Woodall will be long remembered.

There were so many babies being born all around Oakland that the doctor couldn't go every place he was needed and carry on his practice in town. It was commonplace under those circumstances for the doctor to select a strong and willing lady in these communities to be trained in birthing babies. Also, the doctor knew that some of the families out in these rural areas just couldn't afford to pay any money at all. The midwife was willing to take whatever the family could give her.

Midwives were taught the basic things they needed to know, and then they were allowed to watch the doctor deliver some babies. When it was clear that the woman knew how to bring little ones into the world, the doctor gave her a little satchel with all the needed medical supplies. She had a new status as a midwife.

One of my first cousins was delivered by Mrs. Woodall who visited Mom Bea often. She not only delivered babies, but she also healed people when they were sick. She would take bitter weeds and boil the roots and have them to drink it. White and black people came to her house. requesting her help to deliver a baby. She dropped whatever she was doing, even though she had children of her own; fetched her little satchel; and went with them. Sometimes she even stayed overnight to make sure the baby and mother would be all right. She even walked to the homes when she received word she was needed. Her pay was a piece of meat from the smokehouse or other food. A total of $5 was the most money she was ever paid.

THE DREADED CASTOR OIL

I suppose my earliest memory was a bitter one. To this day, I can see my mother place a bottle of a clear, greasy liquid on the hearth in front of the fireplace to get warm. I soon realized that they were going to give me a dose of the contents. Warming it was designed to make it taste worse. Surely mortal man has never concocted a potion more dreaded by children. I was sure that parents enjoyed seeing their child squirm and resist taking it. Seems like I remember a little gleam and smile on their face when they were ready to give it to me. There had to be some perverted pleasure in holding a child down and forcing a dose. Even now, I don't know what in the devil it was for.

At the time, they called it castor oil. I've not met a person yet who didn't have a story to tell about their experience of terror when they were growing up. It was not just my parents; all parents administered this mixture to their helpless, ailing children. Evidently, this misconception about the all-purpose healing powers of castor oil began around the 1900s to be handed down from one generation to the next. My research has found that this unsavory medicine was actually given to children who suffered from any ailment whatsoever.

From literature, I accumulated only a partial list of conditions for which it was given: constipation, pain (anywhere), deodorant, as a "personal" lubricant, hair oil, warts, menstrual irregularities, and an additional assortment of health issues ranging from bladder problems to inducing labor contractions. People fell for these claims for over half a century.

And it had another use called a castor oil pack. These were made by pouring a small portion of the horrid liquid onto a piece of flannel and placing it on the area of your body you were trying to heal. A piece of plastic went over the pack and then a hot water bottle to heat it. I experienced the full range of treatment inflicted upon me as a kid. And you will never convince me that it was tasteless and odorless.

My mother used to tell the story that one day she had put the bottle on the hearth to heat up with me nearby. She had to go elsewhere in the house, and while she was gone, I leaned over and pushed the bottle over on the hard surface. Of course, the bottle broke. When she came back in the room, I pointed to the bottle and so innocently said, "Broke, broke," as if I had nothing at all to do with it.

My little research on this famous (or infamous) remedy found that its use goes all the way back to ancient Egypt, where they gave castor berries mixed with beer to children. That's a horrible thought that kids had to take this stuff for all those years. For most of its history, it was used internally, but now it is recommended only for external use. Oh, now we learn this! If that had only been known when I was young. And did you know you can still buy castor oil?

I learned that a fellow by the name of Edgar Cayce was responsible for all this misconception, and he was the one in the United States who popularized its use. Then I discovered that Mr. Cayce was a psychic, of all things. Here is what I think: I think he just dreamed this one night and mistakenly thought he had a heavenly vision of a cure-all medicine. He perpetrated its use on thousands upon thousands of vulnerable little children like me.

I don't know, maybe it cured lumbago; I don't hear people complaining about that anymore.

―◄○►―

BACK TO WHERE I WAS BORN

Later in my life, I decided that I wanted to make my way back to the old home place near Oakland, where I was born. That was my time for nostalgia. Sort of like Alex Haley wanting to know about his roots. I had to park the car on the narrow road on the rural route and ask a nearby resident where the Old Robinson Place was located. I was disappointed when he said that the old house had burned down several years before. But I still had to see for myself.

We walked across some spring branches, some hollows, and some hills until we finally found where the house had stood, though it seemed to me that the creeks and branches didn't have as much water in them as they did in those early days. I tried to imagine what life was like for my mother and father with no other house in sight. I stood there silently trying to get a glimpse of the day when my parents lived there—the sounds, the words, and the emotions. One could see the location of the cellar underneath the house where food products were kept. There was the slope down the hill to a spring, the source for our water. In my mind, I could see my mother toting two full water buckets up that long hill to the house. Remnants of an old sandstone chimney lay in ruins. All these scenes impressed on me like never before the hardships they experienced trying to simply make it in life, surviving from one day to the next.

It dawned on me that Old Dr. Donaldson had to come all the way from Oakland and then walked to the house to deliver me. I wondered what that experience waiting for him must have been like for a woman having her first child and for an anxious father. The doctor's only supplies were what he could carry in his medical satchel. I thought of all the possible vulnerabilities, but luckily, I was born healthy, and my mother survived childbirth.

I looked around for some relic to carry home that would remind me of the place from whence I came. A sandstone rock became that piece of history. It had helped to hold up one end of the front porch. I polished it and placed it on the hearth in my home, where it has been ever since. Every time I look at it, it reminds me of "gravel and grit" that I associate with my upbringing. It is said that for any group to maintain stability, they need symbols of group unity and with which they can all identify. That old piece of sandstone from that old log house that heard me laugh and cry as a baby is my symbol and my inspiration.

I can never remember when I was ashamed of our not having much material things when growing up. It is sad to me now that only after all those good folks who made such a difference in my life have gone on to their eternal rest that I've come to more fully appreciate their daily efforts. Lord knows that they tried all day long and into the night to provide table food, a little warmth in the house, and enough money to pay bills.

COTTON FIELDS BACK HOME

After I was older, mother told me the story of what happened one day when I was still an infant and when Daddy had tried to plant a cotton crop while working all day on the road crew. It came time to pick the cotton, and Mother had to help him before bad weather set in. She took a quilt to the field and spread it under a shade tree at the end of the rows. I was placed on top of the quilt while she picked a row of cotton. She checked on me each time she returned and by looking back at me every minute or so.

After her first row of cotton, she noticed something underneath the quilt poking up its head. After jerking me up and taking up the quilt, she discovered that she had placed it over a snake without noticing. It scared her so badly that she made a little bed at the end of her long cotton sack and put me on it, so I traveled down the cotton rows in high style.

Creative ways had to be developed to deal with cuts and scratches and other work hazards. Some cotton pickers took an old pair of gloves and cut out the ends of the fingers to avoid the sticking burrs. That didn't always work. Over the years, I still remember seeing the women's hands bleeding from the cuts. With blisters from hoeing and manicuring every stalk of cotton, which appeared to be a foot apart, with a bending and aching back, my mother could stand there and admire each stalk in all its stately glory. She was certainly not one of those "lick and a promise" type people who hoed. A passerby might reinforce her effort by saying, "Y'all sure have a nice stand of cotton."

HIS BLOOD WAS SEPARATING

The worst time we needed a doctor was when a cottonmouth snake bit my father's ankle. Daddy, Elizabeth, Joanne, Grandmother, Big Puppy (my dog), and myself went down below the house near a bottom area that had a spring branch to pick some wild grapes. They were up high wrapped around a small tree, so Grandmother carried the ax so we could chop down the tree to get to the grape vines. Grandmother planned on making jelly with them. Daddy was carrying the single-shot rifle as people didn't go off into snaky places without a gun. Big Puppy started barking at something near the tree. We mistakenly stopped his barking when, in fact, he was warning us about the snake. As we were looking up at the vine, suddenly, my father fell to the ground. He had stepped on the snake that bit him. The snake wouldn't let go, and my father had to take his pocketknife and cut the snake loose. My grandmother thought the snake was going to strike again, and she threw the ax at it, after which it crawled away. The snake could just as easily have bitten me. After cording his leg with his belt, my dad hobbled on one foot all the way back up the hill to the front porch.

I still have this scene vividly in my mind. My mother poured coal oil over the bite. McKnight, our neighbor, was called over to the house because everyone knew he kept a sharp pocketknife. But McKnight was too anxious and nervous to split his ankle open. That was all we knew to do. When Dad limped toward the house, Elizabeth cut across the field to another neighbor's house, Tom Nelson, who had a truck. Tom was a good friend of Dad, and they were about the same age. He came quickly to take Daddy to town to see Old Dr. Donaldson. My grandmother, Mother, Daddy, and Tom all managed to get in the cab together. After the doctor examined my father, he told Tom to put Daddy back in the truck and to not stop until he reached the hospital at Charleston to see Dr. Paul Googe. He told Tom that Dad's blood was already "separating," meaning a series of life-threatening symptoms. Luckily, they already had some antivenom medication at the hospital because someone else had been bitten the day before.

My dad was quite sick, but he managed to come home fairly soon. I remember him staying in our one room of the house all day for about a month until he healed. I was cautioned to leave him alone during the day. I didn't know anything about this at the time, but he was severely depressed. There he was with wife and child, living with his in-laws, not able to work and hurting inside and out. Dad had a lot of pride, and down deep, he always wanted to find a place in his life where he could get ahead.

When Daddy was able to walk, he went down to that hollow with a hoe where he was bit, looking hours for that snake. My uncle, Clarence McAllister, claimed that he had a mule that could sniff out a snake. He brought that mule over to the Coulter Place and rode that mule all over that bottom but never found it. Dad never found it either. This was the first time that my father almost died. It would not be the last.

THE GERMAN PRISON CAMP

One of the strongest American values has been self-sufficiency. It is expressed in the statement, "I want to make something of myself." That was my father's determination.

Camp McCain
Grenada County, Mississippi

World War II had started, and it brought new jobs to the surrounding communities. Dad heard that there were jobs at a new military installation near Grenada called Camp McCain. It was one of several that sprang up in Mississippi during the war. Troops for the army's Eighty-Seventh and Ninety-Fourth divisions trained there before being sent into combat in Europe. As many as fifty thousand troops prepared for war there at the peak of its expansion. It became a site not only for basic military training, but they also tested bomb-dropping mechanisms and other maneuvers and bivouac purposes.

The site required people to build the buildings and do the maintenance and provide for a multiplicity of services at a camp housing that many soldiers. But it also served as a prisoner-of-war camp for captured German soldiers. At one point, there were more than 7,700 prisoners. Part of the buildings included small apartments for the personnel while they worked there. My father heard about this opportunity, and since he was turned down for active duty in the military, he applied for any job they thought he could do. This was his way of making a contribution to the war effort.

Our apartment was small, but it was the nicest place we had ever lived. We grew to know many other families with small children. But the one thing I remember most was that every day at a certain time, the German prisoners marched on the other side of a fence in our backyard. I was amused by this scene, not really knowing much about the horrors and consequences of war. I noticed that every day one of the German soldiers looked at me, and he said something each time he saw me that I couldn't understand. He always waved and smiled and seemed to be friendly. One day he stopped and came a little closer to me before a guard made him get back in line. Later, we heard that he had made me a little toy he wanted to give me. Someone who knew this prisoner told my mother that he had a son about my age back in Germany that he missed terribly and wondered if he would ever see again. He said that I reminded him of his son, and that was the reason he was so nice to me. That must be one of the harshest realities of war for any soldier in any army, being on the other side of the world, away from wife and your little children, wondering every day if they are safe and if you will ever hold them close again.

PROMISE OF A BETTER LIFE

Dad heard about a wealthy man from Memphis who had bought a large farm east of Oakland. He also bought a house on that road between the farm and town, which had a lot more privacy to it, where he stayed when he came down from Memphis. I never knew the exact details, but Dad was able to get hired as the manager of the farm. He was given an old truck to drive, a fairly nice house to live in with a front porch, a fireplace, and a wood cookstove in the kitchen. We even had a good water source and a well-constructed outhouse. Mr. Cress, the owner, built a fine barn and started Dad out with some cattle and hogs. Dad's work was to raise cattle and hogs to sell. Hay was gathered for the barn, and most every piece of farm equipment Dad needed, Mr. Cress provided. But the best part was that Dad could also raise his own cattle and hogs along with Mr. Cress's. This provided Dad with a great opportunity to make some extra money for the first time in his life. We were living in high cotton in the Land of Goshen.

An American Classic

Those were happy days for us. Dad could drive the old truck to town when he needed, and we could visit family. Mother could harvest vegetables from the garden. And she could even take her vegetables into Oakland to a cannery, which made the whole canning process much easier. That was when we even acquired a battery radio for the first time. Mother and Dad had their favorite programs. They enjoyed listening to the Harrington Sisters sing and listened every morning to the *Buck Turner Show* out of Memphis. Their favorite song was "Cool Clear Water."

> All day I face the barren waste
> Without the taste of water, cool water
> Old Dan and I with throats burned dry
> And souls that cry for water, cool, clear, water.

My father did hard, grueling work every day, attempting to build Cress's farm into a successful operation. He lifted and strained way beyond his strength. I remember him telling my mother about a cow that had died, and they were afraid the cow had some contagious disease. Normally, these large animals were buried when they died, but if disease was suspected, their carcasses had to be burned for the safety of the other cattle and humans. At the foot of the hill below the house, Dad piled planks, limbs, and stumps over the dead cow. He poured some burned oil on the carcass. I had to stand at a distance, witnessing something like this for the first time with wonderment and fear. I trusted my dad to always do the right thing, so I just accepted this event as something that had to be done, even though I didn't fully understand.

TABLE SPREAD

Isn't it amazing how some scenes from childhood stay with you the rest of your life? When I was little, one memorable day occurred when we were visiting a bereaved family on the Coffeeville–Oakland road who had lost a loved one. That's what neighbors did. Again, this was before there were state regulations relating to how a dead body was prepared for burial. Some families just couldn't afford the use of a funeral home, so everything was done by the family at home. There were still some men in the community who knew how to construct a burial box—a skill, which had been handed down from one generation to the next.

I didn't see a casket anyplace, so while the men sat on the porch and talked, I wandered around the house, looking for something to do. For some reason, I decided to go back into the house through the backdoor. Upon entering to my great regret, I opened one door unfortunately, which led into the kitchen. Right before my eyes was the most horrifying scene I guess I had ever witnessed. No young child should have ever laid eyes on something like this. The poor deceased fellow had been stretched out on the kitchen table, completely naked. About a half-dozen women appeared to be going about their work in a serious manner. Right off, I knew I wasn't where I was supposed to be. Of course, I was run out of the kitchen, but it was too late. I had witnessed this scene that would forever stay in my mind. I learned later that the women were preparing the body for the burial box, and it involved washing the body real clean and putting the burial clothes on his body. These, evidently, were the delegated women who had the solemn duty to perform this needed task. And as far as I could tell, before I was abruptly run off, they were doing an admirable job. I guess what I never could understand was why they chose the kitchen table for the place to lay the body. Lord, have mercy! How on earth could that possibly make sense? Can you imagine having to eat a meal on this table after seeing that? I would have gotten choked and sick to my stomach for sure.

GOOD TIMES DOWN ON THE FARM

Mr. Cress had built two large ponds on his place and stocked them with largemouth bass and bream. He loved to fish using a fine rod and reel with all his fancy lures. We knew not to disturb him when he was fishing. We were allowed to fish the ponds, but our fishing equipment was somewhat simpler than his. We had long cane poles and used whatever bait we could find, such as worms, crickets, grub worms, grasshoppers, and chicken livers.

One of the ponds was just below our house, and we could hear the bullfrogs at night, singing almost in rhythm. Small pleasures of Southern living kept me grounded in my own world. On hot summer nights, the windows were raised in hopes some cool fresh air might blow through to my bed. At night, there were so many frogs croaking, making that deep, hoarse sound, that they resonated like sweet harmony found in some child's lullaby. The crickets and tree frogs joined right in, and in some unexplainable way, that rhythmic cadence was reassuring and quickly eased me into a sound and restful sleep.

Mother took our single-shot rifle one morning and shot so many frogs they filled a washtub. Now eating bullfrog legs was an absolute delicacy. For the first time, I learned how they would jump in the frying pan and was quite amused at that. I never understood the biological explanation of the jumping though.

Once, we caught a turtle down close to the pond, and Mother made turtle stew out of it. As I recall, it was pretty good. Haven't had any since though. I was always afraid that that turtle's head would snap and get one of my fingers.

MR. CRESS'S LADY FRIEND AND GOSSIP

We knew that Mr. Cress always brought a lady friend down from Memphis with him to his house about two miles from his farm Dad was managing. I always thought it was his wife, but in later years, I learned that she might not have been. Of course, there was much gossip about her. All I knew was that she seldom left the house to accompany Mr. Cress. He didn't live there except on occasional weekends. The gossipers were upset because all their gossip couldn't hurt him. This is why gossip was so prevalent in small Southern towns. They knew that their gossip could do great damage to the reputation of someone. They knew their power and used it as a means of social control. Rumor or the threat of rumor and gossip were means used by some to demonstrate their influence. These words expressed the fear of rumors:

> Don't do that. Don't you know people will talk? Why, it wouldn't take two hours for that to spread all over the community, and then what would we do? No telling what people would say, and once it gets started, there is no way to stop it. We have to be careful, knowing what people will say.

In the matter of Cress and the lady he brought down from Memphis, introduced as his secretary, an absolutely unexpected revelation came to light. The limited number of high-society women in Oakland accidentally discovered that the evil, immoral adulteress could play bridge. Desperate for more women to participate in these carefully constructed and beloved bridge parties, this previous woman of ill repute was now invited into the elite circle of Oakland's upper crust. She was now a welcomed, lovely, and delightful socialite from Memphis who was gracing the afternoon rituals of Oakland's leisure class. Suddenly, her bridge skills trumped any previous notions of indiscretions. The conversations were something like this: "Why, I thought that woman . . . now don't be too quick to judge . . . once you get to know her . . ."

Gossip today has lost some of its earlier success. It doesn't do the damage it once did, though there are still many people who need gossip as part of their daily nourishment.

Telephones, where available, fueled the gossiper's insatiable hunger. Monday mornings were the time for folks to get caught up on all the rumors and unusual things said and done. It was the responsibility of each one to pay close attention over the weekends.

Afterwards, some people made their long lists of misdeeds and rumors of misdeeds. They inquired at church on Sunday, which was the prime source for new and juicy gossip. Then on Monday mornings, the phones rang off the wall so everyone could share all that they had heard. Hearing all the dirt in the community somehow made some ladies feel less guilty for all their own missteps, which they never admitted.

Some of the churches had a time in the service when members could come forward to be rededicated or restored. One of the implicit norms here, understood by all, was that you never, heaven forbid, ever specified what your sins were. People knew full well that things would be much worse for them if they started confessing shocking revelations. You had to speak in generalities by saying things like, "Well, I have not been as faithful as I should, and I have said and done some things, and I want prayer and everyone's forgiveness." Then the preacher prays, others congratulate the confessor for their courage and change. Actually, you cannot win in either case here. Not stating what it was that you said or did just aroused the curiosity of the gossipers. Then it became their quest to find out the details by asking around until they had at least some clues about your transgressions.

Preachers preached against gossiping till they were blue in the face, and it didn't even make a dent in the amount going on. I've attempted to explain that gossip is culturally ingrained in the South. It has always been a part of our way of life. It is even part of the daily nourishment. And that will always trump whatever is taught in the Bible.

One particular type might be called *overt gossips*. They have no reservations whatsoever of telling everything they know about any person in the community, never considering the harm it might do.

Guess what I heard. Well, let me tell you something.
The way I heard it . . . I think you should know . . .
Now I know you would want to know this . . .

But there were others who felt they must somehow morally justify their gossip. To them, this was accomplished by prefacing their gossip with certain expressions. This seems to clear the conscience and make it okay. These might be called the moral justifiers of gossip.

You know I love her to death, but I know she does
the best she can, but . . . Now I don't mean any harm,
but the poor woman . . .

By beginning the gossip with these clarifications, no guilt was ever felt.

Other "gossip qualifiers" were often used to feel morally superior:

As long as I can remember, he has been that way. She
is just following in her mother's footsteps. You would
think they would know different. I reckon they just
don't know any better.

SATURDAYS IN OAKLAND

In those bright and sunny days at the Cress Place, I seem to remember a lot of good times. Even though the work that Dad did during the week was hard, the weekend was different. Saturday was the day to take a bath, dress up a little, and go to town. Kids were usually given a small amount of money, maybe a nickel or dime, to spend on small pleasures such as ice cream. Main Street was always crowded with people who both shopped and enjoyed the social life for that day. You could get caught up on happenings in and around Oakland. In those days, all the stores were open for business, and there were many customers, both black and white. Some folks came in wagons and mules and parked at a place across the street from the stores next to the railroad track.

Going to town on Saturday was a nice reward anticipated during a week of busyness and hard work. This tradition was great financially for the businesses and enjoyable for the common people who came to socialize and buy the necessities. The act of walking the short front street was a ritual for some involving showing off some new clothes or presenting yourself as somebody. Herron's store was one place I remember because one could buy most anything there in one place, maybe a forerunner of Walmart. One could also buy his or her coffin there. Some folks swapped eggs for food. Others brought live chickens to exchange for needed merchandise.

The other store I remember was Wells Drug Store on the corner, where I purchased my ice cream cones. Doc Wells was the pharmacist with a moody disposition, meaning that customers both black and white had to be careful around him. Local blacks needing items from his drugstore knew that there was a side door through which they could enter. Everyone knew which door was for whom. Wells had a black man called Forty to do the dirty work around the store, sweeping, lifting, and running errands. He and other black workers also worked at their house, mostly in the yard or taking care of small children. Most of the successful business people hired one black man for these jobs, perceiving them as their possession but allowing them to have various perks that made it worthwhile for the black men to have such jobs. These men often endeared themselves to the family who took care of their basic needs in their old age.

Doc Wells allowed people to put their medicine or other products on their bill. When they returned to pay their debt, he gave them candy as a motivator. That gesture must have worked quite well because he boasted that he only had one debt not collected (because the man moved away).

Wells's wife, Viola, was the ultimate Southern lady, active in community work and described as a big Methodist and leader in all the respectable women's clubs. Being regarded as the "Hostess of Oakland" meant that she took the lead in giving bridal showers, afternoon teas, and receptions for other people of the same social standing. She volunteered for whatever the need and, consequently, was highly respected by most everyone because she knew how to get things done by calling on friends for donations to good causes. Doc and Viola had a large imposing home with a wraparound porch. People were overheard to say "The Lord only knows how she and Doc Wells got connected."

By the 1960s, Oakland had no business and economic future for the same reason as many other Mississippi towns. The few wanted to keep their own comfortable living exclusively to themselves. The cost of preventing black people and poor white working people from having much of an opportunity to get ahead came at a great price. One day driving through Oakland around 1964, I stopped to show my wife where I bought ice cream as a child. The drugstore was barely hanging on. With no other customers in the store and us not being recognized, Doc Wells's son, who now ran the store, kept a close eye on us, perceiving that we were not from around there. At this time of social unrest, some Mississippians became suspicious of any stranger, thinking that they were possibly outside agitators. I attempted to be cordial but received no positive response, even after

I introduced myself. We left the paranoid atmosphere thinking how sad this reception was. Not long after that, the store closed forever.

OAKLAND'S FRONT STREET VERSUS BACKSTREET

There was a seamy side of Oakland that was off-limits to proper women and young children who were never to be seen there. It was called backstreet because it was behind the stores. Any number of pleasures were available that one could not find elsewhere. Nearby, Jimmy McCracken had a store that sold items to the school children during the week. Having a jukebox in the store allowed some of the students to go in and dance. But he was bad to drink, and sometimes in his drunkenness, he took his gun outside and shot up in the air. People grew used to it and just assumed that McCracken was drunk again. His living quarters were on one side of the store. He had a wooden leg, and sometimes his wife took it away from him just to prevent him from acting out.

There were some other living quarters on the backstreet where a couple lived that had daughters who, shall we say, made themselves available to men in town. They had a very workable strategy each Saturday when there was a crowd out on front street, especially in the morning time. These daughters dressed rather flamboyantly and seductively. At various times, they went out on the street, where they could be seen by the men as they sashayed from one end of the street to the other in their red dresses. That might be called throwing out the bait, setting the hook, or setting the table. You can pick your own preferred metaphor. From that time on till late into the night, they had plenty of business. In fact, sometimes there was so much business they had to take appointments, or men had to wait in line.

Of course, the wives knew about this place and usually kept a close eye on their husbands. The most welcomed words the men could hear was "I'm going to be in here for a while looking at this cloth and the dress patterns. You just go on and get all your business done. And when you are finished, you can come back in here to get me." It was hard for the men not to flash a big smile upon hearing these words. There were times, however, when the wives couldn't find their husbands and figured out that they were back at that cathouse. Some women were known to have gone back there to the house, banging on the door and demanding to know where her husband was. In my mind, I can just see her grabbing him by the ear and leading the wayward back to more proper surroundings. In those days, women did not have as many options as they do today. Because of a lack of ability to be financially independent, they learned to tolerate some amount of naughty behavior for the sake of their futures and that of the children.

Front street and backstreet were worlds apart with different cultural norms operating. On front street, normal niceties, appropriate language, and proper decorum were expected. On backstreet, a different set of behaviors was allowed. One of the strongest, implicit norms was that you never revealed who you saw back there. Fighting was frowned upon because that would draw too much attention. Occasionally, the sheriff conducted a "walk-through" so the "respectable" citizens would think he was doing his job.

The water fountain on Main Street said, FOR WHITES ONLY." Black folks had to go to backstreet, where there was a water spicket. Nearby was a log cabin, which was a café during the week and a club on weekends. Buck and Minerva's sold sandwiches to white kids who would come down there from school. But on the weekends, it was turned into a place where blacks could go and party. It was a place to forget your troubles and enjoy a little of the good times being around other people that you knew. Sometimes the fun was called juking and jiving, where there was much laughter and noise. Whites were not welcome. It was said that one could get whatever you wanted, sort of like "Alice's Restaurant."

In some towns in the South, on certain days (usually Saturday) in some of those clubs, blacks and whites *could* mingle and party together with no resentment or problems. It was a carefully, socially defined situation in which the usual cultural mores (must and must-not behaviors) were suspended. The quality required of whites to be present was that they possess at least some amount of "soul" and could "chill." The larger white community usually were not aware of these places. It was a matter that was kept quiet by those who were enjoying the interaction.

Not just today but also even back then, there was always a house where men could go, pay a little money, and enjoy their pleasures. Often, the house location changed, but the town marshal and sheriff always knew where it was. Often, they knew for their own personal and practical reasons. The amount of tolerance and allowance for these "houses of ill repute" was truly amazing!

One such place existed between the Coffeeville Road and Highway 32, where a woman and several daughters accommodated mainly a clientele of service men stationed at Camp McCain, a military base, near Grenada. The daughters had been trained in the art of profiting by seducing men. Even the mother participated in this ancient profession. The boys somehow reached Oakland, and a taxi service took them out in the country to the location. It was said the taxi driver made a small fortune doing this for the service guys. I wonder if he waited in the taxi for them until they returned. The greeting at the door was from the mother. "Come on in, boys. If my daughters can't satisfy you, I will."

◄◉►

ANGEL SIDE AND DEVIL SIDE OF OUR NATURE

We've always had two parts of our nature operating: the angel side and the devil side. Each one is sitting on a shoulder and saying into our ears, "Come on, do it," and from the other shoulder, "Don't do it." Psychologists say that the battle going on between these two competing forces is constant, and whatever compromise we work out determines our character and personality. My own opinion is that we are never completely consistent.

In the South, we have always had an overactive conscience, which means that when we deviate, it bothers us a lot (usually). When some have "gotten religion," they are religious to an extreme. But when they fall, they tend to fall hard. The truth is, we are all fallible human beings and vulnerable to err. The reformer Martin Luther framed it this way: *Simul justus et peccator*, meaning we are both saint and sinner.

Our culture taught us that sins of the flesh (drinking, stealing, fornication, cussing, and carousing) were the primary sins that usually affected the conscience more. Our culture traditionally taught us that our treatment of some categories of people was really no big deal and not worth agonizing over. Therefore, we never saw people weeping, repenting, or crushed over their participation in or approval of violent or discriminatory acts designed to keep some people degraded.

Southerners have made great efforts to try to reconcile these two parts of our nature. As Emmanuel Kant postulated, we all have this sense of a "moral ought." Brother, that has always been keenly felt by us reared in the South. At another level of consciousness, however, we are also painfully aware of our sometimes aberrant and shameless behavior. Perhaps this is why remorseful drunks always want to sing gospel before the night is over. For some, working out a congruent solution becomes an impossible task, even though we keep trying. Whitfield Hospital for the mentally ill was full of people who never could accomplish this, and eventually, the stress drove them insane. This is why preachers preaching on God's grace gave forth such a comforting feeling.

But some preachers were legalistic, relegating to hell all that didn't keep God's commandments by dotting every jot and crossing every tittle. The commandments were many, and every Sunday, the preacher kept adding to the list. When you thought he had run out of commandments, he began to make up some more. (Such as the Pharisees who thought the Law of Moses was not strict enough on fasting, which only required it once a year, so they imposed fasting every Monday and Thursday.) Commandments were found everywhere: the culture, the community, the family matriarchs and patriarchs, the school. Some conscientious people tried their best to measure up to this impossible standard, only to never feel like they were righteous enough. Eventually, such a system drove people either crazy or right out of the church.

Quite a large percentage of society's talk centered on this philosophical issue. William Faulkner and Tennessee Williams became literary geniuses telling the stories of this incongruence. Much of the dialogue in movies such as *Cat on a Hot Tin Roof* and *Long, Hot Summer* dramatized this constant effort toward some kind of reconciliation between these two natures. And in the end, all to no avail.

In those years when I was young, I was protected from the realities of that other part of Oakland. I wouldn't have understood even if I had known. Since those youthful days of innocence, I've discovered much more about our fallibilities.

THE WALTONS OF MISSISSIPPI

For most of my growing up years, I lived in an extended family involving three generations. We either lived with my grandparents or were nearby. That meant there was always someone older in my life that I could pester. Living in an extended family held a lot of positives. I knew every one of my many first cousins, which is often difficult because of our use of bilateral kinship patterns. We could always romp and stomp with one another, and this added a lot of enjoyment.

Joanne and Elizabeth, Mother's two youngest sisters, were still at home. This was an opportunity for me to make my presence known when their boyfriends came courting, which was totally unappreciated by my two aunts. Just for pure aggravation, I poured some water on one of the boys, which required thereafter a family meeting to discuss my bold and outrageous behavior and the appropriate discipline. My mother and grandmother were in charge as they were the recognized ruling matriarchs in the family. I just knew the death penalty was imminent. The only thing that saved me was their Christian upbringing that allowed me yet another second chance.

With such caring family members always there to validate my worth in so many different ways, it never bothered me being the progeny of plebian farmworkers. I also lived near people we called cousin and aunt but who were not actually biological cousins and aunts. But they maintained that status in my life, which added even more security and caring.

I enjoyed living on the Cress Place partly because my grandmother and grandfather Helm moved into a house about a mile from us. They lived next to the second pond that was on the back side of the place. I could go over to their house most anytime. Joanne and Elizabeth, their two youngest daughters, were a little older than me, and I enjoyed their attention. We were living on the sunny side of life. My granddaddy always rose at four thirty every morning to start his day of hard work, trying to provide food and to keep the house warm in the wintertime. Late in the afternoon, he cleaned up and took a straight chair from the house and sat in it out under a shade tree. He smoked his Country Gentleman tobacco and cooled off from the day's work. It was one of those few moments when he could just sit and enjoy this small pleasure. That was when I liked to talk to him about all sorts of things he was doing in his life. He was patient toward me, and he never complained or begrudged anything about his life. I thought of him then as an old man, though he was only sixty-three. Already, the toll of his hard labor was making him appear older. That was not uncommon during those days.

Granddaddy liked to roll his own cigarettes. He could get a bag of loose tobacco of Country Gentlemen that rolled about thirty cigarettes for ten cents, while a pack of twenty machine-rolled cost about fifteen cents. You see, my granddad knew how to "go savin'." He was probably not aware that women in North Carolina who needed extra income were hired to sew drawstrings into those cotton tobacco bags he was buying. Some of those poor women made as many as a thousand a day, for which they were paid fifty cents. Most of those women earned an average of five to thirteen cents an hour.

For those experiencing economic difficulties, it wasn't much, but it amounted to something. It bought a loaf of bread and something out of which to make a sandwich.

With Dad managing this farm, we were doing better financially than we ever had. This meant that occasionally, I received something extra special, especially at Christmastime. The first thing that I can remember that I really wanted Santa Claus to bring me was a red wagon with sideboards on it. My anxiety over the possibility of getting that wagon was only matched by Ralphie wanting that Red Ryder BB gun.

I never knew for sure whether I would get it until Christmas Day morning. When I saw it, I said, "I see red. It's exactly what I wanted." What I didn't realize at the time was the joy in the hearts of my parents that they could get that wagon for me, and their seeing that it excited me was a great reward. I used it some to clean up the yard by putting sticks in it and hauling them off. But mainly, I hauled stovewood to the back porch that my mother needed to start a fire in the old wood cookstove.

FRONT ROOM PLANK

I went over to my grandmother's house every chance I could. There was a path through a pasture, over fences, over a creek, and up a hill to their old house. Joanne had accidentally dropped one of her hair barrettes through a crack on the front room floor, and it was located on the ground beneath the house. She needed that hair barrette, so she and Elizabeth came up with a plan. They could raise a plank off the floor, and I was small enough that they could drop me down through that opening to the ground underneath the house where I could retrieve the prized ornament.

The plan was working fine except they failed to take into account that it was the spot where the dogs slept at night near the chimney to keep warm. So the moment my feet hit the ground, fleas engulfed my whole body. I'm sure I was yelling as they raised me back through the opening in the floor. They took me to the front porch, where they stripped me buck-naked. Finally, the fleas were swept away with a broom, and I could redress. I don't recall if we ever retrieved that barrette.

Many years later, after I was married and had two children, I told this story to my yuppie son and asked him if he could imagine having fleas all over his body. He said, "Actually, I wasn't thinking about that. What I couldn't imagine was having a plank on the living room floor that you could raise up enough so that someone could crawl down underneath the house."

OUR FRIEND AND HELPER GEORGE

When Daddy needed some extra help on the farm, he could always find some men who needed the work. But he did have one black man who lived in a shack on the backside of the place. George helped wherever he was needed and was always ready to go the extra mile. We all liked and relied on George frequently. He was single, and he didn't know how to cook. It was obvious that George wasn't eating well and needed more nourishment, so Mother and Daddy invited George to come up to our house at suppertime for a good hot meal. Mother always prepared him a glass of sweet tea, a large plate of food, and dessert. He ate it sitting on our back doorstep. Seemingly, he couldn't thank Mother enough for the fine food he had for supper.

Finally, George found a wife, and she moved in with him in his little house. He appeared to be a lot more jovial after that because his wife could cook. George was a religious fellow and was a member at the Philadelphia M. B. Church, which was not far down the road. Dad had the truck Mr. Cress provided for him to use on the farm and to go to town and other places. From time to time, Dad let George drive his truck to church. Once, when there was some special activity, George invited Joanne, Mother, and Daddy and me to go to church with him. We accepted his invitation, and he was delighted. When we arrived at the building, we all sat on the back row, but George wanted us to come and sit close to the front. While it was not unusual for white people to attend services at a black church, we remained on the back row, where I promptly went to sleep.

Sometimes white people drove up close to a window, which was open, and just listened to the preaching and singing. The members expected this, so they appointed two young men to come out to the car and invite them inside, where they were always welcomed.

There was nothing in my culture that ever motivated me to raise the question as to why black people could not come to the white churches until I was a graduate student in college. I was, what you might say, culture bound, which meant that I had never been exposed to enough objective insight or discussion that would help me escape from my own social blindness. I do remember hearing some men talking about the need for "N— to stay in their place." But again, I never made them explain where that "place" was and the humanity behind that reasoning.

—◄o►—

"LET'S MAKE SOME MUSIC"

The highlight for us during those days in the middle 1940s was going over to Jim and Edna Conner's house usually on Saturday night, where some men made music, and folks danced. This was a family that lived on a road that went around the back of the Cress Place. The Conner's two sons, John and Bill, could play musical instruments, my uncle Clarence played the bass guitar, and there were always some men from Coffeeville who came over to play. The house where the music was made was beside where the Connors lived. They moved out all the furniture from the front room and the one right behind it. This allowed plenty of room for the musicians and those who wanted to dance.

The kids stayed in one of the back rooms of the house until we played down and went off to sleep. The kitchen table was always full of food, and through the night, the guests came back to partake of the fine Southern cuisine after getting a little tired. There was always a break when the music makers went back there to eat something. It was often said that a good time was had by all.

No matter how hard you worked during the week, no matter how many troubles you had, there was this unwritten rule that on Saturday, you laid it aside and attempted to enjoy a little slice of living. You had to allow a little enjoyment and happiness to penetrate your life on Saturday. No one was allowed to express his or her worries or fears on Saturdays. It was an escape into another world with friends and family. It was one of our survival techniques. To this day, I remember the songs they played. One instrumental tune that always motivated people to move onto the dance floor was "Under the Double Eagle" and the song "Goodnight, Irene." Iconic blues musician and singer Huddie "Lead Belly" Ledbetter first recorded this song in 1932. White people did not know the origin of the song, but they loved to sing it:

> Goodnight Irene, goodnight, Irene
> I'll see you in my dreams.

Everyone joined in when "Corinna, Corinna" was played. I can still see people smiling at one another and singing. All deprivation and hardship in life were momentarily forgotten to have at least a little time to enjoy the lighter pleasures of life.

> I love Corinna, tell the world I do. I pray at night
> She'd like to love me too. Corinna, Corinna

And no one could forget another Leadbelly song "Birmingham Jail," an old tune with many variations of unknown origin:

> Mail me a letter, send it by mail,
> Send it in care of the Birmingham jail.

The music and dancing usually continued till midnight when people started home. The nights were darker back then. Occasionally, you could see a small light from a coal oil lamp in the distance at someone's house.

Neighbors who never learned how to appreciate the music seemed to have sour moods. This reminds me of what Shakespeare wrote about the value of music in *The Merchant of Venice*. Lorenzo said,

> The man that hath no music in himself, / Nor is
> not moved with concord or sweet sounds, / Is fit for
> treasons, stratagems and spoils; / The motions of his

spirit are dull as night, / And his affections dark as Erebus: / Let no such man be trusted.

After my grandparents moved over to the Old Leonard Place nearer to Coffeeville, Barney and Bell Caulder moved into their old house at the back of the Cress Place. What classic literary names! They also loved the Saturday night parties and dancing from house to house. Bell was a little heavy on the feet, and when she danced, the floor appeared to sway a little. Barney was just like so many others of that time doing a little farming and just getting by. He also liked to drink, some of which he made himself, but followed a principled rule that he didn't drink in the daytime, only at night. Daytime was for work. They were people with a good neighborly heart and helped anyone in need. Like so many other families with similar backgrounds, I hope they all lived long enough to know that their descendants enjoyed a few more opportunities for success, often never experienced by the parents of that era.

BUCK TURNER BAND AND SAM PHILLIPS

The favorite musical group in our area was the Buck Turner Band from Memphis. Fans such as my mother and father made them popular and rich. Their radio program could be heard all over North Mississippi. They booked shows throughout the mid-South. I remember one special show they did at Legion Lake, which was located about halfway between Coffeeville and Oakland, on Highway 330. The CCC boys had constructed everything there. My dad always liked to go because it reminded him of his contributions to land development in the county.

Everyone looked forward to a musical show on certain holidays, such as the Fourth of July. We were there nearly all day enjoying plenty of food, seeing good friends, and watching some boat races. One night the Buck Turner Band performed for the dance. I was not allowed to go inside, but I could see what was going on from the door. After about an hour, and after several men had gotten fairly drunk, a fight broke out on the dance floor. I was horrified, but my mother made sure that I was out of the way and prevented my dad from going inside. The band tried to get outside by a back door to avoid getting involved. They had a blind guy playing for them, and I could see them trying to direct him out the door. Some of the spectators were helping them escape the scene.

Then I saw something else that no young child should ever see. A man from outside with an open pocketknife went inside and stabbed another fellow in the stomach. He just went up to the man who was engaged in a fight with someone else and stabbed him. I thought that was unfair, sort of like shooting someone in the back. After that, my mother whisked me away, saying, "Buddy, come on and let's go home." Again, like seeing the washing of the dead man's body, I have never forgotten that scene. Some kids had to face the harsh realities of life very early on, too early. Somehow so much innocence was lost too soon. It was an unsettling lesson for a six-year-old to learn that the world had such horrors.

There is an interesting little sidelight to the story though. In 1949, a man by the name of Sam Phillips leased a small storefront at 706 Union Avenue near Downtown Memphis with rent at $150 a month. Phillips didn't have any recording equipment until Buck Turner gave him a two-year loan. Turner had been performing on WREC radio in Memphis and was doing quite well. Without much equipment, Phillips recorded wherever he could get a booking such as weddings, funerals, or religious gatherings.

Memphis Recording Studio's first paying job was transcriptions of Buck Turner's band for the Arkansas Rural Electrification Program. These were distributed to radio stations throughout the mid-South. In 1954, Phillips and his Sun Records decided to record artists and successfully launched the careers of Elvis Presley, Carl Perkins, Johnny Cash, Jerry Lee Lewis, B. B. King, Howlin' Wolf, Rufus Thomas, and numerous others. One could make a good argument that Sam Phillips was one of the most important figures in twentieth-century American musical culture.

Hmm . . . Let's see now! All these musical legends literally changed much of the music world. They got their start because of Sam Phillips, who got his start from a loan by Buck Turner, who was made successful and wealthy by fans such as my mother and father. So do you suppose my family could lay claim to having a little bit to do with the success of all these others? Forgive me, but I like to think that they did.

GOSPEL SONG OF THE HOUR

Where I grew up, those two old natures were always at work within us—the devil side and the angel side. Often in the midst of our parties, dances, and otherwise good times, not ever far from our consciences was the thought that we might be enjoying ourselves a bit too much. Heaven forbid that we should ever do that! So to placate the angel side, we sang a few gospel songs just as a reminder.

Really, this is a trait found throughout the South. The local and area bands and performers full well knew that this moment was always appreciated. "Well, we have come to that part of the program where we gather around the microphone, take our hats off, and sing the gospel song of the hour." Some outsiders thought this was not good because they saw it as a downer after an upbeat show. No, no, no! In the South, singing that hymn made us feel better. You see, it was a kind of a redemption song following a time of too much drinking, too much hilarity, and all the rest.

Local radio and television shows carried on the tradition. Tennessee Ernie Ford even took the practice to a national television audience. Performers always did this on the Slim Rhodes Show out of Memphis as well, with Dusty and Spec. People outside the South wondered how Southerners could stand there a little inebriated and sing "Precious Lord, Take My Hand" or "Amazing Grace." Actually, it was really easy to sing those songs with tears flowing down the face, reflecting recognition of our human frailties relating to strong drink. This cleansing effect lasted all the way to the next show.

Black soul music of the time reflected a greater recognition of the fact that we never escape the pulls of those two natures. White people, on the other hand, kept up the never-ending effort trying to separate the two (all their life).

RADIO HAD SOUL

My parents' battery radio at the Cress Place gave us many hours of pleasure. We learned a lot about a much larger world out there, though not all of it brought happiness. There was music, drama programs, and the war news. Sons are fortunate to have a father present in the home and with whom you could do certain things together. Dad came in late, cleaned up, and ate his supper. Afterward, he and I would turn the radio on to a detective program called *Sam Spade* in 1946.

There was something reassuring to a son to listen to these programs with your father and to be able to comment to each other about the show. There is nothing better than having good conversation with your father when you are young. Howard Duff was a film star who had the starring role as a private eye detective. The show had all the ingredients you could want—action, drama, tough guys, women, wisecracks, and laughs. I could just visualize the scene with all those sound effects. Our imaginations filled in all but the voices. In fact, at age five, I thought the sounds were real. Duff's coarse bass voice made it sound even more dramatic. There was much more to this experience than just listening to a radio show; a family bond was strengthening. Such informal family rituals have always helped solidify the relationships.

The show was sponsored by Wildroot Cream Oil for hair grooming. At that time, men slicked their hair back, which was easy to do with all that oil. And it gave them that Clark Gable look as they knew all the women swooned over him. Dad always kept a bottle to use on his own black hair. To make the hair easy to comb back straight, at night, my dad wore a "pompodoe," which I assume is a regional variation of the French word *pompodour*. He took a worn-out pair of mother's stockings, cut off the upper end, and tied a knot in it to slip tightly over his head. I laughed at him for doing this only once.

I believe listening to that radio made me a better listener, and I know it helped me become a good imaginer. That has benefited me throughout my life. Whether it was baseball, drama, music, or comedy, I found a certain mystique about it, and its intimacy sort of sucked us in. By the 1950s, when we moved to town, my family increased our social status by getting a little Philco radio that ran on electricity.

—◀◯▶—

COMMUNITY COMPASSION AND FUNERALS

Somewhere along this time, my uncle John L. Helm, mother's brother living at Greenwood, died of a brain hemorrhage. He was married and had two small children. He had answered the call of his country during World War II. But the military discharged him because of high blood pressure. Afterward, he operated a Billups service station in Greenwood. It was a tragic and sudden loss for all the family.

The burial would be in the Coffeeville Cemetery, so Mother and Daddy offered to let his casket and visitation be at our house, out from Oakland. Old Mrs. Connor, the neighbor where we made music on Saturday night, knew there would be many people to come and view the body and visit with the family. She did a very magnanimous act by cooking up a lot of food to bring over to our house. In fact, she fixed so much that she brought it all over on the back of a wagon pulled by mules. She was another example of a woman of strength and honor.

John L. was the first one of the Helm siblings to die and the first child of my grandparents to die. He was in the prime of his life, had a good wife and grand hopes for his two boys. I remember the funeral and then the burial at the cemetery. Eunice, his wife, had to have one last look at him before his body was lowered into the grave. Seeing these small children lose their father was frightening to kids like me. What would happen to me if I lost either my mother or my father?

—◀◯▶—

LISTENING TO THE WAR NEWS

On top of all this fear, I was old enough to know that the United States was in a world war. Every family was concerned and worried about the boys fighting and losing their lives in a far and distant land. As a young child, I struggled to understand why we had to be at war.

Late in the evening, some neighbors would come over to the house to hear the war news on our battery radio. Some of them walked; they didn't have a car or a radio. Yet some of their children or kin were in the war. They lived daily with fear and anxiety, asking, "Is he safe? Is he still alive?" They gathered around and listened carefully. In that war, news services were allowed to reveal where the battles were being fought. I knew not to make noise or interrupt. I didn't know it then, but later, I learned that when the announcers said that casualties were moderate, they meant about half of the boys had been killed. When casualties were light, about 25 percent were killed. When casualties were high, most all of them lost their lives.

The names of those radio announcers still ring in my memory. Walter Winchell always began his program by saying, "Good evening, Mr. and Mrs. Nawth Americur and all the ships at sea." At 6:30 p.m., Gabriel Heater came on, beginning each broadcast with "Ah, there's good news tonight!" no matter how dreadful the report.

I suppose my favorite was Edward R. Murrow of CBS News. His tone convinced you that he spoke the truth without any exaggeration. In the early days, he came on with these words: "This . . . is London." He placed vocal emphasis on the word "this," followed by a brief pause before he spoke the rest of the phrase. Another of his famous quotes was his closing: "Good night and good luck." He aroused some critics by his reporting of the liberation of the Buchenwald concentration camp. He graphically described the physical condition of the camp's prisoners that had survived. He referred to "rows of bodies stacked up like cordwood." Some actually wanted him to apologize for the harsh tone of his voice after witnessing such a disgraceful horror.

THE VESTIBULE QUANDARY

Occasionally, soldiers came back to Oakland on leave for a few days, and I was able to listen to their stories. They preferred telling funny and amusing things rather than focusing on the fearful future that lay ahead. Also, they wanted their loved ones to feel happy and not sad, so they told something light.

I remember one of those stories: One soldier told about the first few days after reporting for duty. Most of these boys with him were right from the cotton and cornfields, having never experienced much of the real and expanded world. They were in an assembly hall, getting instructions about the activities of the first few days. The commanding officer announced the events of the day. After reviewing their schedule, the soldiers would reassemble in that same hall later in the day. The officer's final word was "And there will be no loitering in the vestibule." This struck fear into the hearts of all those boys, not knowing exactly what a vestibule was. This soldier said that he didn't think there was a vestibule out on Route 1, Oakland, but he wasn't sure.

For the rest of the day, they worried, afraid that they might loiter in the vestibule and not know it. When it became time for them to reassemble, they began to inquire, "Have you heard whether they caught anyone loitering in the vestibule?" My, what a relief it was to these callow boys when it became obvious that no one had been accused of this serious violation of protocol.

OUR FAMILY SACRIFICE FOR THE WAR

Thomas Eldon Helm was the youngest son of Ethel and Eldon Phillip Helm, Mother's parents, living at Oakland. He had been a daring, unafraid, rambunctious young man who helped Granddaddy and my father try to raise their crops. My grandfather always worked in the fields, trying to provide for eight children. One of the reasons parents had a lot of children was in hopes that they might have many strong boys who could help around the farm as free labor. My grandparents ended up having six daughters and two sons who hated farming. When Thomas Eldon received his draft notice for the U.S. Army at age twenty, he took his hoe to the house and prepared to go to war without reservations.

Pfc. Thomas Eldon Helm (1923–1957)
Oakland, Mississippi
American soldier

Uncle Thomas was sent to Camp Shelby in Mississippi for his basic training. He had only finished grammar school, and his civil occupation was listed as "general farmer." Standing 5 feet 8 inches tall, he weighed only 129 pounds. All his sisters and parents were grieving over his going off to war. Thomas, though, was always the one to calm them down and ease their worries.

Within a year, Thomas was on a ship bound for the Mediterranean Sea. After being in North Africa, his unit went to Sicily. From there, their mission was to establish a beachhead at Anzio on the western coast of Italy, to us a remote part of the world. The Germans had mined the sea around the area, and Thomas's ship exploded. Not having enough lifeboats for everyone, the soldiers took turns sitting in the boats and then in the water holding onto the sides. The Mediterranean has always been known as a tumultuous sea. By his account, the rain, winds, and waves sounded the wrath of the storm-tossed sea. The soldiers were in the water for many hours before they were finally rescued.

Uncle Thomas said it was unclear as to what should be done and where they should go once they landed. The Allies thought that the Germans would pull back to Cassino once they landed, but instead, the Germans counterattacked. Vicious fighting continued from January to April, when it appeared there was a stalemate. On May 11, the Allies launched another weighty offensive, which eventually smashed the Gustav line. This allowed the Anzio force to spread out and advance.

The death toll and the numbers of wounded and sick were devastating for both sides. Americans alone had 2,800 killed and 11,000 wounded as well as 4,500 prisoners, missing, and sick. The estimated German casualties were 5,500 killed, 17,500 wounded with 4,500 captured. Among the sick were about 1,000 soldiers who contracted tuberculosis. In that number was my uncle Thomas. Not only did he have to stay in the waters of the sea a long time, waiting to be rescued, but also once they landed on the Italian shore, it rained every day for weeks. They lived in cold, wet, moist conditions, where disease rapidly spread. Another year passed, and while boarding a ship home, he began hemorrhaging.

Eventually, he was brought to Fitzsimmons Hospital in Denver, Colorado. His condition was quite serious, so much so that the Red Cross sent Grandmother enough money to fly out to Denver to see Thomas. They evidently thought he was going to die. Granddaddy was sick with the flu and couldn't go. One of the daughters, Janie Florence, had gained experience in traveling outside our little corner of the world. She and Grandmother went to Memphis to get train tickets but discovered that they couldn't get them going west for another day. John L., her other son, accompanied them and was able to secure plane tickets. When Thomas finally saw his mother and sister from home, Route 1, Oakland, Mississippi, he gained new strength and purpose in living and survived his close encounter with the pale horse and his rider.

Grandmother would make several more trips to Denver, each time riding a train because she didn't develop any fondness for flying. Aunt Janie had developed experience and skills the other daughters didn't have, such as being able to drive a car, and the courage to learn how to cope in a complex outside world. She taught Grandmother how to get around and to take care of herself a long way from home. Grandmother found a room to rent in Denver and stayed with Thomas all the time she was allowed.

Uncle Thomas was so likable, even as a very sick patient, that he endeared himself to many of the medical personnel at Fitzsimmons. My mother had a box with many of the pictures of the other patients and nurses Thomas had met there during his stay. He often looked at these pictures and had stories to tell about each person. The entire medical staff full well understood the terrible toll this war was taking. Every day they saw the wounded and wracked bodies of those boys brought there from the battlefields of Europe. The spirit of unity, empathy, and goodwill took precedence over despair. The nurses' faithful love calmed the fears, reached down, and dried many a tear.

When Kennedy Veteran's Hospital opened in Memphis, Thomas Eldon was moved there to be closer to home. There, he was beloved by the hospital staff, so they recommended him to have his picture made with the mayor of Memphis and featured in the Memphis Commercial Appeal. On weekends, Uncle Thomas could always expect company from his family. We drove up to Holly Springs to Highway 78 and on to Memphis, where our mission was to bring comfort and cheer to a young veteran soldier who had only a small portion of one lung left with which to breathe following eleven operations. I could stand outside his window for a few minutes, and he talked with me about being a young boy and my future.

He was allowed to come to Coffeeville a few times to stay several weeks. My grandparents and everyone else available anticipated his every need. This was a major undertaking conducted primarily by strong women. My grandmother, the family matriarch, gave her instructions to everyone that there was not to be any fussing whatsoever. His time there would be enjoyable and memorable. The men were to take him to Scuna River some nights, build a big fire, cook some food, and run the trotlines. Thomas always missed these manly activities he remembered growing up. Uncles Evie and Noffy Langham were there with their tall tales. Some men took him squirrel hunting at the back of Elam church. Neighbors Hilliard Griffin and Herman Langham brought him fish and country ham.

In 1957, with Grandmother by his bedside, he breathed his last breath at Kennedy Veterans Hospital. His valiant endeavor was over, and the gathering clouds of sorrow overtook our emotions. We all knew that someday the silver cord would break. But we were never ready to lose such a bright spirit who always thought more of others than himself. Our resolve was to try to let our words be sweetly spoken like his were. He was buried next to his father and brother in the Coffeeville City Cemetery. He was thirty-four years old.

SOLDIERS WITHOUT UNIFORMS

Everyone doing any constructive work was made to feel they were helping the war effort. Farmers were reminded of their contribution on an inspirational page in the 1943 Sears, Roebuck and Co. catalog:

> You also serve—you who stand behind the plow, pledged to feed the Soldier, the Worker, the Ally, and, with God's help, all the hungry victims of this war! You also serve—you who farm, you who pray and sacrifice. You'll feed the World even if it means plowing by lantern light, and harvesting by hand— even children's hands—even if it means putting up the trucks and going back to covered wagons once again . . . The U.S. Department of Agriculture Urges you to: See your County USDA War Board. Meet your 1943 farm goals. Keep tractors working. Take good care of your machinery. Conserve your trucks. Turn in your scrap. Buy War Bonds. Farmers must

win the Battle of the Land with the machinery they already have.

Of course, we had a Sears and Roebuck catalog, and this message did make my farming grandparents feel good. Granddaddy was surprised to discover that others had plowed by lantern light just like he had done. I vaguely remember some older men regretting not being able to do more to help out. One fellow said that he wished they would take him because if nothing else, he could tote buckets of drinking water to the front lines for the boys. These were the ones who never expected to live on flowery beds of ease while others fought to win the prize or sailed through bloody seas.

In later years, one World War II veteran I knew told about how his outfit had whipped the Germans someplace in Italy when they were given word that the war was over. He said, "We were mad as hell because after what we had done to the Germans, we were ready to go and fight the Japs."

People didn't dare complain about rationing or other sacrifices. If you did, someone quickly reminded, "There's a war going on, you know!"

TRUE AMERICAN HEROES

Defining the true American military hero has been a quest for every generation since the American Revolution. None have improved upon the original words of Thomas Paine, author-soldier of the Revolution, who referred to "John Smith, the rent payer" as a greater man than the generals who got the glory. Later, George Lippard, in the 1840s, borrowed those thoughts from Paine. Ever since, the description has been slightly changed to fit the times. Author Gary Nash in *The Unknown American Revolution: The Unruly Birth of Democracy* (2005) quotes the lines from Lippard.

Here is one of the later versions: "In World War II, as well as the wars that went before and those that have come afterward, the true hero is the common soldier, the man who knows firsthand the constant terrors of war. So often, it is the general or the politician who receives all the glory of the battles. They are the ones revered so much in poetry and history, but not so much the common soldier, the rent payer in the trenches dodging bullets and blasts. Yes, the commanders and generals and presidents who are wise deserve their due, but so often, we forget the poor soldier who came from the heartland, from the fields, the factories, and the streets, whose skull bleaches in the sands. And when he dies, there are no piles of white marble over his last remains. Yet he was the one who suffered the most, endured the most, worked the most, and died the hardest."

But the most remarkable thing about these soldiers of World War II is that they didn't complain but rather saw what they did as their patriotic duty for their country and their families. Uncle Thomas became virtually a skeleton, breathing on one-fourth of one lung, but never did I hear one word of remorse or regret. On the contrary, in our family, he was the one, from his veteran's hospital bed, to be the source of encouragement for the family to the very day he died in 1957. The one who went through hell was the one who could heal the broken spirit and tell his loved ones not to be dismayed, whate'er betide.

Once, I heard him say that nearly all the soldiers had a Bible verse they memorized that they quoted to themselves every time they were in mortal danger or in a nighttime prayer. One of the verses he mentioned was taken from Isaiah 54:17 NASB: "No weapon that is formed against you shall prosper." Another one he recalled: "By this I know that Thou art pleased with me, because my enemy does not shout in triumph over me" (Psalm 41:11 NASB). And this one meant a lot to him: "The Lord is my rock and my fortress and my deliverer" (Psalm 18:2 NASB).

I found a large magazine-sized feature, published by a local newspaper, which showed pictures of Yalobusha County soldiers serving in the war—all white, which included my uncle Thomas. African American soldiers from Yalobusha County served also and thought that their service to the country might make a difference in their life chances once they returned home.

Johnnie Roland (1922-2018)
Coffeeville, Mississippi
"I fought for my country both overseas and
right here in the United States."

One such soldier was Johnnie Roland of Coffeeville, who entered the army at the age of twenty and fought in some of the hottest battles in Europe. Once, his unit was cut off during heavy fighting with the Germans. Everyone thought they would all surely be shot, but eventually, they were able to join up with Patton's Third Army. He mistakenly thought a grateful nation would embrace their efforts and afford them equal rights upon arriving home.

Birbon Brooks (1921-2016)
Oakland, Mississippi
"It has always made me feel real proud
to have helped liberate Paris."

Another was Birbon Brooks of Oakland, who served in England and France. He said that it had always made him feel extremely proud to have helped liberate Paris from the Germans. He said, "I put my hand on the Eiffel Tower to be able to tell my family." One of his war stories was about volunteering to take some food to the soldiers on the front lines. Once, right after he crossed a bridge, it was bombed. When there was a shortage of men, they would send him to fill in. On Christmas Eve night in 1944, he was in a train wreck going into the United Kingdom that killed many soldiers. After more troop movement, he said he was somewhere near the border of Russia when he boarded a ship on the North Sea to come home.

LEFT BEHIND

The days of mules and horses, breaking plows, and harrows gave way to new technologies during and after World War II. Those landowners with collateral could get the loans necessary to purchase new farm equipment such as tractors and plows. Consequently, there was an explosion of productivity and wealth among those who were already on third base. But the farming revolution bypassed us because we didn't have money with which to make money. Granddaddy rented a small farm and had small crops, a few cattle, a garden, and with that, we "got by." We could see the progress of some neighbors who owned good farming equipment, but we were left behind.

My grandfather and other farmers, some sharecroppers, were overheard talking about a new government program that subsidized farmers for not farming their land. These men were perplexed over such a policy, shaking their heads and wondering if the government knew what they were doing. These dirt farmers on rented ground sure couldn't understand it. They usually ended any discussion by reminding others that it didn't matter to them anyway since they were not landowners.

III

EVERY ROAD HAS A BEND

Curse God and die . . . though he slay me, I will hope
in him . . .
through all this Job did not blame God . . . have I not
wept for the one whose life is hard?
Was not my soul grieved for the needy?
–Job 2:9; 13:15; 1:22; 30:25 (NASB)

E{ARLIER, WHEN DAD} was bitten by that poisonous snake, he almost died. As kids, we like to think that our parents will live into old age. Hardly did I know that my daddy was about to go to the very brink of the river of death for the second time. I was six years old and in the first grade of school at Oakland in 1947 when the wind began to shift, and the road began to bend.

My dad felt so proud to be a farm manager, living in a fairly decent house on the main road with a farmhand to help him. For the first time, we could see the road running in front of our house and the cars that passed by. More than that, he could see the potential of his making a really good living off the hogs and cattle he was raising for himself. He talked about how his herd would increase and how he could sell them off from time to time. It seemed that finally, the wind was at his back, and the future was bright.

Then he began having serious stomach problems, and Old Dr. Donaldson sent him to Grenada, where there was a hospital. At this point, Dad was jaundiced with hollow eyes and little strength. He was diagnosed with, as I recall, infectious peritonitis. The stomach had been perforated and was causing a great amount of infection in his body.

While my mother stayed with Dad in the Grenada hospital, I was sent up to Uncle Clarence and Aunt Alice McAllister (Dad's sister), who lived only a mile or so up the road from us. They tried to reassure me that Dad was going to be all right and sent me to school every day. Mother came home once to get some clothes but didn't stay long.

Surgery was performed on my father that removed part of his stomach, but it didn't stop the infection. The hospital doctors didn't have strong enough antibiotics to treat the infection, which was now circulating throughout his body. My dad was dying. At the time, I didn't know how serious it was. Someone came and brought me to the hospital where he was a patient. Back then, they wouldn't let small kids go into hospitals for any reason. But my father insisted on being able to see and talk with me. They put a gown and facemask over me, and I remember how thin and weak he was. He told me that he thought that I had been a good boy and that he was proud of me. He wanted me to do well in school and try to make something of myself. Then he began to speak about getting well and coming home. And he told me what all we would do together when he got there. In the meantime, I would have to help Mother with all the chores to do around the house.

Only many years later did I realize that my dad was about to walk that lonesome valley. The thief in the night was lurking near. As I saw him in that hospital bed, the star began to dim that lately shone. My mother was discouraged, thinking all was lost. But God was about to move in an unexpected way.

The doctors told Dad about the infection and that they couldn't stop it. But they said they knew about a new antibiotic medication that had been discovered at Rutgers University in 1943. It was called streptomycin. During the war, with all the wounded soldiers, a desperate need developed for stronger antibiotics. They found out that the new drug was effective in treating tuberculosis earlier that year in 1947. The doctors thought they might be able to get some at their hospital. And by the grace of God, they were able to obtain the new drug. My father was one of the first civilians to be given streptomycin that might save his life. And it worked!

Maybe it was for me that he recovered. Maybe my mission was determined that day. Maybe God planned that I might grow up with the guidance and influence of my father and do something in life that was worthwhile.

By the time he was able to return home, Dad had been in the hospital over a month. No sooner had he begun to feel better and could get around some than the bad news started arriving in the form of hospital and doctor bills. And just like it has for so many others over the years, one major illness took everything we had. My father always, throughout his entire life, paid his debts in the name of pride and honor. He would "go savin'" if he had to, but just debts were paid. That meant he had to sell all his hogs and cows at once to come up with enough money to pay the bill. We were left with nothing more than a few pieces of furniture and a wood cookstove.

HARD CANDY CHRISTMAS

We held on a few more weeks through December. Somehow I knew not to ask for things for Christmas. Long before Dolly Parton sang about a "Hard Candy Christmas," I had one. We didn't even have a Christmas tree. The mood in the family was somber and bleak. The sky was o'ershadowed with blackness; no shelter or help was nigh. To this day, I remember the despair and sense of hopelessness. On Christmas morning, I didn't know what to expect. We hadn't talked about it much. In the rocking chair, there was a large stick of peppermint candy that had to be broken into pieces to eat. And there were some of my favorite candy bars. Mr. Cress had already decided that Dad was too weak and sickly to manage his beloved farm, so we would have to move away. Life's stormy billows rolled again. But somehow we pressed on. Our grit would bring us better days and a brighter future. No one talked about jumping off the Tallahatchie Bridge, but we did need someone to throw out a lifeline.

By this time, Grandmother and Granddaddy Helm had moved to the Old Leonard Place closer to Coffeeville on the Oakland–Coffeeville road. They offered to let us have the one room that was on the right side of the house. It had a chimney flue, which could be used for a wood cookstove. The dirt road up to the house crossed over what we all called a bad place, which carried us over a creek bed that usually had water running over it. We had to take many tree limbs and put them out over the shallow place to prevent getting stuck. When it rained, we had to leave whatever vehicle we were in next to the main road and walk to the house.

—◆○▶—

FARMING ON THE SHARE

While my dad was still recovering from surgery, neighbor Gaines Walker told him he could use some of his bottomland to raise some cotton on the share. There was nothing else Dad could do. Again, it seemed that the wind was blowing against us. Dad rounded up enough equipment, mostly by borrowing, to engage in a profession that, as far as I know, was never spoken of in any positive manner except by the landowners.

Sharecropping had a long history in the South, going back mostly to post–Civil War. The planter class had large plantations and a lot of farmland. At the same time, the freed slaves were ill-prepared for an independent life, being uneducated and impoverished. After the war, even the big landowners didn't have a lot of money for wages. So out of this condition arose the sharecropping system.

The sharecropping family only brought their own labor. Most everything else was needed from some other source. Equipment and seed were provided by the landowner, who also advanced a little credit to the families for basic living expenses. These items were usually purchased at a country store, often owned by the landlord. It was the owner who kept up with the accounts and selling the crop. In return, the workers, who were confined to serf-like conditions of poverty, received about half of what was made on the crops. By the time the debt was paid at the country store and other bills, the family discovered that they would have to start all over the next year. Various types of abuses abounded. The point was to create a situation where the sharecropping family had to continue the following year to simply have a place to live and at least some amount of income. This kind of arrangement was called peonage and was a system of perpetual indebtedness. Some called it unofficial slavery. Even though a common cliché was "Move to cotton country and get ahead," the response I frequently heard was "There is no way in hell one could 'get ahead' sharecropping."

The 1930s saw increased mechanization, which, along with a depressed economy, put millions out of work. Gradually, large landowners replaced their sharecropping tenants with tractors. One planter in the Mississippi Delta bought 22 tractors and 13 cultivators and then evicted 130 of his 160 sharecropping families. Farming on the share or living on rented farms was the setting into which I was introduced to the world.

In 1948, my parents became a part of that system of survival. In the fall, when picking time rolled around, everyone who could pitched in and helped—Grandmother, Joanne, Elizabeth, me, and Mother, all of us. The thing I remember the most was that the rows seemed like they were a mile long. Being seven years old and having to pick cotton was not my favorite afterschool activity.

Grandmother put a sweet potato in the ashes in the fireplace, and by the time I came home from school, all I had to do was to add the butter! How could I be so blessed to enjoy such a delicacy? After picking one row, what I liked to do most was running over to this spring branch running alongside the patch and jump in a water hole. The others went in with me at times. Then we heard Mother shouting for us to get out of that creek and start picking again. The most cotton I ever picked in an afternoon after school was thirteen pounds.

One scene is embedded in my memory of that time. Late in the afternoon, when the sun was setting in the west and shadows of the night began to appear, I could see my mother and father in the planting and growing stage still hoeing that cotton with just a glimmer of light long after everyone else had gone to the house. They hoed not only in the sunshine but also in the shadows. There had to be some occasional respite from the backbreaking work. At different times, they straightened up, stood there for a while, gazing off in the distance for a few moments. After a sigh and a deep breath, they went back to the task at hand. I didn't know then what their thoughts were. I was shielded from their despair. Now so many years later, I think I know. Was it really true that one's labor was never in vain?

Those thoughts make me appreciate so much the poem by the famous poet Edwin Markham in 1898, "The Man with the Hoe."

> Bowed by the weight of centuries he leans
> Upon his hoe and gazes on the ground,
> The emptiness of ages in his face,
> And on his back the burden of the world . . .
> How will it be with kingdoms and with kings—
> With those who shaped him to the thing he is—
> When this dumb Terror shall rise to judge the world.
> After the silence of the centuries?

◄O►

PUBLIC WORKING

In 1949, we moved to Water Valley, where Mother and Dad found public jobs, which were being rapidly created in a post–World War II economy. Many of the returning soldiers attended college for professional training on the GI Bill, thereby paving the way for their children to have a better life and future. Thus, a more stable working class and the development of the middle class were created. The principle of "working hard" and "playing by the rules" seemed to open other doors, at least for white people. Higher education was the means by which future success could be achieved. "We're working for our children" was the oft-heard comment.

Mother was hired by Rice Stix, a textile factory that moved South in search of cheap labor. My father looked for work every day in town. Our preacher told him about a job at Happy's Cleaners. Someone heard our despairing cry. He secured that job because he was willing to work for so little. Together, their paychecks paid the rent, bought groceries, and helped Dad buy an old car. But it was a start—two jobs, two incomes, food on the table, and hope. The bruised reed was not broken, and the smoldering wick was not snuffed out.

For Dad to keep his job, there had to be many people wanting their clothes dry-cleaned and pressed. Next door was J. T. Cox's Shoe Shop, a common service at this time. Both owners found out that they could get more clothes to clean and shoes to repair if they picked them up in surrounding communities and delivered them back. One of those pickup places was at Taylor Grocery between Water Valley and Oxford. Tom Cox, my boyhood friend, and his uncle Jesse went over there to pick up these clothes and shoes for more business. My dad cleaned and pressed the clothes, and J. T. repaired their shoes. Today Taylor Grocery is a famous restaurant serving fine catfish dinners.

We had a second-story, three-room apartment in the Old Redwine house on Clay Street. What I remember most was that off the back porch was a bathroom with a tub, commode, and sink. We weren't sure we deserved such accommodations. Morris Dalton and his wife lived on the first floor, and in the evening, Dad and Morris talked for hours, and I sat by them and listened. Two of mother's sisters also were hired by Rice Stix, and Elizabeth came up and lived with us for a while.

⸻◆⸻

PASS THE MOLASSES

My parents thought they could do better financially if they moved back to the Old Leonard House, where we formerly lived with my grandparents but who had now moved into the town of Coffeeville. They continued to drive to Water Valley every day to work. What I remember most was that the coming year would be a great financial struggle for us.

We lived in one room of that old house with a wood cookstove. The only heat source was from that stove. The old coal oil lamp provided some dim light in the room. Some nights we would finally arrive home in the old car to enter this cold room. The cold mornings and getting out of bed to dress were even worse. At least during the night, we could pile a lot of quilts and coats on top to keep warm. I was always glad to get to the school building so early because I could get warm from the steam heat.

So began our most difficult winter. Both my parents were public working in Water Valley and arrived home around dark. They worked hard for pathetic, subsistent wages by the hour. They were constantly reminded how lucky they were to have a job and that they should be satisfied with what they were making.

We didn't have enough money to buy many groceries. I don't know of anything worse for a child to experience than to know that there is not enough food. There is no shame or regret greater for a parent to know than that they are not adequately providing, even though they were working hard every day. No one who works hard all day should live in poverty!

There was never any quit in my parents. Sure, they struggled to ward off the depression and fatalism. But "tomorrow was another day" and another opportunity to search for an open door. We had always heard, "Plow your row all the way to the end." I'm convinced now that they were inspired by Scarlett's angry promise: "As God is my witness, I'll never be hungry again." As I recall, the sun never set as low again in our lives.

My uncle Bo and aunt Earline Fly had seven children, and they always planted a lot of sorghum and made up cans of molasses for the winter. They gave my parents several cans, knowing that we really did need them. It seemed in my memory that we had molasses to eat most every night for supper. Mother fixed molasses about every way she had ever heard. My favorite was biscuits, butter, and molasses and getting to sop the plate. Nothing could be wasted. Those cans of molasses got us through the worst winter I can remember. Later, I found out that one reason they were saving was because of something they wanted to buy for me.

THE WESTERN FLYER: THE CADILLAC OF BICYCLES

All the other kids my age already had a bicycle. They were not only a lot of fun to ride, but they were also status symbols. My parents, like so many other parents of the time, were working and saving because for them, it was really all about the children and their future.

There was a Western Auto store in Water Valley. One day my mother and I went into the store for some reason. I wandered over to the bicycle section just to look at these marvelous wheels of joy. Mother asked me if I saw one that I liked. I was reluctant to say because I didn't want her to feel that I expected them to buy me one under our present circumstances. There was one cream-colored with red trim that caught my eye. She said nothing else, so we left, and my memory of it quickly faded.

Several weeks passed. One afternoon, my parents brought this bike up the old road in front of the house tied to the back of the car. That was the nicest present I had ever received. To this day, I can see the big smile on my mother's face and the sense of pride in my father. I often wonder now in the long years past whether I thanked them enough.

—◀◯▶—

RUNNING THE GAUNTLET

The word around the Coffeeville Elementary School at the beginning of the fall term in 1951 was about the upcoming "belt line." Today some would call the ritual a form of hazing. But this was school-sponsored and overseen by the superintendent! All freshman boys had to run down the wide sidewalk in front of the school, one at a time, with senior boys lined up on each side. Using their leather belts, they hit the freshmen boys on their rear ends as they ran by. Therefore, it behooved the freshmen to run through the gauntlet as fast as they could. As a nine-year-old bystander, I didn't think it was all that amusing. The seniors seemed to enjoy the annual ritual. But the freshmen, for the most part, saw it as an opportunity to prove their toughness, even though it appeared that some were covering up tears. One unwritten rule was that the freshmen were never to show any hurt. By the time I became a freshman in high school, some authority figures somewhere eliminated this rite of initiation for safety reasons. Frankly, I didn't mind.

CIRCUMCISION: A MARKER OF SOCIAL CLASS

As I grew older, I learned some unusual things about socioeconomic class, how important some people regarded it, and the symbols by which they chose to measure it. I came along at a time when hospital births were increasing (though I had a log-house birth), and the doctors convinced parents of an extra service they could render on the helpless infant and for which they could charge. Parents were told how circumcision performed on the male child promoted cleanliness and how this procedure would be something well received and appreciated in later years. The rite of circumcision goes back to around 2400 BCE in the land of the pharaohs. In ancient Egypt, circumcisions were not done in infancy but done when the child passed from boyhood to manhood. After experiencing such pain and suffering, I'm sure they wondered, "Who in the devil made up such a requirement?" It had to be someone with a sadomasochistic personality.

The practice evolved throughout the Mediterranean countries, but the Greeks were not as impressed. The ritual was revived with the advent of doctor-attended births in more recent times. At first, only the wealthier parents could afford it and allowed the mutilation, but eventually, other parents approved of it so their child would be perceived as "normal." By 1960, around 80 percent of newborn males were circumcised at birth. So the mark became a status symbol for boys, which began to make some feel superior somehow.

During some low-level schoolyard discussion among nine-year-olds about this infrequent topic, I carefully avoided participating until I could tap into a more reliable information source: my mother.

I finally came out with it: "Mama, was I ever circumscrewed?"

"You must mean 'circumcised,' Little Buddy." (In later years, I think I preferred my own mispronunciation.)

"Well, most of the other boys were bragging about how they had it, and I didn't know. One boy said that he had never had it done to him, and the others made fun of him."

Mother explained, "When you were born out there on the Old Robinson Place, Old Dr. Donaldson said he preferred waiting a few days, but we never took you to his office to have it done."

After she said this, I just never commented in those schoolyard discussions lest I be abandoned to some third-world country if someone found out. My greatest fear in my young and innocent imagination was a thought that I might be called an uncircumcised pagan. Really, the answer to my supposed dilemma was an application of something Erma Bombeck once said: "The solution to ring around the collar is wash around the neck."

One of the most amusing things about Judaism was how much the Jews revered this practice in biblical times. Of all the 613 laws listed, when Christianity came, this was the one practice they wanted to retain. I think their attitude was "If I had to go through it, they should have to go through it too." I am so thankful that at the Jerusalem Conference in Acts 15, they concluded that God gave no such commandment.

My, my, my! I've often wondered why they were so proud of this physical mark. It didn't show! Can you imagine a religious argument with an idol-worshipping pagan, and one says, "Look here! I'm an orthodox, Israelite Jew, circumcised on the eighth day! You can't top that!" I'm glad that under Christianity, there were other more spiritually meaningful ways to demonstrate one's faith.

WHITE TRASH

When a town boy argued with a country boy on the schoolyard, the town kid might say, "You need to get on out there with all the other white trash." These were considered fighting words, and someone would say, "Who're you calling white trash?" Then the fight would be on. Again, this was yet another discussion to be taken up with my parents, who wanted to make sure that I nor any of our family had been called this. We knew we were not high class, but we were not white trash.

If we were ever referred to as white trash, I never knew it. But some countryfolk acquired that label when rumors developed about some poor family committing some impropriety. The term had racial overtones. The thought process went something like this: we know black people are trash, and some white people are no better, thus "white trash." Occasionally, the term was used loosely to refer to all poor white people. The term was more likely given to those who were poor and either lazy or engaged in some sin of the flesh. I've always been amused by the fact there is no corresponding term for the wealthy and their questionable lifestyles and behavior. Erskine Caldwell's *Tobacco Road* (1932) forever defined the term. This novel portrayed a destitute Georgia sharecropper family concerned about hunger, and sex, and feared they might fall below the social status of black families. Caldwell's descriptions were described as "sick" and "lurid."

◄◉►

EVER-PRESENT POCKETKNIFE

I don't remember exactly when it began, but I understood there was a time in every Southern boy's life when he began to carry a pocketknife. To not have a sharp one in your pocket was to invite unflattering evaluations of yourself as a young boy. You never knew when you might be challenged to a game of mumblety-peg. The first time I played it involved throwing the knife down as close to your shoes (or your bare feet if you were still going barefooted) as you could. If the other player threw his knife closer, the loser had to pull up his knife, or "peg," out of the ground with his teeth. There was an exception to the rules that said if the knife were to actually stick in your shoes (or feet), you were the automatic winner. Supposedly, this proved your obvious bravado and deserved all glory despite the foot pain being endured. The game was quite popular in the nineteenth century and in the first half of the twentieth century. A lot of social bonding took place between the combatants, and many a father grew closer to his son playing the game.

A variation involved flipping the knife away from your foot, and you had to stretch your foot out to that point. You kept on throwing it farther out and stretching even more. You always had to be able to pick the knife without any other part of your body hitting the ground. The point was to see who could stretch the farthest and still pick the knife. The consequence for the loser was still having to pull up the dirty peg with your teeth.

Uncle Clarence McAllister and I began to swap knives sight unseen. I had a stack of knives, and the point was to pick the worst one to hold hidden in your hand. When you challenged someone to a knife swap, they had to play regardless of the knife they had in their pocket. When I knew he was going to be around, I always went ahead and put the bad one in my pocket. The assumption was that at any given time, the other person had a knife in their pocket. I always seemed to get the nicer knives. In retrospect, I think Uncle Clarence was letting me win. He didn't mind; he just enjoyed seeing me get a good knife.

I think I figured out what my uncle was doing. Over the years, I had spent a lot of time with Uncle Clarence and Aunt Alice. They took me in when Daddy was sick in the hospital in Grenada for a month. Since they lived nearby, he stopped to spend time playing with my dog and me because I had no siblings out there in the country. He knew that a boy's pocketknife was a status symbol. He wanted me to have the finest-looking knife in school. He found a cream-colored one with pearl on each end and won it on a bet, swapping, or God knows how. Then he let me get it in our little swapping sight unseen game. I kept that knife for many years and enjoyed showing it off. It is only now in my latter years that, looking back, I realize what a nice and considerate thing he did for me. I wonder if he ever really knew what that knife meant to me and how grateful I was to him.

That habit of carrying a pocketknife, learned long ago, has stayed with me to this day. I've even lost a few at checkpoints where knives were not allowed. But the ever-present knife is there in my pocket, a symbol to remind me of something special that started when I was only a kid.

◄O►

VALUE OF GOOD NEIGHBORS

Then there was the afternoon when I forgot to stay at Morris Lambert's service station to wait for my parents driving home from work at Water Valley and got on the school bus. I thought about it before the bus got home, but I wasn't about to mention this to Mitchell Brooks, the bus driver, who hated any interruption to his schedule. I just went over to Mrs. Lillian Brown's house, across the road from where we lived, and told her what had happened. You see, we were a y'all people, neighbors one of another. "Why, Little Buddy, don't you worry about a thing. I'll take care of you until your mother and daddy get home."

She gave me something to eat and turned me loose to play with her watchful eye not far away. I looked constantly for the car to drive in across the road. It was a healthy thing for my character development that I truly empathized with my parents, knowing how frightened they would be when I was not at Morris Lambert's service station. I'll bet they were praying that I would be home when they arrived. But right then, I was in the care and keeping of a good neighbor.

When Mother and Dad drove up to our old house, Miss Lillian, as we called her, practiced her yelling across the bottom, telling them that I was over there and all right. Her careful caring for me was just the expected thing for a good neighbor to do.

Back then, it seemed, we had a lot of primary friends who were confiding, trusting, caring, personal, and helpful. These were the people you contacted at 3:00 a.m. if there was a crisis. Over time, with society becoming more diverse, complex, and demanding, most relationships became secondary, characterized by being impersonal, businesslike, and formal. We may know a lot of people, but they are mostly acquaintances, just taking care of business. Ideally, it was intended that the social institutions of the family and the church be primary groups with primary relationships.

◄O►

MAMA SANG A SONG

Whispering Bill Anderson recorded a song titled "Mama Sang a Song," in which he tells about early hardships and how his large family made it through those times. Mama's songs helped soften the pain and suffering of our little family. I can relate to that song because my mother did the same thing when I was a child. She knew how important it was to shield me from the harshness of our lives. Those songs soothed a troubled soul. Ludwig van Beethoven (1770–1827) was right when he said, "Music can change the world."

I think my mother inherited this talent from her father when she was small. My granddaddy, it was told, sang to all his children when they were small to comfort them in times of deprivation. In those early days, Granddaddy sang bass, Grandmother sang tenor, and everyone else would sing the melody. When they were sick, he would entertain them with the stories of Uncle Remus, stories passed down through the generations. The central figure was Brer Rabbit, who used his wits to survive in extreme circumstances. These stories have an African American origin during slavery times but may go all the way back to Africa. Granddaddy knew how to act out the story to the amusement of a sick child.

◄O►

COUNTRY PATHS AND UNPAVED ROADS

Back then, there were several paths leading away from the house. These paths took you to the garden, the barn, the outhouse, the chicken coop, the field, and the neighbors' houses. They were beaten down places to walk, sometimes with twists and turns. Mother always told me to stay on the path because if you did, you would eventually reach your destination. I could always make my way back to the house by following the path. Life is like that, isn't it? We benefit from those who have traveled this way before. Venturing off the path could lead to trouble. Today we don't have need for these paths, and few feel any nostalgia for them.

We even walked those paths at night. We seldom had a flashlight, so we used a lighted lantern or a torch from a pine knot on a stick of burning wood. When there was a full moon, you didn't need any additional light, and the paths were easy to follow. Even though I was warned to watch out for haints, I don't ever recall being bothered by one. I recall many a night visiting with the neighbors till bedtime and walking home on those paths through the woods and pastures. The paths led to friendship and good times at someone else's house.

Those paths always led back home. There is something magical and reassuring about that thought. We could always go back home in those days. For some of those rural folks, there was fear in going very far from home. "If I ever get on the other side of Toccopola, I don't know where I'm at." Never a word was spoken more truthfully than these: "Mid pleasures and palaces though we may roam, be it ever so humble, there's no place like home."

Most of the roads in my growing-up years were unpaved. Traveling was not quite so easy. Getting stuck in mudholes happened so frequently that we usually went prepared. Everyone knew what to do when we were stuck. The division of responsibility was clear as we all did our part to get us on the way. Usually, we still got to where we were going.

"Unpaved roads" can be a metaphor for the hardships along life's journey. Not having inherited land, a recognized pedigree, social credentials, wealth, or privilege meant that we had to achieve success the old-fashioned way—we had to work hard to earn it. At times, others requested to see our calling cards. Not having many simply delayed the process a little. Not being born with the proverbial silver spoon in our mouth meant we just had to look harder to find a way. The grit made us strong, but more than that, it gave us a sense of empathy and justice. We thought if you don't have these qualities, you are not much of a person.

It was empathy that caused us to reach back with a helping hand to those who came after us who needed a little guidance and a hand up. I've always thought that was a good thing instead of letting each fend for his or her self. Some people said, "Let them sink or swim." That philosophy never seemed quite humane or Christian to me.

FARM FACTS

For some, saying grace at meals is a ritual often without any real appreciation for the food. In my family, the appreciation was real. Though most of the time we had plenty of food, we also knew what work and effort it took for that food to be on the table. Appreciating it more caused us to enjoy our daily bread even greater. One explicit norm was that we were not to take more onto our plates than we could eat. If food was on the plate, we had to eat it. Wasting food was an egregious act of misbehavior. Knowing how hard they had worked the ground and how hot that old woodstove had gotten, I think my parents would have cried seeing food wasted.

When living off the land became a way of life, part of the coping mechanism was finding every little piece of enjoyment one could find. From watermelon seed spitting contests to the vegetable garden, we could find them. One bit of fun was making a whistle out of a squash stem. We learned first you had to be careful not to let those squash prickers cut you. You wanted to find a large, long, and firm stem. One that was limp would not make a good whistle. Once you found one, you cut it off close to the ground and then trim off the leaf and cut off about two inches from the small end. You had a long hollow tube that was wider at one end. You cut a slit in the narrow end about one inch in length. Then you put the wide end in your mouth and blew. It made a lot of noise that my grandmother didn't like to hear. She let us blow on it for a while until she grew tired of it. At least it was a fun diversion away from the usual work.

Some people observed a gully off the road and made a remark about soil erosion and how someone should do something about it. I must admit that some folks would throw their junk into nearby gullies. More respectable people didn't think highly of this practice and never did it. Rain resulted in land degradation, which was a great loss to farmers whose living was in the soil. But children like me had a different perspective.

For us, gullies were seen as great playgrounds for capricious play that could be sculpted into magical kingdoms. Alice, Dorothy, or Peter Pan had nothing that we didn't have in gullies of all places. When you lived out in the country, you had the means to create your own fantasies in a real, material place, often scorned by grown folks. Kids from the city just didn't know what they were missing. We learned to use what we had for our enjoyment and pleasure. Not many others thought highly about our stories of playing in the gully.

The imaginary scenes we could create were endless. Probably, the most common play activity was cowboys and Indians. The protrusions, crevices, and holes provided secure spots where we could hide and shoot our toy guns. We could recreate some of the scenes from the movie we saw at the Saturday morning matinee. The mixture of sand and clay allowed us to mold and shape different structures and objects, thus sharpening our imaginative skills. We could make cars, boats, wagons, barns, houses, and even Noah's ark. The soft dirt and slopes made it possible for us to run from the bank and slide down to the bottom of the gully. Of course, sand, clay, and mud were caked onto our clothes and bodies. We were colored orange from the top of our head to the toes of our feet. My mother did not allow me to enter the house until I had stripped off naked, washed off, and left the clothes and shoes in a pile outside the house. Actually, the best time of all was playing in gullies after a big rain. But I was only able to do this once or twice before my mother decided that was more mud on my clothes than she could tolerate.

Older adults said, "You boys are just making it worse for it to wash out even more." I never really believed them and tried not to let that deter me from my majestic creations.

In the absence of store-bought toys, we made our own and used nature to provide opportunities for joy and excitement. There were times when I felt sorry for town kids not having access to such pleasures. Though I'm sure they felt the same about our supposed deprivations out in the country.

We were constantly on the lookout for long grapevines that extended way up into the trees. If we found one over a creek or ditch, how much more joy awaited! To us, Tarzan and Jane never swung higher or had as much fun as we did.

Store-bought toys were only items we could dream about having someday. So we became ingenious by creating ways to make our own. We could take two clothespins, dismantle them, and make a toy gun that could actually shoot a piece of the pin when we pulled the "trigger." When there were several cousins visiting, we found Grandmother's basket of clothespins and make several of the "guns." "Bang, bang, bang!" We chased one another around the house shooting and then reloading. I can still hear Grandmother shouting to all of us that we had better be careful lest we shoot somebody's eyes out. She let us play till we played down, and then she made us all remake the guns into clothespins and put them back in her basket.

Other toys could be carved out of wood with a sharp knife like swords, pistols, and bows and arrows. We could make eye masks like the Lone Ranger and capes like Superman. I doubt any town kid had any more fun with the store-bought items than we did with our homemade toys.

When listening to Southerners talk about their childhood, watch for references to behind the barn. Sooner or later, you'll hear something that happened there. For some, it was one of those spots remembered because so many life-changing events took place there. It was there where we tried new experiences or engaged in something revealing about ourselves. It was one of the first places my mother looked when she couldn't find me. For boys like me, it was that secluded, private area where we could be alone in our thoughts. Maybe we just needed to get away from it all for a while. Or decide how we were going to face some mistake we had made such as being caught gazing at women's bloomers on the clothesline.

The one thing I remember out behind the barn perhaps better than others was the time I attempted to smoke a cigar I found. What was the pleasure that made men enjoy them so much? I had to know! I had to do it quickly, lest someone find me after smelling the smoke. Just as I smoked it in a hurry, I quickly got sick as a dog. A play buddy said my face turned white as a sheet. I wanted to vomit but couldn't. I remember thinking, "Lord, just let me recover, and I'll do better." Maybe this early bad experience was the reason I never took up smoking.

Everyone who has ever had a barn with a hayloft in their background has stories to tell (or maybe not) of the good times there. Again, we put our creativity to work, and out of the hay, we constructed hiding places, rooms, beds, and other stuff. Finding a hen's nest and some eggs or a cat that had her kittens up there were exciting discoveries to share with Mama. The occasional chicken snake didn't prevent us from going back again and again. The privacy of the hayloft provided us with our own make-believe world away from the watchful eyes of adults.

Another enjoyable thing was later on in the year when the garden was not producing much anymore, tomatoes could still be found. After getting in from school, I would take a salt shaker to the garden and find a ripe tomato and then sprinkle salt on it and eat it right there. Brief, momentary moments of pleasure like that made the day more durable.

Putting out a garden at the Old Leonard Place involved an elaborate division of labor in which all of us participated. Together, we could do a lot of work in a short period. We raised far more than the "three sisters of corn, beans, and squash," as the Cherokees referred to them. When the garden came in again, everybody had a job to do, from picking, gathering, shelling, shucking to hauling. The work at the house involved the porch and the hot kitchen, where the canning took place on the wood cookstove. Sometimes my grandmother put up over four hundred jars of vegetables and fruits for the winter. Usually, I couldn't get away to go elsewhere, though I would try. The activity I despised the most was shelling butterbeans.

I would shell for an hour with only a handful of beans in the pan to show. Shelling peas presented a great opportunity for the women with purple fingers to engage in pleasant conversation.

Looking back, I now appreciate so much more the various ways our matriarchs had to help cushion the blow of deprivation. Some of the older children began to perceive the class differences and wondered, *Why us?* The other kids had better clothing, better houses, more opportunities, and more money to spend. At other times, special hardships threw us backward. The men of the family especially wondered out loud why all this was happening to us. In the midst of working so hard, being honest, and striving, the end of the road showed nothing. It was the women who provided the buffer between us and complete despair. I can still hear my mother and grandmother sigh and say, "Well, I guess this is just our cross to bear. Everyone has setbacks, and this is ours right now." For most, those words seemed to help a little. Mainly, they didn't stew in their despair; they found time, places, and people for a little fun and pleasure.

STATEMENTS I NEVER HEARD

Maybe it was related to the socioeconomic class in which we lived. Our values and lifestyle never fit with these statements:

"I am so bored." I don't think we even knew what boredom was. There was always work to be done.

"It looks like we'll just have to stay in debt the rest of our lives." No, the number one economic goal in life was to get out of debt. No debt could be passed on to the family or church. This was perceived as a moral issue. Banks were not trusted by that generation. The day we were debt-free was cause for a huge celebration.

"We just don't have anything to share with those needy neighbors." No matter the limited resources you had, there was always something to share with those in need. We didn't even have to have a reason to give of our blessings. We considered it just simply being neighborly to give them something to carry home—a mess of greens, jar of preserves, something from the smokehouse, or a doily.

"Have you decided which college you are going to attend?" College, any kind of college, was out of reach. Parents had hopes for the younger children. You might hear something about maybe being able to go to Northwest Junior College for two years. While being able to attend some elite university was taken for granted by some families, we bragged about someone in our family graduating from high school.

"I think we should just let Hitler have his way in Europe. It's really none of our business." Everyone I recall talking about the war spoke of America's involvement as something we had to do, especially after Pearl Harbor. The war would involve sacrifices by everyone, and that generation understood that. We unified as a region and as a nation.

"Why, you can just wear your everyday clothes to church." No, we wore our best clothes, whatever that best was.

"I don't like to fish or hunt." Even the women liked to fish. Often, both these activities were out of necessity—putting food on the table.

"I don't understand all these people trusting God." We all had to trust and believe there was something higher than us, guiding and directing us who understood our failures and who would forgive. Otherwise, the way would grow dim and the shadows would o'ertake us.

LOSS OF INNOCENCE

Most every grown person can point to an event, a revelation, or some disappointment in a person that brought a new understanding about the world around him or her. At age ten, I thought that all people were honest, trustworthy, would do the right thing, and help out when needed. That was the way we were, and I thought that neighbors, friends, and family were like that too. I couldn't imagine people being deliberately cruel.

All that naive thinking was shattered one day when a neighbor, unprovoked, shot my dog, Big Puppy, in the hip. Now to understand the profound hurt in my heart over this incident, you have to know what my dog meant to me. I had no brothers or sisters and no neighbor children close enough with whom to romp and stomp. But that didn't matter much because Big Puppy and I had our own games and could go most anyplace we wanted. He was always waiting patiently for me to come out of the house to do something together. Wagging his tail and watching alertly, he figured out what we were going to do. Once he did, he knew what role he was to play. If we were going into the woods or down a trail, he knew to run ahead to make sure the way was safe. If he thought he heard something, he stopped just like a bird dog to show me where to watch out. There is nothing to compare to a dog's situational awareness. Their ears and nose cannot be fooled. I had seen him take a snake in his mouth and sling it so viciously that he killed it. Nothing would hurt me when he was along. He was indeed my best friend, my protector, my companion. He never wronged me. He was there to bring joy to whatever I chose to do.

One day I overheard some folks telling about buying their dog some dog food at a store. I was not aware that such a product was sold in stores and with the ingredients dogs love. This got me to thinking that maybe I could reward Big Puppy with such a treat since all he had ever known was leftover table scraps. When I inquired about this possibility with my mother, she said they might be able to purchase a can to my delight. I remember serving him myself, and Big Puppy ferociously gulped down that store-bought delicacy. Afterward, he came over to me, rubbing his head next to my legs. I knew he was telling me how grateful he was for the pleasure of such a once-in-a-lifetime moment.

What I learned most about Big Puppy was that even though my parents or others might be put out with me, he still liked me. Your dog will love you when no one else will. Your dog is the greatest example of unconditional love. An old Polish proverb says, "The greatest love is a mother's; then comes a dog's; then a sweetheart's." Mark Twain once said, "The dog is a gentleman; I hope to go to his heaven, not man's."

So that one afternoon, Big Puppy came up from the pasture howling and crippled on one back leg. He had been shot by a neighbor, a first-class hellion, who lived across the road. In fact, we heard the single rifle shot just a few minutes earlier, and we knew where it came from. He had been shot above his left rear leg. We had three vacant rooms in the old house, and we put Big Puppy down on a lot of papers while I pled for Mother and Daddy to make him well. We had no veterinarians in the area, and people with our limited resources just couldn't afford their services anyway.

My mind was swirling with questions. *Isn't the world always fair? How could a human being do this to my dog and to me?* Surely a man could not be so mean that he would shoot a little boy's dog. The reality that this had happened gradually began to sink in, and I was in a moral dilemma. What should I do? Turning the other cheek just didn't make sense to me. Finally, the justice side of my nature kicked in—the fighting side of me. Daddy had a single-shot rifle, and I knew where he kept the bullets. Even though I was only ten years old, I already knew how to shoot a gun. "An eye for an eye" sounded like the appropriate solution. At least it fit with my emotions at the moment.

While walking down the pasture to cross the road where the man lived, not far from the Burney house, Daddy caught up with me and said, "I'll go with you." I didn't know what his plans were, but mine were to shoot the man's own dog. He probably knew that, which explained why he took the bullet out. The man came out of his house when we walked up. When he saw the rifle, he became a little leery.

"Why did you shoot my dog?" I blurted out.

"Your dog was sucking eggs."

That was always a serious charge in rural areas, similar to accusing someone of being a horse thief in the Old West.

"My dog has never sucked eggs. We've had chickens and chicken coops and hen's nests all our lives, and he has never bothered the eggs."

My father confirmed that Big Puppy didn't suck eggs.

I could not hold my tongue seeing his belligerent attitude: "You had no reason to shoot my dog. How could a man call himself a man and shoot a kid's dog? How would you feel if I took this rifle and shot your dog for nothing? And you shot him in the hip. He'll never get well." Of course, I was crying when I said all this; just couldn't help it. I had come face-to-face with the coarse, shameful, gravel side of life.

Daddy knew I had gotten it all out of my system at that point, so he told me that we would just go back home. Neither one of us said anything until we reached the house. I spread some paper on the floor on the back room, once used as the kitchen when my grandparents lived there. Mother and Daddy examined Big Puppy's wound and quietly tried to explain to me that he was suffering, could not get well, and that it would be best to put him to sleep. Well, I knew what that meant, and I would have none of that. "No, we will put him down on this floor, feed him and give him water, and put medicine on his hip." I was hoping against hope that maybe, just maybe, he would get well.

My parents relented, and I frequently checked on his condition. Sometimes I stayed there and told the stories of our adventures together. He occasionally opened his eyes and blinked his eye like he remembered the experience. But in a few days, Big Puppy died. We buried him on the edge of the woods, near some big red oaks. Daddy said he would dig the hole, and when I learned that he was just going to put my dog down in that hole next to the cold dirt, I said, "No, we will build him a box." So my dad patiently helped me build a box with a bottom and some siding. We found some planks that could be used for a top. In the visions of my mind to this day, I can see where we buried him. I never wanted another dog after losing Big Puppy.

My world had changed. I never quite trusted other people like I had before. I often wondered what people's motives were. I was a little more protective and sometimes even suspicious. That man had destroyed my idealistic and trusting feelings. When people told me about Jesus's final judgment day, that never quite satisfied me. Why can't people do the right thing in the here and now?

For some kids growing up, their loss of innocence might be other traumatic events: child sexual, emotional, or physical abuse; the sudden loss of a parent; witnessing something awful that no child should ever see. I like what James Thurber, a twentieth-century humorist and satirist, wrote: "In his grief over the loss of a dog, a little boy stands for the first time on tiptoe, peering into the rueful morrow of manhood. After this most inconsolable of sorrows, there is nothing life can do to him that he will not be able somehow to bear."

After Big Puppy died, I was never again as carefree and comfortable in my feelings of security and trust. It was like passing from one chapter of life to another. I was a lot more serious about things. I knew that whatever the circumstance, I had to stand up and assume my place of responsibility. That didn't mean that it was always fun. And I missed Big Puppy standing there by my side and still do. That is why I, and many others, believe that "all dogs go to heaven." And when I cross the chilly waters of Jordan and dwell on a new earth, I'll see him running toward me, and we will have glorious times together again.

—◀○▶—

"ONE OF THESE DAYS, YOU ARE GOING TO CROSS THAT RIVER"

Where we lived, the front porch was a place of reflection and speaking from the heart. Late in the day, after the men cleaned up from the day's work, they stretched out on the porch to rest their weary backs. I joined them to see what words of wisdom I could pick up. There was usually a calm and yet serious demeanor coming from those with a distant look in their face. Looking down that long road in front of the house all the way to the main road, each one philosophized about the present and the future. Simple analogies were used by my grandfather to offer lessons about life and living: "You see that 'bad place' down there where the road crosses that spring branch? We're on this side, and you have to get across that 'bad place' one way or another to get to the main road that will take you places. That's the way it is in life. There's always some hard places and times to get over to get to the main highway."

Even at my young age, I could understand that. My granddaddy continued: "Sort of reminds me of that time in the Bible when Israel was wandering in the wilderness trying to get to the Promised Land. To get over there to all that milk and honey, they had to cross a river. That's not easy to do. I crossed the Tennessee River one time when it was iced over, taking my daddy back to Tennessee to bury him. We didn't know if we'd make it or not. We all have rivers to cross from time to time."

As though this didn't apply to them anymore in life, they turned to the younger ones to offer a vision: "One of these days, Little Buddy, you are going to cross that river, and you will get on the other side all the way to the main road, and you will go places." I understood that to mean that I was to engage in a glorious gallantry of bravery and chivalry while pursuing a noble course. That older generation often gave this kind of encouragement to the younger ones coming along. For some of them, there were just too many rivers to cross in their experience, too many dreams of their own that were lost to get where they wanted to be. But there was always hope for their descendants that they would someday get to that other side.

Words like those were like a song because they moved my soul. They still dwell in my heart, and I wonder if, after all these years, he would think that I ever really crossed that river. I like to think that he would.

IV

FAMILY TIES (1948–1950)

Tell your sons about it, And let your sons tell their sons,
And their sons to the next generation
—Joel 1:3 (NASB)

LIVING WITH MY maternal grandparents at the Old Leonard
Place on the Oakland–Coffeeville road with Joanne and Elizabeth
still at home were some of my happiest years. We had no electricity
and no indoor plumbing. We didn't mind because we had never had
those luxuries before. We drew our water from an old sulfur well.
To this day, I still refer to "drawing water" for a bath.

Granddaddy seemed to live in his own world, involved in his
daily tasks of tending to a few cattle, some mules, pigs, a garden, and
numerous other chores. He was a small man, only 5 feet 7 inches tall
and probably weighed no more than 130 pounds. Every morning he
was up at four thirty, and his work took him till dark. This circadian

clock, involving his getting up and going to bed at the same time, was something he evidently learned early in life, and it never left him. In the evening, he cleaned up on the back porch at the washstand, where the water bucket and dipper were. My grandmother required everyone to be clean before eating supper around the table that Granddad constructed for meals. Through the hard daily labors, it was truly amazing what my grandparents brought to the table in the form of homegrown vegetables, fruits, and meat from something caught, plucked, or skinned.

Small farming couples had several children in hopes that the boys would be able to help with the backbreaking work. Small farming couples had several children in hopes that the boys would be able to help with the backbreaking work. As it turned out, his two boys preferred moving on to other opportunities in life. That didn't mean that the six daughters were excused from farmwork. On the contrary, each one learned early there was manual labor to be performed, and they were expected to do their part. By the time we lived with them on the Old Leonard Place, only Elizabeth and Joanne remained at home. The other sisters—Stella Ruth, Maye Earline, and Janie Florence—had married and moved elsewhere.

Eldon Phillip Helm was born in Morgantown, Kentucky, in 1882 in the Little Muddy community. His Helm family had a long and accomplished history in the state. His great-grandfather, Lt. John Helm, fought in the Revolutionary War. His grandfather, Moses Helm, moved to Butler County, Kentucky, between Morgantown and Bowling Green. My grandfather had asthma and heard wrongly that moving South would help. While in Union City, Tennessee, he married Ora Allen, who died giving birth. Her body was placed on the dining table, where the doctor made the incision in an effort to save the baby, but it was too late. His wife's father, a wealthy landowner, begged my grandfather to marry the deceased's sister so he could inherit his plantation. After refusing to do so, he later explained, "She was uglier than homemade soup." Even though he never would own a piece of God's good earth, he never regretted not marrying the man's daughter.

His life was a testimony to the value of finding work, any work, to provide and survive. Once, he was a cook for the workers building a highway from Nashville to Knoxville. Later, he drove a Dray Wagon, which delivered supplies from store to store and town to town and also drove a horse-drawn hearse. We still benefit from the labor and sweat of these working-class people.

Eventually, he made his way to Coffeeville, Mississippi, where he met my grandmother, Ethel Langham. One of his favorite topics was discussing his recollections of living in Kentucky. He always wanted to return to visit the familiar places of his youth—the old home place, the Little Muddy Presbyterian Church, and the old school building where he attended—a wish that never came to pass.

Other than his rolled cigarettes, his only other open pleasure was listening to the Grand Ole Opry on Saturday night after he was able to secure a radio that ran off a wire and post. His favorite performer was Roy Acuff. He identified with him so much that when Acuff's father died, Granddaddy sent him a sympathy card. Now he didn't mail letters to just anyone. Acuff sent him a letter, thanking him for his thoughtfulness.

—◄○►—

THE AX MAN

Meals were cooked on a woodstove requiring a big pile of split wood and kindling near the kitchen. On a regular year-round basis,

Granddad hitched the mules to his wagon, and he and I went off down a field road to the woods, where there were numerous red oak trees. He would find a tall straight one to chop down. Once it was laid on the ground, he took his double crosscut saw and started trying to saw the tree into short logs that could be split with his ax. The saw waved back and forth on the other end, making it almost impossible to use. He asked me to "just hold it straight and I will do the rest." His ax was always sharp, and that fresh red oak easily split into stovewood. He kept Grandmother a good supply of the necessary fuel for her cooking year-round. Even in the heat of the day, he was always ready to bear the burden.

My grandfather possessed a remarkable skill in making wooden tools such as rolling pins, ax and hoe handles; wooden bowls; and most any other tool that was needed on the farm. Neighbors called on him frequently to make them one of his wooden gems. When he went to town on Saturday, he took his crafts that he had made to sell. It was a means by which to make a little extra money. All my life I knew him to be a skilled hewer of wood and drawer of water. Additionally, he made most of the furniture used by the family. When a daughter married, he made something the couple could use. Using planks with a burled finish, he constructed a kitchen table. One of the first things he had to do when they moved from one place to another was to build an outhouse or a chicken coop. What was more impressive to me was how he took care of his tools. He did not put up his hoe or shovel dirty. He hand-sharpened his tools, and no man living could beat him. This was a trait of that generation and also the veterans of World War II who carefully took care of their work tools. They were put up in their proper place and kept clean and oiled. That was all a part of that feeling of self-reliance and self-sufficiency for which they were known.

OUR HUNTING CODE

Much of our meat to eat was from animals and fowl we could clean, skin, cook, and eat—deer (usually shared with us by those who had a deer gun), quail (from those who had a shotgun), fish, squirrel, rabbits, raccoon, possum, chickens, and most parts of a hog. We only had a single-shot rifle, which limited the type of hunting we could do. My granddaddy taught all of us that you didn't shoot an animal and leave it wounded in the woods. No true Southern gentleman would do such a thing. If you shot them, and it wasn't fatal, you had to search to keep them from suffering.

One day he came to the house in a hurry after going rabbit hunting with his rifle. He had shot one, but it ran away, and he couldn't find it. Every one of us—Grandmother, Joanne, Elizabeth, my mother and father, and me—all had to go help him look until we found the rabbit.

◄〇►

GRANDDADDY'S LITTLE CHURCH SERVICE

Granddaddy seldom went to church with Grandmother and the two younger daughters. They would get all dressed up and all the while fuss at him for not going to church: "It is shameful that we have to go by ourselves. Don't you know that all the ladies in the community will be there with their husbands? And I'll have to make up some excuse for you again." Granddaddy did not argue; he just let them go on and on until they just gave up.

One Sunday, he knew that my mother and daddy were gone someplace and forgot, I suppose, that I was in the house. After the women all left, he went to the front room where Grandmother kept the family Bible on a table on top of a pretty doily. He took the old Bible, sat in the quietness of the house, and began to read:

> The Lord is my shepherd, I shall not want. He makes me lie down in green pastures; he leads me beside the still waters. He restores my soul.

He closed the Bible and gently placed it back in its usual place on the table. Then as men often did when they prayed, he knelt on one knee and began,

> Lord, I pray for my family, all those that have married and got children of their own, for John L. who has passed on, for Thomas who is suffering up there in the Veteran's Hospital in Memphis, for the young ones still at home. Lord, I pray that their life might be good and maybe not as hard as we've known it. Lord, may the crops be better next year so I can provide more for them. Keep us all in good health so we can enjoy your blessings. Amen.

Afterward, he sat in the old rocking chair near the fireplace for a while. Then I heard him sing this song in his aging, cracking voice:

> If I could hear my mother pray again, if I could hear her tender voice again! So happy I would be. It would mean so much to me. If I could hear my mother pray again.

I dared not let him know that I heard him. It would have embarrassed him because he didn't show his emotions before others.

Men just didn't do that in those days. I wondered about what I just saw. I decided that maybe Granddaddy's little church service might have been more spiritual than the one at the church building.

Sometimes the word would go forth to my Fly family cousins and all of us living with my grandparents that Granddad needed all the free hands he could get to help him hoe corn, cotton, or the garden. So Gerald, Harold, Jimmy, Joanne, Elizabeth, and I gathered, having brought our own hoe. We were all eager to get it over and done, but before we could begin, we had to listen to Granddaddy's lecture on the spiritual ramifications of our work. "Before we start, just remember: "You pray for potatoes behind a hoe handle. You can pray for your daily bread, but God is not going to hand you a loaf from heaven. Now let's get to work."

There were times when neighbors experienced some interruption from putting out their crop such as a death in the family, an illness, or something that prevented them from hoeing out the crop. In such times, my grandfather would get four or five of his girls together to help finish the neighbor's hoeing. On one occasion, a neighbor looked at the youngest of the girls and said, "I didn't know that you could hoe." Joanne replied, "Why, I sure can. I'm the best hoer of the bunch." While the other girls giggled, my granddaddy, who didn't often speak, turned to his daughter and said, "Well, you may be, but you need to find a different word."

◄○►

LESSONS FROM STRAY DOGS

We had two old stray hound dogs someone left unwanted on the road, and they found their way to our house. They were decrepit, scrawny, dirty, mangy, and had never been trained to hunt. Joanne and Elizabeth picked them up and threw them in a water hole in the spring branch, where they cleaned themselves by furiously shaking off the water. In the wintertime, they stayed mostly under the house next to the chimney to keep themselves warm. Around suppertime, they made their way to the side of the porch by the door into the kitchen. They patiently waited for the table scraps. They could bark and howl, but I'm sure they had never caught a rabbit, alive or otherwise, and were of little help until we fattened them up and gave them some attention.

When I think of those stray dogs we took in, I make the analogy that says our country consists primarily of stray dog immigrants. Unless we are Native American or were brought here in bondage, we descended from immigrants who came here, many of whom were unwanted by their own countrymen. These common working people from European countries experienced the indignities of Ellis Island, but seeing the Statue of Liberty for the first time gave them hope for a new and better life.

FALSE HOPE FROM MEDICAL PROFESSIONALS

When health problems developed and a doctor was required, we placed a lot of trust and faith in their knowledge and skills. Once, Elizabeth and Grandmother took Granddaddy to see a doctor in Coffeeville. They were really concerned about his condition and were eager to follow the doctor's advice. They came home stating that the doctor instructed them to give Granddaddy poached eggs for breakfast. All the adults in the house were gathered to see if anyone knew exactly what a poached egg was and how to fix it. For the next several days, it was the task of everyone to find out what it was so we could help Granddaddy get well. After about three days, Grandmother thought she could do it. She cracked the egg into a bowl and poured it into a pan of boiling water. "Now don't stir it," someone reminded. When the outside of the egg was white and the yoke was still creamy and soft, he was to eat it at that point. I remember he gagged, but all the girls insisted that he eat it because it was actually believed to be some sort of magical cure the doctor told them about. After about a week, Granddaddy said he would not eat them anymore. He said, "I can just eat a raw egg occasionally." We never understood that the reason for the advice had to do with decreasing the amount of grease in his diet, when hog lard was used in cooking most everything we ate.

My father had a similar experience when he was dying: The renowned doctor in Oxford told him that he should stop eating bananas. He explained that all of us whose lineage went back to Northern Europe (which was true of most white people of Anglo-Saxon origin) had inherited a physical makeup more receptive to the foods our ancestors ate. He reviewed the type of fish to eat such as crab, salmon, cod, etc. but not crappie, bass, or catfish. Black people were more adapted to eat corn and bananas, but white people should totally avoid them. My father, who loved bananas, refused them, sadly thinking this might save his life.

News of neighbors and family dying, the cemeteries, the funerals, the mourning all created the solemn awareness of that inevitable hour for each person. Funeral homes took advantage of the common fear that one might die and his or her family might not be able to pay the expenses. This circumstance would most certainly be an embarrassment upon the family. The thought, frequently expressed, was "You may need to get some burial insurance." When my mother passed away, we discovered that she had one of those policies that she had been faithfully paying on for over thirty years. Her benefit after thirty years was $600.

THE EASTER SEAL DILEMMA

We had to walk about a mile from the Old Leonard House to our mailbox on the gravel road. Once, a piece of mail put the whole family into moral anguish. The letter was from the Easter Seal Society and contained address labels and stamps with their logo. They wanted a contribution so they could help the little girls on crutches pictured on the stamp. The recipient could keep the labels and stamps to use for themselves. This caused grave concern for all of us and was discussed at length. The issue was whether we could keep the labels and not send in a contribution, which the family couldn't afford. It was finally decided that we had to send the labels back and apologize for not being able to give them money. We scrounged around and found enough for postage, and my mother wrote the letter of apology.

Looking back on this event, I do so with admiration for the profound sense of wanting to do the right thing in my family and yet anger against companies that tried to make money playing on people's natural sensitivities. The intent of sending the labels in the first place was obviously attempting to make people feel guilty for not sending them money. I guess this is why I wouldn't make it as a businessman because I could not engage in this type of exploitation.

GET THOSE CARDS IN THE MAIL

When there were formal weddings in the community, which was not often, a special obligation fell upon the married couple. The rule was understood by the older people who had sacrificed to purchase a nice gift for the newlyweds. The new couple only had a small time frame in which to send out the thank-you notes before uncomplimentary remarks were made. If five days passed without anyone receiving a card of thanks, an uneasy feeling began to set in. Normally, a week was considered a generous period for expressing formal thanks. If a week passed and still no card, unflattering comments emerged. "Well, I thought that surely we would have received a card by now. You'd think that they would be more grateful and write a note." Parents of the new couple were aware of the expectations and often encouraged them to be sure and get the thank-you notes in the mail. If two weeks to a month passed and still nothing received, the couple was usually regarded as thoughtless ingrates. Once this egregious act had been committed, it had irreparable harm because it took their friends and family a long time to forget the slight.

INVASION OF THE POLITICAL MISSIONARIES

Occasionally, someone "from money," usually a willing lieutenant in the cultural preservation army, would drive up the old dirt road to the house. Going house to house, this person carried copies of some book in their hand to give to us uninformed folk after explaining that they had come across this really good book telling us why we should be electing the right people to office. (The frequency of these political missionaries coming by was second only to those selling burial insurance.) Supposedly, these books would convince us unwashed masses to maintain Southern solidarity by voting for candidates that would unify us on the issues of race and welfare. Well, they didn't say it exactly that way.

One of the books was *Weep No More, My Lady* by W. E. Debnam, which was a Southerner's response to some words by former first lady Eleanor Roosevelt. Historians know that Mrs. Roosevelt was greatly concerned about the plight of people everywhere trying to overcome the devastation of the Great Depression. Once, she said that she saw "too much poverty and unhappiness" in the South. Mr. Debnam felt obligated to defend "our way of life" by denouncing the widowed Mrs. Roosevelt as a "hideous bucktoothed crone." How dare anyone depict life down South circa 1950 as anything other than an egalitarian paradise!

After reading books like these, we were told that the values of racial superiority, fear of the government and communists, and the need to oppose any form of racial integration should be reinforced.

I don't recall that we reacted toward these "gifts" with very much enthusiasm. Why, we didn't even have any progressive candidates running for office. To be successful (get elected), they all had to try to outdo the competition by promising outrageous things in their effort to preserve the status quo. So my folks were polite, took the book, quietly laid it aside, and went back to work.

We were culturally conditioned to believe that aristocrats (large business and landowners) controlled access to jobs and other scarce opportunities for a better life. Therefore, it was important for us to show deference. We feared missteps, which could doom a family to failure with significant economic consequences. So we showed our friendliness, agreed with their assessments of how fearful we should be, and bid them adieu.

WIDOWHOOD AND REMARRIAGE

Certain terms I heard growing up have simply passed away. In some cases, they are gone because they never were appropriate or were prejudicial or offensive. Really, I don't know how the term "grass widow" would be taken today. Most people would not know what it means. In fact, when it was used in those early days, there were different meanings attached. I'm not even sure if anyone ever knew exactly what it meant when it was used in my neck of the woods. If you were to look up the origin of the phrase, you would find it could possibly refer to an abandoned mistress, the mother of a child born out of wedlock, a woman whose husband was temporarily absent, or simply a woman who was divorced or separated from her husband. I always thought it referred to a widow who had been put "out to pasture." That is, her courtship and marriage days were over, so in solitude and in private pleasures, she would live out her days. On second thought, no doubt this term would be considered offensive if used in that context. So don't go around calling women a grass widow! You could get seriously hurt!

I often wondered where those unwritten rules came from about how long a person had to be in mourning after losing a spouse before they could go out or remarry. Nothing stirred the community gossips more than learning about a widow or widower dating too soon. If a person violated this old folkway, the gossips attempted to make it into a real community scandal. "Why, it is downright disrespectful to Sister Louise—God rest her soul—that Leroy would turn right around and remarry." And one of the daughters might say, "Papa, how could you possibly be going out with that woman? Mama has only been dead for seventeen years."

This very old societal rule was reinforced in the classic movie about the South during the Civil War, *Gone with the Wind*. Mammy reminds Scarlett that not enough time had elapsed between the death of her husband and her going out with Rhett Butler. Those unwritten social norms remained at some level of our consciousness.

THE NORM OF RECIPROCITY

My social observation was that most people followed the norm of reciprocity in their relationships with others. The term refers to returning good for good and ill for ill. If someone did a good deed toward you, you must return it in kind to keep the relationship balanced. "No, it's our time to have you over. We were over at your place last." Some people were very careful in their efforts to return an equal amount of hospitality and services. One woman said to her husband as they were leaving the home of the host family, "I just don't think that their eggplant casserole was equal to our fried chicken."

The norm was reflected in our language. "We've just got to have them over. They have been so nice to us." Someone made the astute statement that we knew more about giving than receiving. It was hard for us to receive without thinking that the giver wanted some favor in return. Sometimes we felt uncomfortable until we could repay.

CLEANLINESS IS NEXT TO GODLINESS

Growing up, I always thought that this phrase came directly from the Word of God. I think that was part of my "Sunday learning." Why, I even thought it was one of the Ten Commandments. "We may not have the finest clothes, but there is no excuse for not being clean." Once, I stayed overnight at my aunt's house, and my mother reminded, "And don't be peeing off the front porch." She had a rather expansive list of proper behaviors and ways to stay clean.

I still have a vision of my grandmother poking clothes in a black washpot over a fire in the backyard. I can see Joanne and my mother scrubbing clothes on the rub board. The clothes were all spread out on the clothesline. Andirons were on the hearth, ready to use even in the hot summertime. Those clothes smelled and felt so fresh and clean. I've erected a clothesline every place we have lived. I still prefer to wear clothes that are clothesline dried. They tell me today that I am supposed to prefer the new technology. My grandmother and mother who had to do all that backbreaking work might agree.

Another aspect of cleanliness was how our yard looked, which always had flowerbeds and sandstones and nothing to distract. My grandfather felt that the time called laying by meant time to clean off the ditch banks and roadways and to get rid of brush usually with a joe blade. While Uncle Thomas was home before the war, he made a little extra money by cleaning off ditch banks for neighbors.

Many people living out in our part of the county had only taken a bath in a creek (in the summertime) or used a number two washtub, about two feet in diameter. Before allowing the kids to take a creek bath, the parents made sure the water in the creek was running down stream. One must never use still water, which might be stagnated. These creek baths were by far the most fun, and having fun in the water took priority over actually getting clean. Towels, soap, and other clothes were brought from the house. Having different times to go to the creek always segregated the boys from the girls. Grandmother monitored this pretty closely. For the girls, there was always the ever-present possibility that some boys were hiding in the bushes, satisfying their voyeuristic curiosity.

A pan of water was heated on the woodstove and poured in the tubs already filled with well water, usually on the back porch. Sometimes the tub was placed out in the bright sun to warm it a little. I always felt sorry for the younger children because the rule was that they took their bath last after everyone else had used the water for God only knows what. By the time the smallest child got their chance, the water was dark and dirty. A saying evolved out of this circumstance: "Don't throw the baby out with the bathwater." In other words, don't throw out the good stuff with the bad stuff. Being an only child, I didn't have this problem.

My uncle Clarence and aunt Alice McAllister had the upscale bathtub (at least they thought so). Uncle Clarence bought an oval galvanized tub forty-two inches long. This meant that he could not only sit in it but could also comfortably get his legs in it. It didn't bother Uncle Clarence at all when some jealous person told him the tub was actually a water trough for horses.

Our first exposure to a shower bath came from a rather unlikely place. In the summertime and in the midst of a good rain, the drops fell from the roof at the eaves of the house. Where there was a valley in the roof, it poured down in gushes. We stripped down as much as allowed and stood ready with soap while the cool water showered down upon our bodies. Ah, the creative ways we found to experience a unique joy!

◀◯▶

SONGS OF THE BIRDS

Late in the afternoon while we were sitting on the front porch, in the distance came the mournful sound of the mourning dove. It was like the bird was crying boohoo and mourning because of the loss of someone. Automatically, upon hearing the sound, you felt down and sad. If there were any depressive issues going on in your life, this sound somehow exacerbated the sorrow. This was not the sound you wanted to hear when the heart was weary and the day was long.

We were startled one day when my grandfather, who seldom spoke his feelings, said, "I wish that damn bird would shut the hell up." You see, he started the day with only a certain allotment of words to speak for the entire day. If he had used up his allocation by 4:00 p.m., then he was nonverbal the rest of the day. We were speechless for a while, amazed that he had finally indicated how he felt about something. We were all on the porch, and my cousin Harold Fly, who always kidded Granddaddy, said, "Whoa, the old man has spoken! Okay, bird, did you hear that? Guess you'd better shut up now."

Other bird sounds were more positive or assertive, like the owl, mocking bird, whippoorwill, or bobwhite. But the depressing sound of the mourning dove stayed with my mother all her life. When it became necessary for her to live with us in her last years, I noticed that while sitting on the back porch, looking over an open area, she could hear the sound of that bird. Slowly, she would raise her head, looking in the far-off distance. I could see the sadness in her eyes. She was remembering times long ago when she wept amid the fires of pain.

Offsetting the sad feeling the mourning dove gave our family, right at dark, the bobwhite quail began to whistle, calling to the mate. The call continued as if the mate was bashful and didn't answer at once. The whistle went *bob, bobwhite! Poor bobwhite.* Someone would say, "Listen to that bobwhite calling for its mate." The imagery was much more positive and reassuring that life goes on, and we must too. Farmers knew how valuable these birds were for eating the injurious insects and the seeds of weeds. We scattered seeds on the snow for them in wintertime.

OUR DUCT TAPE

Today many feel they can't survive in life without keeping some duct tape around the house. We know of its many uses. Well, we had our own form of duct tape when I was growing up. Early on, it was called baling wire as in a thin form of wire used to bale hay. But it had numerous other uses. I've seen it used to repair a door about to fall down, a barbed wire fence, plows, parts on a car, chairs, furniture, mule gear, chicken wire fence, toys, bucket handles, shoe laces, coal oil lamps, and latch doors, just to name a few. In later years, baling twine sort of took the place of baling wire. Everyone I ever knew out on that Coffeeville–Oakland road always kept baling twine around. It became such a part of my life; I've never felt since that I could do without it. Wherever I've lived, I've had a big ball of it hanging on the utility room wall. To me, it has been so useful to have around that I've assumed than any man would appreciate having some, so I've given these big balls of twine for Christmas gifts. I'm amazed to discover that some men just don't get it and fail to appreciate such a thoughtful gift. Well, they are the loser here; I'll just keep on having it around and find myself often saying, "Oh, I've got some baling twine for that." That doesn't embarrass me in the least to have some to go along with my supply of duct tape.

"GOING TO THE HOUSE"

Certain expressions indicated the feeling that the house was a haven. After a long day's work, eventually, you could bet that someone would finally say, "I don't know about the rest of y'all, but I'm ready to go to the house."

> Where you going? I'm going to the house.
> Okay, if you can't do that right, just go on to the house.
> Here, take this to the house when you go.
> How far did you take it? Why, I took it all the way
> to the house!

Taking something to the house was a rewarding and commendable thing usually. "I'm sure glad you brought that to the house." In the evolution of that term many years later, a football coach turned it into a metaphor for scoring touchdowns and said to his running back, "Now when you get the ball, I want you to take it to the house!" The player knew exactly what was meant. That is why, for some guys with the football, the end zone is like a magnet; the closer they get there, the harder and more determined they run. Some players have a knack for getting the ball across the goal line, while others have to struggle. A lot of people don't know that the origin of that term goes back to farming days in the rural South. Today it is widely used in football jargon even in the NFL. We in the South originated that term, or at least we think we did.

In my senior year of high school in the 1950s, this expression was greatly popularized among the students: "I'm ready to go to the house." The intent for each student was to say it at the most inappropriate time, whereupon there would be much laughter. At our graduation exercise, when all the school dignitaries took their place on stage in front of the students, Bully Wells stood up and announced to the class that he was ready to go to the house. That incident won the award for saying it at the most embarrassing moment for the school.

THOSE MALODOROUS OUTHOUSE BLUES

I was ten years old when we moved into a house in town that had indoor plumbing. My parents were in their thirties before they were exposed to such luxury, and my grandparents were much older. In prior years, we were used to the common little house behind the house for our private business.

Ah, the legendary seats of comfort were arrived at by following the well-traveled dirt path out from the back porch. The proverbial Sears and Roebuck catalog was not just something to snicker about in later years; in its time, it was an ever-present and absolute necessity. One could see pictures of items for their wish list and be grateful that the paper was a lot smoother than the corncobs.

Outhouse stories have been told for centuries and will continue, I suppose, since you can order one today off the Internet. I learned to be cautious approaching one and, once inside, investigated every nook and cranny for snakes, spiders, lizards, and wasps. If people got on the bad side of the neighbors, mischievous boys turned their outhouse over, sometimes with the neighbor in it. When staying overnight with a family, it was wise to find out ahead of time which path led to the outhouse. One could easily get confused or even lost in the dark with paths leading to the old barn, to the chicken coop, to the well, to the spring, to the garden, or to the field.

Basically, an outhouse was just a wooden shack built over a hole in the ground with a wood seat constructed over it. The roofs were sloped with the lowest portion above the sitting area, leaving adequate headroom. Making sure there was an adequate outhouse was the first thing Granddaddy did when the family moved to a different place. Usually, he didn't have much lumber and building materials, though he always ended up with one that was adequate for normal use (meaning a one-seater and assuming, sometimes wrongly, that one size would fit all).

Like so many other things, outhouses could actually become a status symbol, indicating your social class. "I'll tell you one thing. They may not be very sociable, but they sure have a fine outhouse." In other words, there were some that were fancy and some not so fancy. The richer folks had plenty of good lumber and tin for the roof and could build a real commodious outhouse such as maybe having two holes, a larger hole for adults and a smaller hole for children and small ladies. The main symbol of a high-class outhouse was the symbol of a half-moon sawed out in the upper middle section of the door. Actually, it had the practical purpose of providing light from the outside and helping with ventilation. In the ones I remember, we could see outside through the cracks between the planks.

In some places, outhouses were called the backhouse. Once a county person came out to this man's house and said, "I'm here because you are late paying backhouse taxes."

The man responded, "Well, I don't know why. We haven't had a backhouse in five years."

Many a fine plan and thought have been shaped sitting there in deep contemplation. Thinking that, this is not an ivory palace, and

I'm not pavilioned in splendor, and at first, you might think your works in vain. But after a while, your soul is revived. Time spent there provided a rare opportunity to be alone in one's deliberations about life and responsibility. One did not expect this to take place in such an odorous atmosphere. So when that outhouse door opened into the sunlight like a breath of fresh air, it was a new invigorating moment to look up and be reminded that we have a charge to keep, and you carry on for another day.

MY SHELTER IN THE TIME OF STORM

During those proverbial "dark and stormy nights," we had a ritual led by Grandmother and my mother. Living in this three-generational extended family meant there was an elaborate delegation of responsibility for every event. Different family members were assigned responsibilities to handle during a storm coming over from the Southwest.

Grandmother was the one designated to start the process of preparing for safety. She made the decision based on what she saw from the porch when lightning brightened up the cloudy sky. She read the dense clouds, listened to the rolling thunder, and gauged the wind like reading tealeaves. The first question was always "Are all the children in?"

Mother had always been delegated work in the time of stormy weather to carry out Grandmother's instructions. Once it was felt we needed to prepare for the worst, everyone had to get out of bed and dress with several layers of clothes. Putting on your shoes was an absolute must, along with any headgear available. Mother explained that this would help one bounce around if we got caught up in the wind, and this might lessen the probability of getting seriously hurt. I never could imagine what "bouncing around" really meant. While Granddaddy went to the barn to check on his old mules, we gathered in a hallway until Grandmother decided we could go back to bed. One of the places we lived had a storm cellar dug out on the side of a bank near the house. Great fear came over me when we were admonished to get to the cellar, which absolutely was a worse and scarier place to be than in the actual storm. After going back to bed, we still had to keep on our three layers of clothes (in case we bounced around, I guess), but we could take off our shoes. Ah, when the clouds had passed over, I knew there would be sunshine in my soul the next day.

I never feared those storms when these two strong and brave women were in charge of our safety. No mama lion ever protected her pride any better. When other helpers fail and comforts flee, these women could perform wonder-working power.

ALL THE WOMEN WERE STRONG

Most all the women I remember during that time were strong, meaning that they knew how to defend themselves both verbally and physically. They feared neither clouds nor winter's chilly breeze. They possessed the physical skills and had broad enough language skills to make a forceful point, provided the occasion called for it. Or at least that was the case out where we lived. After we moved to town, there was more emphasis on being ladylike since the environment didn't call upon women to be as assertive or strong.

Mass media have always played a powerful role in our socialization: learning all the do's and don'ts of our culture. A song I remember on the radio that created a lot of amusement was "Pistol Packing Mama," written by Al Dexter and recorded by Tex Ritter and many others, including the Andrews Sisters.

> Lay that pistol down babe, lay that pistol down;
> Pistol packing Mama, lay that pistol down.

Everyone enjoyed listening to that song and teasing Grandmother about her gun skills. Women, I believe, learned that occasionally it was okay for them to hold their spouse in line when he wandered and strayed in sin's dark valley.

My grandmothers, Ethel Langham Helm and Beatrice Tribble (Mom Bea) Price, were strong in their abilities like other matriarchs of our area. Vital roles in the family and on the farm were filled with their willingness and love. At any moment in time, they could tell you what you should be doing. Their unique work was courageously accepted while faithfully standing by her man. It was not beneath the dignity of these rural women to put on their broad-brimmed sun hats, roll up their sleeves, and get their hands dirty in the fields and around the house. Some of their names are filed away in my memory bank: Lillian Brown, Vera Prichard, Edna Conner, Fannie Burney, and Shirley Walker. It would take a long time before these Southern matriarchs would be romanticized and set apart for their tenacity and grit.

These women were the forerunners of multitasking women of today. They knew how to wring off a chicken's neck; skin a squirrel, possum, raccoon; hitch a plow to a mule; shoot a rifle; make a garden and gather it; preserve enough food for the winter; get flowers to bloom; milk cows; wash clothes in a pot; draw water from a well; cook over a hot woodstove; keep a clean house; count her blessings at church; and take young children into her lap and console their worst fears and hurts. At night, she could sing a hymn to mellow the spirits of grizzled farmers and young children. These mighty matriarchs of Mississippi majored in being models of mettle and maturity. In my mind, the magnolia marvels were majestic memorials to the values of mercy, merriment, and magnanimity. Their memoir would never reveal moodiness, murmuring, moping, or mendacity. Rather, their manifold motivation in life mostly was to mend the mysterious misery often surrounding them and to merit the modest praise that too seldom came their way. There should be a monument someplace that honors their memory and myriad other women like them.

The gender expectations didn't leave out the men. We had to avoid any activity regarded as sissy stuff and portray the big wheel and sturdy oak image. Public displays of affection had to be kept to a minimum. One of the consequences of learning all about the manly expectations was that fathers and sons were not to show much affection for one another. When you saw your mother for the first time in a long time, you gave her a big hug. You shook hands with your father. After I went away to start my career and returned home for visits, I could tell that really, both of us wanted to do more than just shake hands. Finally, after seriously thinking about what all my father had gone through in his life and what he had done to help me along the way, I began to see how absolutely foolish those cultural norms were. The next time I saw him, I pulled him in close and gave him a hug, and he hugged me back. Thereafter, the barrier had been broken, and we always embraced afterward. That change was something I've never regretted.

SPECIAL ACTIVITIES IMPORTANT TO US

Visiting Cemeteries. "Why don't we go over to New Hope and visit the cemetery? It's been a long time since we were there." This was done on a fairly regular basis, visiting a variety of cemeteries in various parts of the county, walking amid the ancient and the honorable dead. We didn't just visit our family graves, but we looked around at others, especially the more recent burials. Often, other visitors were there, and the occasion quickly turned into a nice social event.

As a young boy, I admit I didn't get the thrill from the gathering that others experienced since all of us cousins were not allowed to run around and play games. Looking back, I now can see the value of families coming to the family gravesite. You stood in the silence and serenity of a sacred sanctuary amid the stones, some ancient in design with inscriptions that kept alive the memory of a life well lived. The social and spiritual benefit of this activity created respect, goodwill, and a sense of togetherness so often lacking in a more impersonal world.

Sunday Afternoon Visiting. This was the time to visit friends and family. It was easy to do because visitors were always welcome. Most often, it was the older family members who got the pleasure of company. But once the family matriarch and patriarch had passed away, this Sunday afternoon ritual became rarer and rarer. Back then, there was no need to call ahead; very few even had telephones. One could drive up to a house and just walk in. You were not asked what you wanted. No one wondered why you came. Often, there were other visitors there, sitting on the porch with other men or with women in the house. There always seemed to be a pie or cake in the kitchen of which you could take a slice. You just blended in with the rest of the folks. The occasion was more delightful because other cousins were there with whom you could play rough and tumble games. Sometimes people stopped to visit because of the inviting scene outside—a lineup of cars and trucks parked in the front driveway. I can hear it still, "Y'all don't rush off. Stay a little longer." More than once I heard it said, "We sure do need to get back to see the old folks while they are still alive."

Watching Traffic Go by from the Front Porch. We could identify the driver and the make and year of a traveler's vehicle. While going to town, you could see other families out on their porch doing the same thing. If someone drove by going fast, we wondered what was the matter. No stranger ever drove by without it being known by someone in the community. That was the earliest form of a Neighborhood Watch program.

The mailbox on the main gravel road was almost a mile from the house. Some people would leave enough money in the box to buy a stamp for a letter. But our family was afraid to do that, so usually, my mother, grandmother, or Elizabeth walked over to the road to wait for the postman and to give him the money in person. There was a strange reassurance that life was on schedule when we saw him drive by during the winter months.

Going to Funerals. Knowing the day and time of funerals was important information to share. One of the latent functions of these funerals that no one actually spelled out was for the social benefits. They were one of the few places where women could go publicly and dress up.

"Are you going to that Smith funeral?"

"Yes, I think I will. We've known them a long time, and I haven't seen their children in years, even though this will be my third funeral for the week."

I remember going only to end up staying outside because there wasn't room inside the church. "If you go, you better get there early because the building will fill up."

Most of those funerals were in church buildings, not funeral homes. This was before funeral homes decided to make services convenient for themselves. The church building funerals, though, were more personal, family friendly, and not so orchestrated.

Comments before, during, and after funerals were so amusing that they have stayed with me through the years:

> Well, John Lee (the deceased) had a big turnout.
> Yeah, I wonder what kind of a turnout I'll have. Well, you know it is a lot better when it's on Sunday.
> Papa would have really enjoyed this.
> You'd think Emma Sue would know how to dress for a funeral.
> I thought the preacher did a nice job. He said everything he could say about the deceased.
> After I heard what all the preacher said about Uncle Ned, I wasn't sure I was at the right funeral.
> Well, I enjoyed Trula Beth's sweet potato pie after the funeral better than anything.
> Did you hear about the time the preacher stepped off in the grave?
> I counted twenty-seven wreaths of flowers.
> Why, that preacher says the same thing at every funeral. He just changes the name.
> It's sure nice to see you but not under these circumstances. We need to get together more often.

Seems like the only time I ever see you all is at a funeral.

They really put Verty Lou away nice, don't you think?

Wife: I thought Erlon Ray looked so natural.

Husband: What is so natural-looking about a dead corpse?

OUR FAMILY READER

I've always felt nostalgic about those painting scenes depicted from yesteryear showing an old farmhouse, lighted by a coal oil lamp, and all the family gathered around listening to one reading a classic book. The children are spread out on the floor, where maybe some have gone to sleep. Others are in chairs or on a bed, absorbing and visualizing the story being read by the most capable reader in the family as she sat near the lamp and had a good fire going in the fireplace. Ah, such warmth and interest in the great literary works.

There is a scene in the movie *Gone with the Wind* when the men have gone on a late night vigilante raid of Shanty Town where Scarlett had almost been ambushed but was saved by her father's ex-foreman, Big Sam. Scarlett, Melanie, and some other worried women gathered to wait on their chivalrous men seeking to protect Southern womanhood. To allay their fears, Melanie began to read out loud from Charles Dickens's *David Copperfield* until some of the men returned from the daring raid in which Scarlett's husband, Frank Kennedy, was killed.

Our family reading sessions were not nearly as dramatic but accomplished some of the same purposes. My mother was the designated reader who had also been grandmother's surrogate (as the eldest child) in efforts to keep all the other children in line. Mother helped all of them with their school lessons and was the best reader in the family. I remember some of those nights quite well. Poor ol' Granddaddy didn't stay up that late, but the rest made themselves comfortable to listen to Mother read whatever was available. She borrowed a copy of Margaret Mitchell's *Gone with the Wind* and read it from beginning to end over a period of weeks. At my age, I never understood the love triangle portion. Sometimes she read one of George Schmitz's coon hunting stories from the Coffeeville newspaper or maybe a story out of our schoolbooks. Other times, there was only the Bible from which to read the twenty-third psalm or the beatitudes.

FISHING TALES

Catching, cleaning, cooking, and eating fish we caught, all in one day, was an important meat source for us. Catfish from Scuna River, caught either by grabbling, setting hooks, or cane fishing, was always a nice treat. Mrs. Vera Pritchard lived only about a mile from our house, and she and her husband had a fishing pond at the back of their house. Vera let me come over and use a rod and reel that my daddy had. Gaines Walker let us come over to his pond and fish for bream. The spring branches around the house always had some small perch to catch. Joanne, Elizabeth, and I sometimes took a straight pin and bent it into a hook, found some line, and believe it or not, we caught fish even with a tree limb or small branch as our pole. Using cane poles was a step-up from our level of fishing. Grandmother had a certain spot off the back porch where she threw the dishwater. We discovered that was the place to dig for worms. Nothing creates more good memories than going fishing.

My mother and Vera Prichard went down on Cypress Creek below Coffeeville one day and caught a dishpan full of brim. When I came in from school, I overheard them say they wanted to go back the next day. Well, I loved fishing a lot more than I did school. The next morning, I conveniently didn't get to the road in time to catch the school bus. So I walked slowly back to the house, claiming to my mother that I just barely missed the bus. Up in the morning, nothing had happened. There was no movement in the direction of going fishing. Finally, it got the best of me, and I asked about it. "I thought you and Ms. Pritchard were going back fishing today on Cypress Creek." That was enough to reveal what had actually happened with my school bus story. Because of some serious reprimand, that was the last time I pulled that stunt.

When fishing with my mother, you were in for quite an experience. She was always a little dramatic and nervous. The main feature of her apparel was a huge broad-brim sun hat. She wanted a long cane pole and a bobber about the size of a small basketball. A small fish had no chance of ever pulling that thing under the water. When she hooked a big one, everyone in the countryside knew it. She pulled so quickly and so hard that sometimes she pulled the hook clean through that fish's mouth. If it stayed on, she landed that fish so hard on the ground way behind her it would almost kill the fish.

My grandmother was somewhat the same with one exception. As long as I can remember, she dipped snuff. Sometimes she took her Garrett Snuff jar with her so she could keep some between her teeth and jaws at all times. Before she threw her line out into the water, she would spit some of that snuff on whatever bait she was using. Some of us wondered whether that helped. She was convinced that it did help, and I must admit, she always caught her share of fish.

Through the years, I've come to really appreciate the influence my parents had on my own fishing pleasures. To this day, I still remember our favorite places in the backwaters of Grenada, Enid, and Sardis reservoirs. There was Billy's Creek, Long Branch, Toby Tubby Creek, and Hurricane Landing. There are not many more meaningful moments for a son than when he is on the fish bank with his parents, sharing the bait.

God knew that fishermen would wonder about heaven and being able to fish. So in Revelation 22:1-2 (NASB), heaven is described as having a river flowing through this "new earth" with fruit trees on each side. I'm betting that there will be fish in that river. Since the water will be "clear as crystal," I might have to switch to trout fishing. Can you imagine anything more idyllic than sitting in the shade of fruit trees, fishing forever? Knowing me, I might try to convince the Lord to put some crappie in that river. Come to think about it, Jesus helped the disciples catch 153 fish one time John 21:11 (NASB). (They must not have had a limit in those days.) I rather think that the good Lord looks kindly on those who love to fish.

Every place I've ever lived, I've found a place to fish. In fact, I believe we would all be happier and healthier if we fished more. A criminal will seldom claim to be an avid fisherman. One of the best things a parent can do is to teach their children the skills and joys of fishing. Some years ago, I ran across a poem by Edgar Guest that expresses my feelings about fishing: "A feller isn't thinkin' mean, Out fishin'."

Variations of the Fisherman's Prayer have circulated for years. I believe this one is the oldest by Pearl Nodge:

Dear Father, give me the strength to fish for many
years to come.
Help me to use good sportsmanship, and also to have
fun.
And when the final cast is made, and the fishing pole
laid down,
I'll say, "thank you" with a smile, Dear God, and
never with a frown.
Please catch me in your landing net to take my final
sleep;
And then, oh God may I be judged as big enough to
keep.

Over the years while growing up, I distinctly recall various
fishing types. There was the style king/queen, people who placed
more emphasis on their appearance than on actually fishing. For
others, fishing was fundamentally a social event in which they
could enjoy each other's company and fellowship. Others couldn't
understand or appreciate the Southern tradition of carrying Vienna
sausage, sardines, and crackers as our bon appétit (though I don't
think we used that French word back then). "Why on earth would
you want to eat food like that on an otherwise pleasant afternoon?"
This food might not have been desirable in other settings, but it was
exotic cuisine on the creek bank. Finally, there were the serious
fishermen who saw the occasion as hard work.

It was there on the creek bank that we created another life
for ourselves, away from some of the more unpleasant aspects of
living. Some of life's greatest lessons were learned there. It was where
relationships were solidified and hearts won and where we really
came to know each other at a deeper level.

GRABBLING

One of my great uncles, Evie Langham, was well-known for grabbling (feeling or searching with the hand) in Scuna River for large catfish. Evie was world class in grabbling, even though the effort was fraught with much danger. Those who had the skill enjoyed the thrill and excitement, while others thought this method of catching fish was absolute craziness, and anyone who would do this was out of their mind. This process was also called grappling, hogging, stumping, noodling, or simply handfishing.

Evie and his brother named Noffy Langham waded into the dark, murky waters of the river and searched for catfish underneath banks, in hollow logs, under brush, under rocks, and even in grassy areas. They grabbed them by their mouths or gills with their bare hands and pulled them out onto the bank. These fish were taken home, skinned, and fried to eat. The art form grew out of the necessity for finding a less expensive way to feed the family.

We were always on the lookout for an old hollow log or stump or any other hollow apparatus that Uncle Evie could use. He would submerge these at certain spots in the river, either marking where they were or just carefully remembering the place to prevent others from stealing his fish. Later, usually during spawning season, he went to his favorite locations in the river and grabbled for catfish. He taught others how to do it, and some people wanted to go with him just out of curiosity.

The dangers were obvious. One could step off into a deep hole in the river or run into a snapping turtle. But the worst fear was confronting a poisonous snake lurking under the water or under the dark bank. Once, I asked him about grabbling, and the only thing he said was you needed quick hands. Well, that was not the only thing needed but the only thing he mentioned.

"Okay, how do you know when it's a catfish and not something else when you reach under that bank?" I asked.

"Oh, there is a simple rule to follow: if the skin is slick and slimy, it is a catfish, but if it is rough, it is a snake," he explained.

"So if it's a snake, what do you do?" He responded, "Do you remember when I said you have to have quick hands? Well, that is when you better get your hands out of there!"

I told him that I heard that one time, he grabbed a snake and slung it down the river. He said it was true, and he did it because he was mad, but he wouldn't recommend that just anybody try that.

Some people used gloves, but my uncles worked barehanded. It appeared they took pride in their bravado doing it this way. Why, it was downright wimpish for them to do it any other way. Both of them rolled up their sleeves and began to show me the scars on their hands and arms where some big catfish had bitten down, tearing the flesh and leaving their mark. What was amazing to me was that they regarded these scars as marks of distinction. It was a status symbol among fellow grabblers. Each scar had its own special grabbling story. Remember that scene in the movie *Jaws* when Sam Quint (Robert Shaw) and Dr. Matt Hooper (Richard Dreyfuss) were showing each other their scars from shark bites? And bragging about them? I couldn't help but remember Uncle Evie and Uncle Noffy. Our Scuna River didn't have any sharks, but it sure had big catfish with sharp teeth.

Most men never involved women in their grabbling adventure unless they had them build a fire and cook something to eat by the riverside. But they probably didn't know about Grandmother's two youngest daughters, Joanne and Elizabeth. My two aunts thought they could do anything a man could do and even do it better, so they organized their own grabbling crew. One of their male friends had put a hollow log in Scuna River at an undisclosed location. One Sunday afternoon, they decided to check it out. Their friend went to one end of the log and Elizabeth to the other end, which was also hollow. They swished the water, trying to run the catfish out, but they wouldn't move. Elizabeth said she had an idea: she would put her long leg down that hollow log and run them out on the other end. To do this, a woman couldn't be all that concerned about modesty at the moment. Two small cats came out on the man's end, but the big one decided to come out Elizabeth's end by swimming next to her leg. That was more than she could take feeling that slimy thing coming up her leg. She started yelling, afraid that thing would fin her pretty leg. "Somebody catch this thing! Get ahold of it!" She wasn't about it to grab it herself. A certain amount of female dignity did offer some limits to her behavior.

"OL' BOYS WHO DIDN'T HAVE A LICK OF SENSE"

When Uncle Noffy and Uncle Evie came around, I wanted to listen in on their tales, some of which were regarded as adult humor. I managed to get within earshot anyway. They usually began their story by referring to "an ol' boy down there who didn't have a lick of sense." One of their stories can only be understood and appreciated by those who know about a Southern delicacy involving crumbling cornbread in a glass of sweet milk or buttermilk.

This ol' boy (who didn't have a lick of sense) went to the doctor, who told him,

Ah, man, you've got some real serious stomach problems. In fact, your stomach is so sensitive there is not much you can tolerate until we get this thing figured out. What I would suggest is to find a woman who has given birth and is trying to wean the child. Often, she will continue to produce lots of milk, more than she needs. Ask her if she will put you some in a jar, and you go by and get it and drink it. That's about the easiest thing you can drink that will stay on your stomach.

Luckily, he found such a woman who was willing to give him her extra milk. "Well, I tell you I'm tired of caking and leaking, so I'll just pump you all you want." For weeks, he picked up his jar of her milk, which was working just fine. One day while getting his milk, the woman said, "Why don't you come on in? I've got something else that will go real good with that milk."

His eyes started getting bigger and bigger with a grin gradually spreading across his face. Finally, he said, "Don't tell me; you've got some cornbread in the kitchen!"

SITTIN' UP WITH THE DEAD

Every time a group of the older men came together to talk or to just rest up, you could bet that eventually, one of the men would have a sittin' up with the dead story.

Later in my life, I came to understand the folkway ritual better. I noticed that when the word spread in the community that a neighbor had gone on to Beulah Land, an automatic and elaborate system of preparation and responsibility was set into motion. It included an organizational structure involving the whole community. This sense of community transcended both religion and social class. You did not refuse to participate in whatever way you were needed. Refusing would show disrespect and could ruin your reputation.

One person was appointed to be in charge of arranging the lineup of men who made sure that the body was never left alone once the person was laid out either at the house or later on in funeral homes. The types chosen for the late night or early morning vigils could be of lesser character than those who were given primetime spots. The time slots were divided according to the number of willing watchers. Occasionally, some of the men consented to stay up from midnight to dawn as long as there was a big pot of coffee available and several men were involved. The implicit rule was that there had to be at least two men to sit, never only one. If a time slot ended up with only one person, a substitute list was readily available to fill the vacant spot.

The history of this tradition and the rationale for this cultural practice of sitting up with the dead was shrouded in mystery. One theory was that if the body was left alone, evil spirits might come and bear it away. Another thought was that in the early days before the widespread use of funeral homes and the body was kept at the house and before window screens, there was the fear that varmints might come in a raised window and mutilate the body. The status of using funeral homes came into being, but many families continued the tradition out of respect for the family and the deceased.

In the heyday of "sittin' up with the dead," the embellished tales abounded. Here is one that I remembered: Cloyce and Idotha Hagan's older brother, Tulan, who lived way off, died and was brought back to Mississippi and to their house for the visitation and the burial. Word spread throughout the community that the family had to prepare a lot of things to get everything ready for these upcoming events. Neighbors began to volunteer their hospitality to make sure everything was decent and respectful, even though the deceased was not from around there. The organizing structure mentioned above was set in order.

Uncle Tulan was laid out in his Sunday suit and tie, and the casket was carefully positioned in the front room. Some flowers had arrived in vases and baskets, really pretty flowers since it was late spring, and everything was in bloom. The couch and chairs were placed around the room for the guests who came to pay their respects. The Hagans were quite pleased at how well the scene looked.

Now one of the reasons they thought about the look of the room was because of the visit from the lady writing up the community news for the local weekly newspaper, Miss Marybelle Pennington. She was thorough in gathering material for her most popular column by attending homecomings, barbecues, fish fries, revivals, weddings, cemetery decorations, funerals, flatbed trailer shows, and any other pig-trot events. She even talked about the weather, the crops, the newborns, the sermon on Sunday, the community prayer list, the vegetable gardens, and how she had been feeling lately. This was in addition to reporting on who visited whom during the week. Being mentioned by her in some flattering way in the paper was quite satisfying because it enhanced your social standing among your friends.

Cloyce and Idotha knew that she planned on visiting their house that evening to pay respects to Uncle Tulan, and hopefully, she would observe how nice he had been displayed with many in the community having come to comfort the family and express condolences. That particular evening, Miss Marybelle had visited several other places and was unsure if she could get over to the Hagans'. On this occasion, the organizer of the willing watchers didn't have anyone slated for the 10:00 p.m. to 1:00 a.m. slot. The only two left were two young boys named Amzie and Mookie; neither of whom had a lick of sense. The organizer thought, *Well, since it's late, there won't be anyone else there, so maybe this will work out without any disruptions of any kind.*

The two boys were none too excited about their assigned duty, and besides, they didn't like the Hagans because every time they walked past their house, Mr. Cloyce had them help him do something on the place. The Hagans weren't too thrilled to have them there either but let them come on anyway. This time Idotha gave them a seat over in the corner and brought in a tub of water with potatoes to peel, a bucket for the peelings, and a clean pan. She had to make up a lot of potato salad for everyone the next day, so she put the boys to work while they sat up with Uncle Tulan. The Hagans had given up on Miss Marybelle coming by, so they went to another part of the house.

The two boys didn't say a word; they just went to work on those potatoes. After a while, Mookie went over to see Uncle Tulan all laid out there with a slight smile on his face and his hands crossed over his stomach. He went back to the pan with the peeled potatoes, picked one out, and took a big bite out of it. Then he proceeded to place the potato with the plug bit out on the inside of Uncle Tulan's hands. Both Amzie and Mookie were looking at Uncle Tulan and laughing when they heard someone come up on the porch. They quickly went back to peeling the rest of the potatoes.

Lo and behold, it was Miss Marybelle Pennington who had finally arrived to make her usual inspection. Cloyce and Idotha welcomed her at the door and graciously invited her into the front room to see Uncle Tulan.

"Well, I sure wanted to come by and pay my respects to the grieving family of Uncle Tulan. I remember when he was just a small boy and when he left us to go off to work. It is so nice of you to receive his corpse and place him to rest here in Mississippi soil."

Idotha said, "We want you to go right in and see Tulan. They did such a nice job on him, and he looks so natural."

Cloyce and Idotha anxiously stood at the door while Miss Marybelle slowly walked toward the casket, noticing the floral arrangements, as she drew closer, calculating the cost and number as she walked. She first looked at his head and the smiling face, and then down to the suit and tie, and then to his folded hands, where pressed between them lay the potato with the big plug bitten out. Miss Marybelle was a little dramatic in her behavior anyway, and suddenly, a frightened look came over her face. Her hand went over her mouth. Then her purse nearly fell off her arm. Her hand and arm crossed over her heart, and she inhaled strongly as if she had lost her breath. She staggered backward. And she screamed, "My god! He's eating a potato!"

The Hagans rushed over to the casket to see what had happened. After examining the scene in the casket, they turned around to look at the boys. Their heads were down and peeling potatoes ninety to nothing, all the while making a concerted effort to keep a straight face.

Cloyce apologized to Miss Marybelle, who had now regained her composure while sitting in a chair, fanning herself. "Well, I must say I don't think I've ever seen anything like that before," Miss Marybelle said while still breathing heavily.

The Hagans were thinking, *There goes a nice write-up about Uncle Tulan.*

Cloyce told Amzie and Mookie that they could go on home and that he would report this behavior to their parents. The boys noticed afterward that Mr. Hagan didn't call on them for odd jobs anymore. That really didn't bother the boys at all.

—◄○►—

"WELL, IT SOUNDS LIKE HE DIED LAST NIGHT"

Communication about who was in the hospital, sick at home, or had died was quite different out on Route 3, Coffeeville, where we didn't have telephones. Dinner bells had several uses and could communicate messages based on the frequency and level of the sound of the bell. Normally, they sounded the message that dinner was ready or that it was quittin' time. One knew about these meanings by the time of day someone rang it. A quick, loud sound meant to get to the house immediately because there must be an emergency of some type. If someone in the household had died, the sound of the dinner bell was slow and with a somber monotone. The ringer waited until the sound had completely gone silent before the next ring of the bell. Neighbors knew that the person in the household who had been on their deathbed for some time had finally gone on to that land that was fairer than day.

Among black American neighbors, there was a slightly different tradition. They rang the bell slowly the number of years the person had lived, no matter how long it took. If the deceased was eighty years old, then it rang eighty times to honor the person's long life. Occasionally, white neighbors didn't appreciate this interruption all that much. Eventually, you could hear someone say, "There is just no need to ring that bell for half a day."

DINNER ON THE GROUND

"And after church, we'll be having dinner on the ground." The first time I recall hearing that, I was confused as to just how and where we were going to eat. I soon learned that the food would be out on the church grounds but served on tables. The dinner was held on the Sunday of the summer revival, which was usually the latter part of July or the first week of August. There was a male reason for this timing. The crops would be laid by, and this allowed the men more freedom. However, they didn't take into account that this was when the garden was coming in demanding time to gather, cut, slice, shuck, shell, and can over a hot woodstove for the women. They had to do that during the day and be dressed up and fresh for the revival meeting that night.

And then there was that expected night when you had to entertain the preacher for supper. "You girls better get this house cleaned up and help me in the kitchen because we've got that preacher coming, and his wife is as highfalutin as they come."

Probably no other event has spawned more jokes than this one. Having the preacher in your home also provided an opportunity to demonstrate one's skill and knowledge in spiritual matters, thinking, I suppose, that if the preacher were impressed, then surely God would be. After the dinner, one lady asked her son, "Johnny, why don't you go in my room and bring out that book that Mother loves so much?" Why, Johnny knew which one she loved so much, so he brought out the Sears and Roebuck catalog. That must have really happened because I have such a vivid image of how she looked when Johnny came back in.

On Sunday after services, the ladies of the church took the lead in setting the table with all the food brought. Their potato salad was made a little different then since there was no refrigeration in most homes. It consisted of creamed potatoes, pickles, onions, and hard-boiled eggs. There was always plenty of lukewarm sweet tea. Occasionally, some man brought a big block of ice that was set in a large pan. Using the ice pick, you could chip off enough that everyone could have a little ice to go with their tea.

Once the food was ready, certain unwritten, implied rules were observed. The proper sequence of events involved allowing the preacher and any dignitaries present to go first through the line. The sermon had fed the soul, but now it was the stomach's turn. The other men followed and women poured them tea and watched the table to clean up any spillage. The small children were helped to get their plate. Finally, the women could go through to feast on the leftovers but were still on call if needed by the men. People ate wherever they could such as some chairs brought out of the church, on tailgates of trucks, or of course, on the ground. In later years, some churches decided to make the eating area much more convenient by having a covering over the tables, making benches, and even putting the tables on a slab of concrete. That was considered high living or, as we say now, "styling."

These were days before casseroles became popular. When the time came for them to be in vogue, men were reluctant to accept them as appropriate food for the male gender. They were considered as "feminine food" and thusly avoided by real men conscious of their masculine status.

It was always amusing to me that each dish was named after the woman who made it: Aunt Polly Sue's thin-crusted fried pies, Miss Omerie's melt-in-your mouth rolls, Sister Velma's delicious coconut cake, Miss Georgette's great pecan pie, Grandma Verline's mixed-up beans, Roleen's deviled eggs, and Addie Mae's baked ham with Co-Cola gravy. Preachers had to be careful in choosing between two of the same kind, especially where there was competition between two women. A wise and prudent preacher always put a little of both on his plate. Often, though, it was impossible to please everyone. Someone usually expressed disappointment that he didn't choose their creamy banana pudding. Once, I actually saw a woman take one of her dishes over to the preacher's plate and give him a serving anyway.

Back then, we were not as aware of potential health problems from devouring large portions of the artery-clogging, high-cholesterol foods we thoroughly enjoyed. There was cured country ham, fried chicken cooked in hog lard, green beans that had been cooked with so much fatback that they looked shellacked, pork sausage, streak-a-lean meat, and crackling cornbread. Brother John gave the blessing and always said, "Lord, bless this food to the nourishment of our bodies." I have since wondered how God handled such a challenge.

It was fairly common for women to have preferred recipes for certain occasions. Observations were sometimes made that what one woman brought was not appropriate food for that event. Different dishes were listed for family reunions, holidays, fish fries, funerals, wakes, prayer meeting, foot washings, creek baptisms, all-day singings, hog killings, barbecues, picnics, tacky parties, quilting days, and even health conditions such as sinking spells, hot flashes, fits, and cravings.

For most rural people in that day, the special Sunday delicacy was fried chicken, quite often referred to by preachers as the "gospel bird." Sunday guests could always expect a huge platter with all the fixins, which usually included potato salad and numerous vegetables from the garden. Often, the preacher was the most common Sunday guest requiring such a meal. The lore abounded of the preacher eating his fried chicken and how people sought to impress him with their favors and praise.

One story circulated for years, so much so that no one knew whether it was even true. It seemed one preacher loved fried chicken so much that once he started eating, he couldn't stop until none was left. The hostess knew of his propensity for eating chicken, so she fried up a heaping pile of the delicious bird. Her arm got tired wringing the heads off so many young chickens. They all sat at the dinner table, where the visiting preacher carefully tucked the napkin under his neck. With fork in one hand and a knife in the other, he looked at the platter of chicken and said, "Well, they all died that we might live," and let loose with a loud guffaw. The old man was definitely not amused. The preacher started eating, and it was so good he just devoured every piece in sight. After the fine dinner, the two men were sitting on the front porch, when an old rooster came around the house crowing.

The preacher said, "That ol' rooster sure sounds proud."

The old man replied, "Well, he ought to. He just had three of his flock to enter the ministry."

SINS: THE BIG THREE

What is defined as sin is variable over time, from culture to culture and from region to region. Well, we had our big sins on the Oakland–Coffeeville road. My grandmother taught us quite effectively that there were several behaviors absolutely forbidden. One was playing cards on Sunday. She sometimes hid the deck so we couldn't find it. There were serious consequences if we were caught violating this prohibition.

I often wondered about the origin of this "sin." I may have found the answer. One day I was thumbing through an old hymnal titled *Heavenly Highway Hymns*, published by Stamps–Baxter Music Company in Dallas, Texas. I found a hymn titled *Ain't It A Shame* (totally unrelated to the Fats Domino song). The verses went something like this:

> Ain't it a shame to joyride on Sunday, / Ain't it a shame, a joy-riding shame / When you got Monday, Tuesday, and Wednesday, /And you got Thursday, Friday, and Saturday, Ain't it a shame.

The other verses condemned working on Sunday, gossiping on Sunday, and lying on Sunday when you had the rest of the week in which to engage in these things. In other words, there were some things that best not occur on Sunday. And my grandmother said that playing cards was one of them.

Another big sin was working on Sunday. If it became known by neighbors that another was in the fields, clearing off a ditch bank or cutting wood, then the talk started, and that neighbor was castigated and ostracized. The gossip would spread until it circled back to the culprit so he would know that he was losing respect with others. The violators were described as sorry, disrespectful, or white trash. The threat of such a rumor stirring was a means of social control that usually resulted in compliance by everyone. Oh, one could take care of the "ox in the ditch" matter but not much beyond that. Sunday was for going to church for the churchgoing types. If you were not one of those, then you had to sit on the porch, visit the neighbors or family, or listen to gospel music on the radio. The enforcer for these Sunday norms was usually the matriarch of the family, which, in our case, was our grandmother. By Sunday night, the rules were relaxed a little bit, and no one objected to listening to the *Amos 'n' Andy* show on the radio.

Included in the big three sins was making homebrew. This is what was called making beer at home as long as you had a few pieces of equipment and the right ingredients. Usually, you had to have some bottles, siphon hose and clamp, hydrometer or thermometer, and a ten-gallon pail. The ingredients (which included malt extract, yeast, and sugar either regular, white sugar, or corn sugar) had to be bought at the store. Some of the brewers avoided the sugar altogether and just used two cans of the malt extract. The finished product, though, was not ready to drink until you had given it enough time to ferment.

The brewers enjoyed telling the story about the preacher one time who was up ranting and raving about people who drank the devil's brew. At one point, he said, "I think all this homebrew, beer, whiskey, and wine, all of it, ought to be carried down here and thrown in the river! That's where it all ought to be." Whereupon the song leader rose and led "Shall We Gather at the River?"

GRANDMOTHER'S BIBLE

I distinctly recall my fascination with Grandmother's large King James Version Bible. I would find it and look through it, mainly because I discovered that it contained much more than just the Bible. The sacred book was a repository of family-related memorabilia with sentimental value. Between the pages and within its covers were several dried rosebuds from family funerals. "That one is from John L.'s funeral, and the other one is from Thomas's, her sons." Also found were important papers, personal letters from loved ones, and an assortment of items she wanted as keepsakes. It was a combination safe, deposit box, and collections of memories.

The most curious item to me was Mama Langham's last snuff stick. No one could remember seeing her without her snuff stick, thus increasing its sentimental value. Often, she directed one of her sons to get her several from old sweet gum trees. She knew how to make the bristles at one end and cut to just the right length. When she was on her deathbed, my grandmother was the lucky one to retrieve the very last one she used. Because it brought back such fond memories, the family Bible became its final resting place.

Families also are wise in preserving these relics that remind us of our identity and heritage. Included might be records of service and accomplishments, medals, uniforms, tombstones, or personal items belonging to a loved one with whom we associate. These ties that bind carry sentiment, good feelings, and good memories,

A FOOT WASHING IN CHURCH

About a mile southeast of our house at the Old Leonard Place was the Gatewood Church of God. During their revival, the services sometimes lasted until 9:30 p.m. We sat on our front porch and listened to the shouting and when people would get the Holy Ghost. I was always amused by this church where the people participated more in the service and were freer in expressing their spiritual emotions, especially when they "got happy." I also learned the difference between just a regular revival and a Holy Ghost revival. The churches I attended were a little more High Church in their formalities. Some of the founders of the Restoration Movement in the early nineteenth century had their spiritual roots in Scottish Presbyterianism. Therefore, our heritage led us to more solemnity, more stiffness, and more seriousness with less spirit.

Some of our neighbors were members at Gatewood, and we always were invited to attend their revival. Evangelist Jackie Sprinkle was the one preacher I remember the most because she always played an accordion and could also play the piano. Though small of stature, she sure had a strong voice that moved the people to greater spiritual renewal.

One summer, the particular night we attended was the designated service for a foot washing. This ritual is based on a story in John 13, where Jesus washed the disciples' feet after they had traveled the dusty trails of Galilee, and no one had offered a basin of water with which to wash their feet. It is quite a compelling story. I would have liked to have been the fly on the wall to see the expression on their faces when Jesus knelt on the floor and began washing their feet. My guess is that they never forgot that experience. Jesus, of course, was teaching a great lesson on how to empty the privilege and become a servant.

Some Pentecostal churches believe that doing this in services strips away pride and creates more humility in our hearts, which we all need. As a kid watching, this really caught my attention. To this day, I remember how much I embarrassed my mother when I mentioned that the water seemed to be getting dirty. Through the years, I've come to appreciate what I saw in my youth in that service. There is so much pride abounding, and for some church members today, it is beneath their dignity to roll up their sleeves and get involved in the messiness of people's lives. They want class, formality, style, and grace to characterize their assemblies. Washing other members' feet might help them get a glimpse into our own human selves. Our hearts (and our feet) might actually get cleaner.

"I HEAR THAT TRAIN A-COMING"

My earliest remembrances of going to church included summertime revivals at the Oakland Church of Christ. It was a long-held tradition to hold "gospel meetings," as some churches called them, usually in the latter part of July. For a number of years, that was the only time we attended when I was a small child. The church building was only a few hundred feet from the railroad track that ran through Oakland. Each night, the Panama Limited train came blazing through Oakland right in the middle of the preacher's sermon. The train made so much racket that the preacher had to stop preaching for several minutes until the train passed through town. Well, all of us kids really got a kick out of that because the preacher always seemed peeved that he had to stop his prepared oration. Every night all the kids listened intently for the glory-land express—the sound of that train coming into town. One night a kid heard it and blurted out, "Here it comes! I hear it!" Several in the audience laughed, but the preacher was not amused.

CREEK BAPTISMS

There was another church of our faith closer to Coffeeville called Sylvan Knoll about three miles west of town on the Tillatoba Road. It had a long history, being established in the early 1900s. There was a freelance preacher named E. C. Fuqua, who proclaimed the Word wherever he could get a crowd together in the county. There were not many located preachers anywhere at that time, meaning that they preached for one church and were paid a salary. A man by the name of Noel A. Pittman came under his influence and was converted. From the conversion of this one man, many others in that community became Christians. It was there one summer night that my mother went before the church and made a confession of her faith. Now our church believes that one should be baptized the same hour of the night, so after the services were over, all the people gathered down at Cypress Creek, not far from the church building, where she was immersed. The next summer, my father was baptized in the same creek. Many believed that creek baptisms were the best kind because they just washed your sins right on downstream, forever gone.

Very few rural churches had baptisteries in their building and usually conducted their baptisms in nearby creeks or ponds. Members brought their lanterns with them to church, often on wagons, and this provided the only source of light. One of the problems with this process was that sometimes the preachers were unfamiliar with the water holes and where the drop-offs were. I heard one man who was to be baptized by a young city preacher say to him as they were inching their way out into the water, "Don't worry, I know where the huge drop-off is." More than once, preachers had to be rescued from the deep water and ended up more baptized than the candidate.

Sylvan Knoll always had large crowds to attend their gospel meetings in the summer. I remember the church building well. It had two doors on the front as was the custom with many of the old buildings. The protocol was for gentlemen to escort their ladies to the left door, parted with them, and then went in the right-hand door to sit on the men's side of the church. By the time we were attending, that practice had disappeared.

If the men were leaders, it was expected that they sit closer to the front, where they might be needed. There was an "amen corner" where the older men sat, and their pews faced the pulpit from the side. These men were revered as the spiritual giants of the faith. This allowed the men to be able to see everyone and everything that went on. Visitors dared not sit in one of the leaders' seats. If they did, they were politely asked to move.

The only cooling was open windows (with no screens) supplemented by handheld funeral home fans. The fans were always in abundance because the local funeral home was eager to get their business later on. Preachers liked to have those fans with the name of the funeral home on them because they felt that it helped remind people that death was coming swifter than a weaver's shuttle and that they had better be ready.

One night a lot of bugs flew inside, attracted by the lights, and were flying around the pulpit. Someone's dogs tied outside managed to free themselves from their leashes and proceeded through the front door and trotted right down the middle aisle. When they reached the front of the sanctuary facing the pulpit where the preacher was expounding, they began to jump into the air, attempting to snare the bugs to eat.

Now in those days, there weren't many special moments for the kids sitting on hard seats so tall your feet couldn't reach the floor. But, brother, this was special to all us kids. There was so much laughter the preacher had to stop, and he looked sternly in the direction of the leaders. They were not used to interrupting the sermon, but several got up and started running the dogs out the back door. At the end of the service, the preacher asked people to come back the next night, "and with the help of the fans and the dogs, maybe we can survive the heat and the bugs."

—◄O►—

MANSION, ROBE, AND CROWN

In the nineteenth century and the first half of the twentieth century, many religious songs were written to appeal to the laboring working class and portrayed heaven as a place where the faithful would receive a mansion, a robe, and a crown. I remember worshippers singing with such fervor those songs that depicted heaven as a materialistic realm where the ransomed would shine and possess a "gold one that was silver-lined." They sang the wish "I want a mansion, a robe, and a crown." Such a description seemed to give them hope that someday they would have a Beverly Hills–style mansion to reward them for a life in which they never had many luxuries.

Many favorite hymns of the era carried this same theme. Another song had the words "to mansions on high a crown there for me" and "'tis riches and wealth His treasures are mine." This sentiment was not new to those generations but has been found in many cultures seeking to satisfy the subsistent farmers or the exploited with the idea that one day things would be better for them in the great by and by. In George Orwell's *Animal Farm* (1946), the character Raven (a bird) tells the other animals about a place in the sky called Sugarcandy Mountain, where they would go when they died if they worked hard. Of course, Raven did not work himself but represented the Russian Orthodox Church, an arm of the state. Presenting heaven in such crassly materialistic pictures supposedly would result in the workers being content with their cheap labor and subsistent standard of living.

People in a hopeless state of deprivation where I grew up were reluctant to demand a fair wage or fair prices for their crops in this life. This is why, I now believe, they always talked in terms of how their children would fare better in their lives than they did and why so many of them strained their backs to provide those children opportunities they never received.

Even today, some are appalled when I tell them that if I ever get to heaven, and they want to put a robe on me and a crown on my head, I'm going to pass. Those songs are like gospel to them and regard it blasphemous not to want them. Actually, "mansions" is an antiquated word from the King James Version of the Bible that simply means "rooms." The image of just having a "room" in heaven is not quite as glamorous or poetic. I suppose my sentiments are more like those of country singer Hank Williams, Sr., who sang, "I don't care for fine mansions on earth's sinkin' sand. Lord, just build me a cabin in the corner of Gloryland."

RAISED ON HELL

As a kid, I distinctly remember that you could bet that on the hottest night of the revival, the preacher preached his sermon on hell. Every preacher had one, and you knew that sometime during the revival, he would pull it out to get scared lost sinners down the aisle. Back then, these sermons and his description of the horrors of hell would not only scare the hell out of you but also make the air seem hotter than it actually was. I would look around the audience, and everybody would be fanning away with those funeral home fans so much in unison it sounded like they were making music. You could almost hear them thinking, *Lord, please, hurry him up so we can get some fresh air.* Afterward, the breeze under the shade trees was always a welcome experience.

Remember that scene in *Gone with the Wind* where Scarlett is fearful she is going to hell and Rhett remarks, "Maybe there is no hell." Scarlett replies, "Oh, I'm sure there is. I was raised on it." Wow! All of us raised in the South can relate to that. Many a parent and grandparent were quite successful in changing behavior in the children by threatening hellfire and eternal damnation. We can still hear those fateful pronouncements that we were going to suffer eternal punishment if we didn't change our language, ways we were acting, or even believing damnable heresies. Those threats struck fear in our hearts and usually worked. If we didn't change, the guilt we felt would go with us forever. Yes, there are children of the South today who can still recall those dire predictions of our eternal fate. And we can still feel a little heat from the flames of hell every time we may be tempted to partake of the forbidden pleasures.

Once a stranger came along (who wasn't from around there) and got into a religious discussion. I heard some of the men talking about his claims. It seemed he described the garbage dump outside the city of Jerusalem in the first century as a place that burned incessantly. He claimed that when Jesus referred to hellfire where the fire was not quenched, he was referring to this awful place called the Valley of Hinnom, where the corpses of the poor and criminals were sometimes thrown following their death.

Oh my! This fellow was now seen as a serious threat to the long-held method of modifying children's behavior by threatening hell. We were warned not to even be around this man listening to his heretical views. Thereafter, he had no audiences and was shunned lest he made deviants of us all.

RUMORS OF SINNERS BEING SAVED

On Monday mornings, the curious wondered what happened on Sunday at the various churches. "Did anything happen at church yesterday?" Who got saved, who rededicated, who got restored, what sins got confessed, who was baptized, what outlandish clothes were worn, what was the quality of the sermons, any funny stories, any new gossip, and what was the temperature in the sanctuary. What really got attention was the news of some community reprobate, alcoholic, heathen, bootleg whiskey seller (not always met with joy), or the nonbeliever getting saved.

This type of church news was reflected by the Oak Ridge Boys in the song about Jesse Taylor (drinker, cheater, fighter, gambler) being baptized in Cedar Creek last Sunday.

> They baptized Jesse Taylor in Cedar Creek last Sunday;
> Jesus gained a soul and Satan lost a good right arm.

THE WEEPING WAILER

Most families during the forties and early fifties didn't allow their small children to attend funeral visitations and the funeral service. I never quite understood why. I suppose they felt that children should not be subjected to grief and sadness and loss. They went to great lengths to prevent the children from seeing a deceased person. Perhaps they felt that the child might become fearful that they might lose their parents to death. I'm sure the intentions were noble.

But I picked up more than my parents thought. Even though I was kept in the background, I observed more than they knew. I even insisted on attending some of the funerals. What was interesting to me was the particular types of preachers who preached funerals and the types among the mourners.

One type of preacher I remember well was the "fill in the blanks" preacher. Funeral services were very easy for them because their church provided formbooks that included all the appropriate verses, inspirational poems, and prayers with instructions on how to use these effectively. Many people thought that this little black book was actually his Bible. Basically, all they had to do was to change the name of the deceased in the appropriate blank space. One preacher had written in so many different names he embarrassingly mentioned several strange names before he got the right one.

Then there was the "It's all about me" funeral preacher. When his sermon was over, you ended up knowing more about the preacher than you did the deceased. "I first met Brother John right after I had graduated from Seminary in 1951 and moved into the parsonage, where we lived for the next four years. I always loved fishing, and sometimes I would invite him to go with me. I was always grateful for him because he was the one that verified that the bass I caught really did weigh six pounds."

The one I dreaded the most was the *weeping wailer*. This was the type of preacher who thought he had failed unless he could get most of the family members and some in the audience to lose control of their emotions and start crying audibly. The funeral home knew to pass out the tissue ahead of the service when he officiated. If all else failed, he started weeping and wailing himself and got to the most hardhearted. He had finally succeeded.

By far the most popular were the *heavenly assurance* preachers. These were the ones that no matter how the departed had lived, he could get them to heaven one way or another. I remember one of these that averaged about three funerals a week. It seemed that most everyone wanted him because they could leave the service knowing that their loved one had gone on to those "mansions in the sky."

Another type that I didn't particularly like was the *eternal evangelist*. This preacher never missed an opportunity to get all the lost saved, and funeral audiences provided him with that opportunity. He turned a funeral service into an evangelistic meeting. Forget about comforting the family, eulogizing the deceased; his main focus was on the living and getting them right with God. The service was certainly not a celebration of the life of the departed but the delivery of a stale sermon outline preached fervently to all the poor, lost souls that might be present.

There were those who truly were the *comforting shepherd*. These eulogized by finding the good in the person's life. It was felt that no matter what the life had been like, they could surely find something good to say about them. Everyone sensed that the service was truly to honor their memory and to celebrate their life and victory. They often reminded families of the loved one that they were now at rest and had "no more fields to plow, no more cotton to pick, no more saws to sharpen, and no more graves to dig."

THE GLAD-HANDER

Among the mourners, there were certain observable types. One was the *walking calculator*. They loved to compare funerals and judged them by the financial costs involved. As she came down the aisle for visitation, she took note of the people and especially any dignitaries present. Once she got in full view, one could just see the calculating start in her mind. Each wreath of flowers was counted and observed for size and cost. She didn't miss a one, even the potted plants. Then she proceeded to the casket, where she started her viewing from the front to the end, noticing any design that might appear on the opened part. Sometimes she even checked to see if the handles were unmovable (less expensive) or the movable types (more expensive).

Not going unnoticed was the deceased's hair, makeup, and funeral clothes.

I always loved to watch the *histrionic performer*. Usually, it was a woman, and her main goal was to make sure everyone knew that she was taking the loss harder than anyone else. To do that, she had to prove it by being the one who cried and wailed the loudest and longest. The performance was carefully timed to coincide when the largest crowd was present at visitation.

You could always bet that the *glad-hander* was there to meet and greet everyone. These were politicians, or aspiring politicians, who viewed funerals as such grand opportunities to meet people and make a positive impression for their campaign.

The *community consoler* was someone good at consoling and who received pleasure in consoling the bereaved. Over the years, they had developed a long list of comforting things to say. "You know they are in a better place."

Some people used funerals to be *fashion showstoppers*. In the South, there have always been fewer social occasions for women to dress up in their best and newest clothes. One of those places was at church services and at funerals. Being one of the few places they could go dressed up, often, the occasion became a place not only just to wear the new outfit but also to compete with others.

FRONT-PORCH PHILOSOPHY IS THE BEST

Many who grew up in the South have told of their fond memories of the proverbial front porch and the many hours of leisure, sitting and conversing there. Most houses had wide front porches with swings and chairs in abundance. At the Old Leonard Place, the house stood perched at the top of a small hill, which allowed us to see across the main road to the Lillian Brown house and the Burney place from the porch. We could see traffic and identify who it was and even where they were going, when the mail carrier ran, who was working in the fields, and any company that might be coming up the dirt road to our house. The late evening sessions on that porch were the ones I remember the most.

The house was awfully hot during the summer, too hot to spend much time inside. When Granddaddy and everyone else came to the house from working all day, it was still too hot to go inside. The first thing to do after quitting time was to clean up on the back porch. That meant drawing some water from the well and washing up right there by the washstand, which was a one-by-twelve board stretched from the outside wall to a porch post. Grandmother never liked people around her dinner table who were dirty. In fact, we had to pass her inspection before sitting down at the table. I recall her often sending someone back to the porch to wash up again. The kitchen was her special domain, and no one would defile it with sweat and dirt.

So after supper, we regrouped on the front porch, with the windows all raised, waiting for the house to cool down. In the quietness and stillness of those times right at dusk, a lot of somber reflection took place. Those moments were similar to those bedtime moments when you are tucking a child in bed. Both you and the child speak to each other from the heart. Same way on the porch.

Nowadays, people usually gather around the kitchen table when trying to figure out how to pay the bills or send the kids to college. But there on the porch, in a bygone era, we shared our mutual woes, and it took from our souls the strain and stress of living. A refreshing breeze blew by, breathing an evening blessing. We not only shared the day's happenings, but often, we also looked beyond ourselves and expressed the deep yearnings of our hearts. A lot of sentences began with "You know, I wish . . ." If there were any words of reassurance to be said, they were freely given. Then the shadows appeared, and the night drew near. Someone would finally say, "Well, I think I'll go on in the house."

It was on the front porch where we talked about the things in life that really mattered. Generally, the talk centered on prospects for the future, a better crop, what the family could possibly have at the end of fall, or a trip to see a loved one. Really, it was always about the children growing up and having a better life. The most significant accomplishment on the front porch was how the parents validated the self-worth of the children. Someone remembered the words of Eleanor Roosevelt: "No one can make you feel inferior without your consent." We were reminded of all the loose ends that remained in life, in relationships, at school, and in the community. Politicians would have done well to have listened to the front-porch philosophy of simple working people trying to survive.

Our language was full of similes and metaphors, but we didn't know that was what they were called. One evening on the porch, someone observed the chickens in the yard. He said, "You know, we're just like those chickens scratching around, trying to find something, anything to eat. They will go anywhere and scratch for a little bite. That's what we do most every day." And like those chickens, we had gotten real good at it.

Once, I recall the men folks talking on the front porch about what they could have been or could be. Their pensive thoughts reflected a faraway, wistful look in their eyes. "I really believe that if I had one of those tractors and some plows, I could really do well. There would be so much more that I could do to produce big crops. I know some land that could be leased and no telling where that would take us."

The men could look around and see that the ones getting ahead were those with land and tractors. Usually, there was silence after such a wish because we knew that this was not probable. But everyone needed to be able to dream, and a lot of dreaming took place on the front porch.

We had ambitions, although some people didn't think that working people like us had any. We were just like others who wanted to matter in life and to "get ahead" and have a little more than we did. I never thought that was a bad thing.

LANGUAGE MYSTERIES

We simplified the great wisdom of the world with pithy sayings: "Warm hands, cold heart, dirty feet, no sweetheart." Someone decided to take that philosophy and make it into something more positive: "Cold hands, warm heart, clean feet, you're my sweetheart." You see, we knew that philosophy could be modified and elevated to a higher aesthetic level of more positive thought. "Kiss me fast, kiss me quick, here comes Mama with a hickory stick." And seemingly, she always showed up about the time you were about to get some sugar. One saying that reflected great intellectual depth was found in this profound piece of literary advice: "When you marry and live in a shack, teach your kids to spit through the cracks." I imagine that many today cannot appreciate just how important this behavior was in keeping a clean house. The boys who wanted to attract the attention of the girls said, "Mississippi rainy, Mississippi muddy. Mississippi girls is all I study." There were actually some girls who found that somewhat amusing.

We discovered that people from up North were blunt and spoke exactly in plain English what they meant. I grew up in a culture that defined politeness as being careful not to offend someone. Therefore, we were vague, spoke in generalities, used a lot of circumlocution, and learned how to determine the truth by reading between the lines. We were more likely to hear "I thought he was mighty peculiar," instead of "He has some beliefs we don't have." The preacher was sometimes described as "gone to meddling." Usually, we figured the preacher must have said something about the women dipping snuff. Preachers learned that preaching "righteousness" and against "sin" was much preferred.

The "sinkin' spell" term was used rather loosely to refer to anyone who often fainted or who tired easily or quickly. One never knew how serious these were, or how real they were, because some used this "illness" as an excuse to get out of work and get to go to the house. "Oh, it's one of those sinkin' spells again. Don't worry too much about it." Often, I heard one of the grown folks talk about someone who was "just having another one of their fits." Fits involved several aggressive behaviors but not exclusively the following: yelling, screaming, hollering, fussing, kicking, stomping, crying, cussing, slamming doors, throwing things, yanking, jerking, and pulling hair. Most everyone knew what "He was feeling mighty peart" meant. It was used to describe others who had been feeling poorly, but now they were fairly peart.

Much of my early education in elementary school didn't appear to be relevant to where I lived. Dick and Jane lived and moved in another world, a world that seemed strange and different from mine. Outside those classrooms, I never heard anyone talk about animals "foraging" for food. Neither did I hear anyone from my socioeconomic class talk about how "famished" they were. I suppose those are perfectly fine words; I just didn't know people who used them. Our textbooks, I noticed, were published in Boston, New York, or Philadelphia. One year, these publishers requested that the teachers give the students a test; I suppose to determine whether the students were learning their material. One item on the test was "Mark the brook." In reality, I knew more about a creek than anyone. I spent a good portion of my time growing up on a creek bank. I knew where the fishing and swimming holes were, how to cross the creek on a log, how to dam up the creek, and how to clear the creek bank. But we never called it the bubbling brook. Maybe in Upstate New York but not in rural Mississippi. So I probably missed that item.

Another question on their little test was "Mark the meadow." I am sure that I knew more about a pasture than anyone. I spent a great amount of time roaming the pasture, chasing cows and horses, picking flowers for my mother, playing ball, looking for guinea nests, and making paths. But never knew I was in a "meadow." I guess I missed that one as well.

One item showed a drawing of a telephone. The question was to state what was wrong about this telephone. The answer was that there was no connecting wire between the receiver and the base. I had to think whether I had seen a telephone before. I recalled being in Harry Gordon's store in Coffeeville once when they were collecting payments for appliances and furniture. I think I saw a phone there and may have gotten that test item right. The assumption, of course, was that surely every student's family had a telephone.

These completed tests were mailed back to some company in the Northeast for grading and evaluation. As they discovered low scores on these culturally biased tests, I imagined them concluding, "My, my, my! These little Southern kids are just not learning. Sad that they are so backward. They talk so slowly! Must mean that they think slowly." I've often wondered if they realized how illogical that reasoning was. Or that they were administering a test unfair to students from a different regional culture and not from the upper middle class.

If these IQ tests were unfair to Southern white students, just think how unfair many of these tests were for African American kids. Once, I came across a testing instrument titled "The Soul-Folk Chitlin' Intelligence Test," developed by black sociologist Adrian Dove in 1971. It is obviously a culturally biased test in favor of those familiar with black, urban life. Once, while teaching in college and knowing that some of my black students had been advised in high school not to pursue college, I administered the test in class. Out of thirty multiple-choice items, the white students had scores of five, eight, nine, or three. Whereas the black students had scores of twenty-five, twenty-eight, or thirty.

FLOWERS FEED THE SOUL

Early every spring, when I see the blooming of the flowers, I remember how my grandmother always made sure we had them all the way to the fall of the year. She taught us to always be on the lookout for some wildflowers that could be brought to the house to be put in an old bucket, discarded pan, or flowerbed or at the edge of the yard. She said the flowers showed people that someone was living there and thriving. It also showed that you were making an effort to "improve" the place you were living on. Sometimes people said that a family "sure had improved the farm or house since moving there." That was a high compliment. Hearing that was a whole lot better than hearing, "They have just let the place run down."

We did our improving by natural means without it costing money. Granddaddy's joe blade cut off many a ditch bank and other places that had "grown up" around the house. We brought black-eyed Susans and Indian paintbrush plants to the house to set out.

To this day, when I smell honeysuckle in the spring, the scent takes me back to an earlier time. It reminds me that this one pleasant experience of nature hasn't changed over the years.

The natural appearance of certain types of blooms could always be predicted. The first flower of spring were the daffodils. (We called them buttercups.) That sounds like a song title to me, "The First Flower of Spring." We need that song to honor the courage, determination, and grit of that flower to be the first to break through the good earth and brighten our yards and our spirits.

Then came the forsythia, plum, red bud, dogwood, lilies, perennials, honeysuckle, day lilies, and later, crepe myrtles, which lasted through the summer. The Old Leonard Place had a row of crepe myrtles down one side of the house. If company came for a meal, sometimes we would cut some blooms (especially buttercups and honeysuckle and crepe myrtle) to put in a jar and put in the middle of the table. Yes, even then, we had some flowers to add to the ambiance of the kitchen. "You make do with what you have." I didn't know it then, but some townspeople and wealthier people thought countryfolk had no pride in such matters.

With the first signs of spring, Granddaddy was more spry with more pep in his step. It signaled new life and a resurrection and a new opportunity for growth and well-being. For older people, the winter months were often a real challenge to survive. Pneumonia brought a lot of misery, along with the cold and dampness, the short days, the long nights, the bleakness and dreariness of some days, and a lack of fresh vegetables. During the early part of the twentieth century, this experience was common among the poor working class. We built a strength within us, the strong will to see the next spring. When we saw it finally arriving, we knew the Lord had spared us over to another year.

I remember the transformation of that old home place after the family had moved. The house was not very livable thereafter, too dilapidated, even though we made it a good place to live. Paths disappeared, the grass and weeds sprang up, and no animals graced the surroundings with their unique sounds. No human voices to break the space. No fun, no laughter, no sorrow, no singing, nothing! Sad really, but I still have my memories and the visions of what it once was but would never be again.

RURAL VERSUS URBAN

Rural people were quite sensitive about what they thought were negative perceptions of them by city folks. Being "country" to some connoted unwashed backwardness. We resented being thought of as only an abstraction; we were real, breathing mortals on life's tempestuous sea, with feelings, pain, love, and hope for the harvest's golden grain. Much of the denigration on both sides was exaggerated. Nonetheless, I often heard how we felt about townspeople:

> We may not afford your fancy food, but we grow so much ourselves that we have enough to share with others.
>
> We may not have your fancy entertainment, but we know how to make our own music and dance on the kitchen floor.
>
> We may not have your fancy cars, but we know how to walk.
>
> We may not have your fancy churches, but we know how to pray and read the Bible.

You live in the city, but our air is cleaner to breathe.

You can have your Debutante Balls, but we can still have a ball.

We may not be in the *Social Register* or *Who's Who*, but we have pride and we do matter.

Yes, it is darker out here at night, but you suffer from light pollution.

We may not have as many things, but we are thankful for what we do have.

You can travel to exotic faraway places, but our imagination takes us far and wide.

We may not have a new truck every year, but we were the ones who invented old pickup trucks.

You may have a warmer house, but you haven't lived until your family sits around the hearth before a roaring fire singing, "I'll Fly Away."

(The glory-land chorus could not have sounded any better as we put a little heaven in our soul.)

THE THREE-DAY ICEBOX

After all the things had been accomplished for a day in town, such as buying some groceries, it was time to head back home on 330 Highway. The last stop was an icehouse run by Frank Hubbard, across from the cemetery. We bought a block of ice that would fit in our icebox at home. The block was wrapped up in a quilt to keep it from melting.

The ice usually lasted till sometime on Tuesday, which meant that we could have meat and store-bought milk till then. After that, if we had meat, it came from chickens, possums, squirrels, fish, rabbits, raccoons, or pork meat from the smokehouse. Ice trucks sometimes delivered in rural areas provided your house was out on the main road. Our house was so far enough off the road, virtually out of sight, that we couldn't get any at other times. Occasionally, if someone was passing into town, we might get an extra block later in the week, but that was rare.

THE MIST OF DOOM

In the late 1940s, everyone in the family was excited when my grandparents returned from town one Saturday with a small hand sprayer for the new agricultural insecticide called DDT. We mixed it with water and sprayed it all over the house, porch, yard, and even the chicken coop. I saw it as a toy and frequently sprayed just for the sake of spraying. We heard so many other people talking about the virtues of this chemical and how effective it was in ridding our space of those pesky insects.

In 1962, Rachel Carson's book *Silent Spring* exposed how this chemical had saturated our landscape and could be causing great environmental hazard to wildlife, especially birds and even cancer in humans. In 1972, DDT was banned because of these claims. Eventually, the ban was credited for the return of the bald eagle, our national bird.

LAP BABIES

Rural families in the latter part of the nineteenth century and early part of the twentieth century were large for economic and cultural reasons.

In conversation about the children, women distinguished them by referring to common images. First, there was the nursing baby that still needed their mother's milk. Often, they nursed right up to about the fifth month or the next pregnancy. Then the weaning process began, and they became a lap child. Many children still remember the comfort and security of Mama's lap. No longer nursing but still had the need for mother's attention. In the ongoing transition to getting older, the knee child was no longer indulged every time they wanted something. They had to wait a little longer as they began to gain a small amount of independence. Finally, the yard child could be let loose and given more freedom. At this point, they might be age five and above. Outsiders might not know the children by name, but they could easily see where each young child was based on the location between the yard and its Mama's lap. Clearly, when these categories were used, everyone knew the stage to which she was referring.

SOUTHERN NAMES

In the first half of the twentieth century, it was virtually a Southern folkway for parents to give a child two first names. Having a first and middle name had several advantages. One of them was quite amusing. The understanding was that if the parent called one of their children by both names, especially if it was said in a stern voice, the child knew they were in some kind of trouble or needed to listen carefully. In mother's family, with seven siblings, this common pattern was evident and often used by my grandmother Helm when one of the children needed a reprimand. There was Stella Ruth, Janie Florence, Sara Christine, Maye Earline, Mary Elizabeth, Eula Joanne, John L., and Thomas Eldon. "Thomas Eldon, you need to quit playing around with that old motorcycle and get on out there in the field to help your daddy." Just the sound of the two names together was enough to provoke attention. You best follow the instructions right away.

Selecting the second name can actually be easy because there are only a limited number of second names that will work, regardless of the first name. One of the following names will most always fit: Lee, Allen, Mae, Sue, Jane, Ruth, Bob, Ann, Ray, Marie, Bell, and Nell. If you choose Pearly for the first name, then Sue works well. If you select Trula for the first name, looking over the list, I would match it with Bell—Trula Bell.

People outside the South have always been aghast by what we name our children. Some children that I knew received their names from motorcycles, NASCAR drivers, and gun manufacturers. Harley and his wife had six boys. They were named Colt, Thompson, Rem, Marlin, Wesson, and Dale.

One day the wife said to her husband, before he left for town, to be on the lookout for some new names since they had a good start on increasing family size, and in fact, she was in the glory land way at the time. He came back in and gave her the following names on a list: Margarine, Jasmine, Gardenia, Chrysanthemum, Vizine, Chanel, and Vidalia.

She said, "Where on earth did you find these names?"

He replied, "Well, I just drove into town, stopped at the grocery store, that flower shop, drugstore, and then by the farmers market before coming home."

The most amusing name story was a woman I met named "Dietary." When I first met her, I had to ask, "I hope you won't mind me asking, but could you tell me the story back of your name? Now not that there is anything wrong with it; I'm just a little curious." She replied, "When I was born, my mother had not decided on a girl's name, but she noticed that all the female nurses had nametags on their uniforms. She decided that she would give me the name of the very next nurse that came into her room. Next in the room came a lady with her tag in clear sight on her uniform. So I've been 'Dietary' ever since." She had accepted her name because she knew her mother loved her and meant well. I guess I admire her for sticking with that name.

Over the years, I've had a little hobby of collecting people's first names that are unique in the South. Most of these names came from the obituary section of Southern newspapers. Many families in the South want to give their child a good Southern-sounding name, but when they check the lists of possibilities, they don't find any that fit. So often, they end up going with the popular TV soap opera names.

As a public service for those looking for just the right Southern name for your newborn, I'll give a small sampling in alphabetical order from this era and from which you might choose (or you might not):

Angelicious, Budgie, Celestine, Dooky, Exie, Finis, Genola, Hook, Izetta, Jaxine, Kackie, Lardell, Mysheba, Noisy, Omerie, Peaberry, Qeurine, Romie, Severa, Tootie, Unetha, Versh, Walterine, Xylam, Yohanna, Zorine

—◀○▶—

OUR FAMILY SECRET

Over the years, I learned that many families had serious secrets. They might include a previous marriage, an extramarital affair, or even their actual ethnic background. There were different types from taboo subjects, rule violations, surprise secrets, dangerous secrets, essential secrets, or even toxic secrets. In some cases, only certain family members were allowed to talk about them. Handling these secrets that were of different levels of severity varied from family to family.

During and right after World War II, soldiers traveling throughout the country were viewed as national heroes. For young women, there was a higher social status associated with dating these guys. One of my younger unmarried aunts got a job in Greenwood, Mississippi, as a proofreader for the *Commonwealth Newspaper*, and while there, she met many soldiers. And for whatever the explanation, she became pregnant. Soon, she had to leave her job because of her pregnancy and return home.

Now my grandmother Helm had used the technique of instilling the fear of God, the threat of hell, and banishment from the family into her six daughters and used such threatening language that she thought would be sufficient to prevent a premarital pregnancy. Such a condition brought public shame and great distress upon a family. But when faced with the reality in 1946, my grandmother became a mother (one of those mighty matriarchs of Mississippi) who dealt with this crisis the best way she knew how.

She gathered confidential information from a few people who had heard about some resources that could help. They spoke in whispers. In December 1946, Grandmother and my aunt went to Memphis, where they first sought boarding at the Salvation Army. They were referred to the "Travelers Aid Society," where a lady made arrangements for her to be admitted to the Bethany Training Home in Oakland (unknown to local residents) until the time for delivery. Also, this person called Miss Georgia Tann, assistant director of the Memphis branch of the Tennessee Children's Home Society, to refer her case. The plan was for her to be admitted to the charity hospital, and they would contact Miss Tann, who would make arrangements for an adoption "by some loving family who could give the child the advantages in life" that my aunt could not.

What my grandmother and aunt did not know was that Georgia Tann was the subject of a state investigation that revealed allegations of fraud, extortion, and child selling. This operation existed all across the state, but the Memphis branch was the one that was exposed by an attorney investigating the agency on orders from then governor Gordon Browning of Tennessee. Reviews of her operation described her as engaging in black market selling of babies for profit. At times, she told the birth mothers that their child had been stillborn. Inmates at a local psychiatric hospital were bred with the guards, thus increasing her inventory. She made her millions off mostly poor women whom she lowly regarded as "breeders" and "cows."

To present the child as acceptable to Jewish families in New York, she inserted her own facts to fit the request. Tann stated on the form that the father of my cousin was Alex Steinburg, supposedly a service guy from South Carolina with "olive complexion," an "American born German–Hebrew who attended temple" in his home state. (Even though his or her mother traditionally determined the ethnic identity of a Jewish person, having only one Jewish parent worked in North American Reform Movements.)

Records indicated that Tann used the same Jewish name for the father in adoption cases seventeen times! Now either this was totally fabricated, or this guy was a most prolific sower of his seed. To make her more appealing to the prospective parents, Tann claimed that her mother was an opera singer, and her father was an actor. Such potential supposedly would prove to the parents that they would reap great rewards because of their "investment."

She sold more than five thousand babies, while many others died through neglect, starvation, beatings, and rape. Many of her babies were adopted by Hollywood celebrities and aforementioned Jewish families in New York. When the investigative net was closing in on her operation, she died of cancer only days after her notorious scheme was exposed. Her nefarious operation has been chronicled in several books, documentaries, an episode of *Unsolved Mysteries*, and an A & E movie titled *Stolen Babies* starring Mary Tyler Moore.

Our lost cousin was sick soon after birth but was flown to New York anyway, where she was admitted to a hospital for eight days after almost dying of dehydration, diarrhea, and malnutrition. My aunt never knew who adopted her daughter or any of her circumstances. With my grandmother by her side all the way, she came home to start her life over.

My matriarch grandmother let her word go forth to all family members that this event was never to be talked about to anyone. It was our family secret—a serious rule violation had occurred. She would see to it that this stain would not interfere in any way with the future of her daughter. All of us knew about it, but we knew never, ever to bring it up. And thus, it was so! My aunt went on with her life, married in 1955, and had three other children.

In 1995, the state of Tennessee changed its adoption policies and allowed individuals to look at the birth records of those who were adopted during Tann's reign of terror. Before contacting the birth mother, the mother had to give her consent. What we didn't know was that our first cousin had seen the A & E movie on *Stolen Babies* and began to think, as she had suspected through the years, that she had been adopted. Through a long searching process, she finally attained the birth records. But she needed more; she needed her history, her identity, her flesh and blood, and her real family.

When my aunt was contacted by the state and asked if she wanted to meet her daughter, she refused. At that moment, she was terminal with a brain tumor, taking chemotherapy, and had never told her husband or her children about her baby girl. I think her decision was unfortunate, and my cousin never saw her mother alive.

The good news is that she was able to locate another one of my aunts, and it wasn't long until our cousin was now united with our family, her half-sister and one of her half-brothers. Once she joined the family, she felt that she had been with them all her life. "It was a perfect fit, and my life changed forever. I know who I am. I know where I belong, and I know where I came from."

SHARING OUR KUDZU

We were told that a special vine growing in Southern Japan would solve our problems with gullies and soil erosion. In the late 1800s, this so-called miracle vine was imported to blanket our landscape, primarily in Mississippi, Alabama, and Georgia, and, at the same time, eliminate our unsightly gullies. By the 1940s, over seven million acres were covered with what had come to be called by that time a scourge upon our beloved land. It had grown virtually unchecked as it spread along roadways, climbing up trees and killing them and other plant life because of its excessive shading.

The invasive kudzu was the "vine that ate the South," someone said. There were other choice words used to describe its destructive path, almost as deadly as Sherman's march across the South: parasite, noxious weed, nuisance, landscape curse. We even attempted to find some positive use for it to no avail except we discovered that goats liked to eat it. Wives objected when their husbands bought herds of goats, only to discover they couldn't eat it fast enough to make any difference. Escaped criminals discovered they could hide in the dense cover, thus evading the law at least for a while.

Relatives from up North came visiting one summer to see their family in Mississippi, whom they had not seen for many years. At one point, the visiting lady said, "My, my, what a lovely vine you have growing here!" not knowing anything about its sordid history. "Why, it's just everywhere I look. You all must highly regard it.""Yes, ma'am, we do regard it, all right."

"You know what I would like to do? I spend so much time in my flower garden this vine would accent my flowers so beautifully. Do you think I could take some home with me to plant?"

"Ma'am, when you leave, we'll make sure you carry back an abundance of kudzu, in fact, all you want."

"You mean I can get it free? By the way, did you all have to stake the vine around those trees in order to get it to grow up on the bark?"

"No, ma'am, actually, it just grew up on those trees on its own."

When the lady and her family left to go back home, her car was loaded with all the kudzu that could be stored. In about two years, the Southern family felt they needed to reciprocate by going up North to visit the family. As they neared the house, something became obvious right away. The kudzu had not only consumed her flowerbed but had also crept up the columns on the front porch. The kudzu had also taken over her neighbor's yards all the way down on her side of the street.

They wondered just how welcomed they would be after this travesty. They were told that concerned citizens in the community had formed an organization in an effort to curb its continued growth. They thought, *Well, good luck with that!*

V

HIGH LIVING (1950–1953)

Because a good opportunity for a great and growing
work has been given to me now.
—1 Corinthians 16:9 (NCV)

SOME LIVING IN rural areas often traveled down a lonely road,
and the way grew weary and long. It was easy to fantasize about some
higher ground. The only place we knew like that was living in town.
I knew some people, though, who resented townspeople generally
because it was felt that they thought they were better than folks living
in the country. Those city dwellers didn't know anything about hard
work and just getting by, people thought. Yet if they had a chance to
move into town, they would do it in a heartbeat.

After Daddy was hired at Happy's Cleaners and Mother worked
at Rice Stix in Water Valley, it was better for us to move into
Coffeeville to cut down on the drive to work. My parents found

an apartment in the Old Johnson Boarding House on Main Street, right beside the courthouse and only one block from Silk Stocking Avenue. In earlier years, this is what Depot Street was called because of several fine residences with long porches, elaborate latticework, and expansive lawns. The term referred to those who could afford expensive silk stockings as opposed to cotton ones worn by the common people. Many towns throughout the South had their own Silk Stocking Avenue.

We were also now living in a two-story house, which had always carried a higher status, even though it had five apartments, and we occupied only two rooms. The kitchen was quite small, but for the first time, my mother didn't have to cook on an old woodstove. We even had a small bathroom that had a lavatory and commode. Man, standing up taking a bath was a whole lot better than the number two washtub. Indeed, for us, we were living in New Jerusalem.

There were certain other amenities we had never experienced. I could ride my bike all over town, walk to school, play sandlot baseball, and go to town anytime I wanted. Three other families lived there at the time, including the George Jones family and Dolly Pate, a lady living alone across the hall. Having neighbors this close to enjoy small talk added to our social well-being. This was living in high cotton for sure.

For us and for so many others, Coffeeville was like the center of the universe. We were only vaguely aware that there was another world out there. If a citizen was in some other distant place, the question might be asked, "Where are you from?" And the response would be, Coffeeville or "Cawful." The other person might then ask, "Well, what state is that in?" We'd be surprised that they didn't already know.

◄o►

ADVICE ON TOWN LIVING

Perhaps surprising to some today, back then, moving from the country to town was a big deal. "Boy, you better be careful. They're going to be watching you to see if you qualify for town living." Below is an accumulation of some of the bits of caution I distinctly remember hearing from various people:

> Always flush. Now sometimes they don't flush, but the social consequences will be more severe if you don't.
>
> Get a haircut at least every two weeks. There are curious people wandering around who actually observe the hair on your neck.
>
> Never admit to eating field corn. They think it is only for animals.
>
> Never tell outhouse stories. They will just frown and gag.
>
> Don't start a sentence with "One time when I was slopping the hogs . . ."
>
> Don't refer to any married cousins that met at a family reunion.
>
> Always close doors behind you, lest you hear the outburst, "Close the door. Were you raised in a barn?" Saying *yes* sarcastically won't help.

You have to get these down from day one. There is no period of probation in which you can learn the ways of city life and behavior.

RESTROOM ETIQUETTE

Daddy knew that I wasn't used to public restrooms, so he evidently felt the need to acquaint his young son on the implicit norms relating to proper do's and don'ts. Of course, I first learned about the use of restrooms in the grade school buildings, where teachers instructed us on their appropriate use. But I later learned that my teachers didn't tell us nearly enough of what we needed to know as men. So my dad filled in the parts that no female teacher ever taught me. I had no idea that these social norms were that important.

Basically, the rule was that men and boys were not to speak a word to anyone else on the inside of a restroom ever, not a single word. Even eye contact was forbidden, Dad said. When he finished instructing me, I decided that any violation of these social rules would result in the downfall of civilized society as we knew it. Dad said that even urinal choice was important: "Always choose the one the farthest away from other users." I may not have understood fully the rationale back of these rules, but I trusted him to know. To this day, every time I enter a public restroom, those instructions are keenly felt and most often followed.

THE SEQUESTERED VALLEY BENEATH THE EMERALD HILL

In discovering Coffeeville's history, one could begin with the time when this area was occupied by the Choctaw and Chickasaw Indians. But as the white man began to invade the territory, the *Dancing Rabbit Creek Treaty* was signed and duly ratified by the United States government. During those days, around three hundred such infamous treaties were signed and were violated at the rate of 90 percent. As more and more settlers came, the tribes, for the most part, were sent westward, and in 1833, Yalobusha County was created by an act of the Mississippi Legislature. The community was given the name after the gallant Gen. John Coffee, a companion-in-arms of Gen. Andrew Jackson in New Orleans and a land surveyor. While a great soldier, he was not a competent surveyor and was credited for drawing the crooked line dividing East Mississippi and West Alabama.

George M. Moreland wrote of his experience in visiting Coffeeville for the first time:

> Seated in its rare dignity and piquant charm deep down in its sequestered valley, the very atmosphere which clings to the sides of its emerald hill slopes seems to whisper of history at Coffeeville. I approached the beckoning portals of this exquisite old town— rare gem in the regal diadem that adorns the proud commonwealth of Mississippi. Guiding my car out of a rural road that leads westward from Coffeeville, at the hill slope, I paused and took one farewell look at the sedate and bejeweled town nesting like a buttercup in a velvety dale in its somnolent valley.

If I understand correctly the meaning of his recherché eloquence, I think he was saying this was a pretty special place. As a young boy, riding a bicycle through its narrow streets with a cool breeze blowing in my face, and still undaunted by the seething, frenzied world outside, I thoroughly agreed.

Coffeeville flourished with economic and social activities. At one time, there were eleven doctors in town. Traveling troupes featuring music and drama came to perform. In the early days, it was reported that there were more taverns and saloons than any other type of stores. Perhaps the most famous was called Bakers Tavern, where locals and travelers gathered for news and entertainment. Gaining a reputation throughout North Mississippi, it housed and entertained some of the most prominent citizens of the state, including Gov. Henry S. Foote, S. S. Prentiss, Jefferson Davis, and L. Q. C. Lamar. The Temperance Movement closed most of the taverns by 1893.

President and Mrs. James K. Polk from Columbia, Tennessee, bought a plantation in Yalobusha County southwest of Coffeeville for farming its rich soil in 1834. He visited occasionally but mainly received monthly reports. After his death, Mrs. Polk continued to operate the farm.

Another claim to fame for Coffeeville was that Burrell Cannon (1848–1922), a man born on a farm near Coffeeville, claimed to be the first to build and fly an airplane in 1902 before the Wright Brothers. Cannon grew up working with wood, steel, and machines and later in life moved to Pittsburg, Texas, where he supposedly made the historic flight. Being a preacher, he was intrigued by the biblical account of Ezekiel's vision of God and strange flying objects propelled by wheels. He called his aircraft *Ezekiel Airship*. This was appropriate because Southerners have always boasted of being a people of "the Word," which tells us that when we take that last journey of the soul, "we fly away" (Psalm 90:10 NASB).

During the Civil War, with Grant setting up headquarters in Holly Springs and Oxford, some of his soldiers raided and pilfered in some of the nearby towns. Only four men remained in Coffeeville: one invalid, two elderly, and a Presbyterian minister. All the others were fighting in the war. The women were left unprotected with the town swarming with hostile soldiers.

Some of the distressed ladies rose up to defend themselves from the disruptions of war. Other women of strength joined them to organize to protect their homes and community. When the Yankee captain arrived, they approached him and demanded protection from his soldiers. The account states, "He received them with every courtesy, apologized for the rude conduct of his soldiers. That night he stationed guards at every home, and personally inspected the guards, both that night and the next morning."

These Southern ladies learned firsthand that war was not a garden party. When the Battle of Coffeeville was fought north of town on the old Water Valley Road, the town women found courage and a strength they didn't know they had. With few medical supplies, these women shrouded the dead and comforted the dying. Many served as nurses to the wounded on both sides as was the case at numerous battle sites across the country.

In 1928, Mrs. W. L. Kennedy read a short history of Coffeeville before a meeting of the United Daughters of the Confederacy. This document is archived at the Yalobusha County Historical Society. One story is of particular interest: One of the dying was a young Union soldier, only sixteen years of age. Knowing that he would not live, he requested that the ladies write a letter to his mother. They wrote it just as he stated it, and they held his hand as he signed it just before he died. Sometime later, they gave the letter, his pocketknife, and a ring to a Union officer passing through town. He promised he would forward it to his mother. No one ever knew whether the mother received her son's letter and personal items. The young soldier was buried in the city cemetery, but over time, the location became unknown as well as his name. The story, handed down through generations, has become a part of the historical lore of the small town.

MIDSUMMER NIGHT'S GAME

On summer nights in Coffeeville, when the atmosphere was still and the scent of honeysuckle was soothing, we could easily round up enough kids to play a game called trail. After a full day of various activities, it was time for a change, so we gathered downtown.

The game was played by first dividing into two groups. The object was for one group to leave without the others knowing which way they went. Group 1 started up a street and marked an arrow in the middle of the street with chalk, indicating their direction. After several blocks, group 1 marked a circle with an X in the middle. Then the group members hid in the vicinity, in shrubs, bushes, under porches, outbuildings, cars, or anyplace around that put them out of sight. Back then, there was never a thought that you might be shot. People seemed to be rather tolerant of kids simply having a good time on a hot summer night. They then waited to see if group 2 could find them.

In the meantime, group 2 started looking after a certain length of time. They followed the arrows until they reached the circle and X. The search was on. Winners were those who couldn't be found. The groups then switched roles for the next trail.

I well remember the night my group won. Oh, how daring we could be! Another kid and I actually found a place where you could crawl underneath the Yalobusha County Courthouse at Coffeeville. I distinctly remember the thought I had: *No one has probably been under here for one hundred years.* We were scared in the shrouded darkness, amid creeping shadows and pesky cobwebs. We kept looking around and wondering what snakes/insects/varmints/ghosts might be around us. But we stayed until the other group gave up on us. Someone working in the courthouse heard the next day that we were under there, and the word was spread in the community that no one had better be crawling around underneath. They didn't have to tell me; I wasn't about to anyway.

I've often wondered about the origin of that game. In my search, I can't find anyone from elsewhere that has ever heard of it. It was one of those games you never forgot about from your youth.

We did not feel that we had to destroy something to have a good time. If we ever destroyed anything, someone told, and the next day, your identity was known all over town. That meant your reputation was ruined. That was about the worst thing that could happen to a person. We were all consciously aware that we should not get on the wrong side of those who enjoyed making moral judgments about your behavior. These behavioral inspectors were always in the back of our minds. We could just see their inquiring faces and their mouths yakking. It was enough to scare the devil away, and even he would not want to cross those folks. This was another example of social control by the threat of gossip.

THE ZIPPER CAPER

Riding bicycles up and down those Coffeeville streets on a summer afternoon, with no worries about the future, was the ideal way of experiencing absolute exhilaration. Usually, it was with the baseball guys, but occasionally, I had the pleasure of biking with my claimed girlfriend, a classmate. We were on Bailey Ave. when she turned into the driveway where her relatives lived. All of a sudden, her five- or six-year-old cousin came around the house yelling, screaming, and crying. She went inside while I attempted to understand the reason for his misery. Upon closer observation, I discovered the poor little fellow had caught his dinger in the zipper of his pants. Now only men and small sons can comprehend the pain and agony wrought by such an accident. Most men or boys, sooner or later, will experience this unbearable pain. It is unfortunate to have a lethal weapon in such close proximity to this most sensitive member. Being able to empathize with this tragedy, I immediately got him released. By this time, other family members arrived to console him over his ordeal. My bike companion and I left the scene without ever saying a word to each other about this most untimely experience of her cousin or the heroic deed I had performed.

THE 1953 BOYS OF SUMMER

They say that everyone at some point in his or her life becomes nostalgic about his growing-up years and the long-ago experiences of childhood. As the years moved rapidly along, I often recalled those days in Coffeeville before we knew how to be stressed and anxious about life's more serious responsibilities. Those were the truly enjoyable years, free and innocent from life's fast lane.

We knew our parents loved us and would provide what we needed, not necessarily all that we wanted. That allowed us to enjoy those carefree days with friends, nourishing memories that would last a lifetime.

My first exposure to baseball was throwing green balls from a bois d'arc tree, sometimes called horse apples. They were about the size of a baseball. My grandmother played pitch with me in the front yard of her house. When the ball started to disintegrate, I just picked another one off the tree. She was really good at catching it and throwing it back to me.

This experience evolved into playing sandlot baseball, meaning the side yard of the Ed Woodall home. Looking back, how gracious and considerate the family was to allow these local boys of summer to use their yard for their youthful summertime pleasure. I remember we learned well the open stance in batting because this prevented the batted ball from banging into their house (most of the time).What a life playing America's sport and listening to Mel Allen announce the New York Yankees' games on a radio! When we didn't have nine players, a sister of one of the players ably filled in. Oscar Ayers volunteered as our coach. We obtained our limited equipment such as bats, balls, and gloves either from Bailey's Store or from Kimbrough's. We didn't have a sack full of baseballs; we only had one baseball each. Every day we decided which one of us would bring our one baseball to practice. We had to protect that ball at all costs. If the ball was lost in the field, it was everyone's task to pitch in and help find it.

The street was right behind the backstop. One day the batter hit a pop fly that went straight up over that street. At that moment, Buddy Fly's cattle truck came by, and the ball fell into the back of his truck bed. Of course, he was not aware of it and kept driving. At first, we were frozen like the proverbial deer in the headlights. Then we ran for the bicycles to chase down the truck driving off with our prized possession. We finally stopped him on Highway 7. What a relief! We simply wiped off the cow manure and went back playing our favorite summer sport.

On one occasion, Mr. Woodall took several of us boys to Memphis to see the Memphis Chicks play. What a thrill it was to see former major leaguer Dixie Howell hit a home run in the old Russwood Park! We even ate at a fancy restaurant called Pappy and Jimmy's, which was a new experience for some of us. But Edward had been there before, and he proceeded to show us how to order.

He became confused, however, and ordered "Fan Tail Cola and Red Rock shrimp." We learned later just how funny that was.

After a while, we decided that we were pretty good ballplayers and ready to compete, so we began to schedule games at Water Valley and Bruce. Now Bruce had a good team, and we really hated losing to them because they were the neighboring town east of Coffeeville.

This was long before the days of organized baseball leagues with rules. First, we had to look like a baseball team, which meant we had to have baseball uniforms. Well, we found that we could get some mail-order uniforms from Sears and Roebuck. So we ordered uniforms complete with our team name on the front of the shirt, the Coffeeville Cubs. Man, they looked sharp on us with our caps and high-top tennis shoes! Now we were ready to play some serious baseball.

But before our first game, Coach Ayers told us there was something he needed to explain. He said since Richard, his son, was going to be the catcher, he would be wearing a piece of baseball equipment for personal protection simply called the cup. And if any of the rest of us wanted to wear one, he would provide them. We wondered, *What on earth is he talking about?* Every young baseball player soon learns of this athletic rite of passage into manhood and has a story to tell about the first time he was exposed to the infamous "cup."

One guy finally blurted out, "Well, where do you wear it?" You see, just by looking at it, it is not obvious either where it is worn or what it is supposed to protect. Richard laughed and said, "Why, you wear it on top of your head, under your cap." He began to parade around with it on top of his head. We didn't figure that was right and thought that he was just clowning.

Finally, Coach Ayers took it away from him and engaged in that initial ritual of educating us on what it was for and where it was worn. Afterward, in unison, these twelve-year-olds shook their heads and said, "No, sir! We really don't think it's necessary for us to wear that thing." So for that season, that was the end of the cup issue.

Things went fairly well for the season, but we still had not beaten Bruce. The last game of the season would be played against them on the field at the back of the Legion Hut. They had good hitters, and we needed some stronger pitching.

The word around town was that there was a kid between Coffeeville and Grenada who was a real hard-throwing pitcher. There was no rule about having to stay with the same roster, so you could add players along.

Speaking of rules, it was generally understood that players had to be somewhere around ages eleven to thirteen. When we approached this kid about pitching that last game against Bruce, we asked him how old he was. He said he was fifteen. We said, "Well, Sunday afternoon, you are going to be thirteen." He appeared to be cool with that, so we were set for our big game.

Sunday afternoon came, and a large crowd gathered. Bruce brought a loud contingent of fans. The game was close, and we played our best game of the year. Our pitching was especially good. I remember that George Ayers had two big hits, and I scored two runs. Coffeeville won the game five to two.

It was one of those moments you wish you could stop in time so you could savor the thrill of victory forever. But time moves on for other victories on other days in other chapters of our lives. When I sang in church, "What a blessedness, what a joy divine," I thought of that game. I hope that wasn't sacrilegious.

I'm reminded of the words of the character Terrence Mann, played by James Earl Jones, in the movie *Field of Dreams* (1989): "The one constant through all the years, Ray, has been baseball. America has rolled by like an army of steamrollers. It's been erased like a blackboard, rebuilt, and erased again. But baseball has marked the time. This field, this game, is a part of our past. Ray, it reminds us of all that once was good, and it could happen again."

—◀○▶—

BASEBALL PLAYERS NOT ALLOWED

At the time, I didn't question anything in the culture, nor did present social conditions bother me much. My grandparents lived up on Number 7 Highway that ran by the school building. The house was on the corner of Kennedy Street and the highway. Right across from their house was an open pasture that was not used. Up on the hill from the pasture on the other corner of Kennedy Street and the highway was a little house where two African American brothers were being reared by their grandparents. That part of town was considered to be part of "the hill." Lloyd and Alfred Brown were about my age, and often, we played a little baseball in that field.

Lloyd wanted to play baseball more than anyone I knew. He saved his money and bought a glove and a baseball. Everywhere he went, he carried his glove with him on his belt. He was always looking for someone to play some pitch. When we played, we used my bat and baseball. There was a batter, a pitcher, and the other one chased after the ball. Then we would switch positions. One day Lloyd said, "I hear you all are looking for a pitcher." I wondered how he knew that.

Before I could say anything, he said, "Listen, man, I can pitch hard, and I even have a curve ball." Maybe he had heard about Jackie Robinson breaking into the major leagues a few years earlier.

I responded, "Well, let me see how hard you can throw." I crouched like a catcher and used a stick for a plate. Using my infielder's glove, he blazed one across the plate so hard that my hand blistered.

"Uh, I tell you what. I'll borrow our catcher's mitt from the team one day, and I'll catch some more."

I borrowed the mitt and after practice took it home to catch for Lloyd. We went to the pasture, stepped off the distances, and started. It wasn't long before I realized that this kid could really pitch and that nobody I knew on our team could hit his pitching.

Looking back, it is quite revealing how growing up in a discriminating culture bound me into that culture, meaning there was never any motivation for me to question the status quo. I didn't say, "Well, I'll see if you can pitch on our team." I'm sure I just went home after agreeing that he could throw hard.

Sometime after that, the team was practicing behind the Legion Hut. When we started practicing, I looked up toward the Hut, and there was Lloyd on his bicycle with his glove, just watching us. I glanced up that way several times, knowing that I couldn't ask him to come on down and play with us. Finally, some white fellow came by and ran him off.

While hitting some fly balls in the pasture one day with Lloyd and Alfred, my ball was lost. Soon, darkness came, and I had to go to the house without the baseball. What I didn't know was that Alfred kept looking for it and found it. The next day, he watched and waited for me to come visit my grandmother. When he saw me there, he crossed the street and came around her house to the back door and knocked. I went to the door, and he gave me the baseball he had found.

Now you see, at one level of consciousness, I knew most of the cultural norms about black people needing to "stay in their place," but I was not aware of all the defined situations that required subservience, such as never looking a white person straight in the eye or using their front door. So when Alfred started to leave, I listened to my heart and said, "Listen, Alfred, the next time you need to come to my grandmother's house to see me, you come to the front door." He didn't say anything and left. Perhaps he understood better than I did about the consequences of violating the cultural morés.

Through the years, I often wondered what happened to Lloyd and Alfred. Once I drove back to Coffeeville and asked around if anyone ever knew their whereabouts. Finally, I was told that Alfred became a preacher and was now deceased. They didn't know what Lloyd did in life, but they heard he was killed in Chicago around 1963.

-◄○►-

DIZZY DEAN AND PEE WEE REESE

After we inherited Uncle Thomas's black-and-white TV set, I soon discovered the weekend baseball game broadcasts with Dizzy Dean and Pee Wee Reese as the announcers. Since Dean grew up in Mississippi, we felt honored to see him succeed in broadcasting after being selected to the Baseball Hall of Fame as a successful pitcher of the St. Louis Cardinals for so many years. Because Dizzy had a tendency to butcher the English language, several education groups attempted to remove him from the broadcast booth. Really, he was just adding flavor and pleasure to the game.

His on-air antics and observations were a welcomed relief to an otherwise boring game. He sang "Wabash Cannonball" and even fell asleep during a broadcast. At some point during one game, he said to Pee Wee, "I think I'll go get me another Falstaff." Once, he said a batter had an "unorsodock stance." Fans worked their weekend schedules around his game. Now broadcasting is almost totally scripted; then, Dizzy was the program. His pitching during the 1930s provided a small respite from the Depression. His announcing in the 1950s and 1960s caused us to have a few moments of joy in a society filled with turmoil and upheaval.

CO-COLA AND PEANUTS

Going down Main Street, just before you came to front street, was Brewer's Store, standing alone. It was sort of like a country store, and they always had nice treats you could buy for change. After playing baseball for hours and being hot and tired, it was time for some refreshments. Several of us would get on our bikes and go to this store where you could get a Co-Cola and some salted peanuts for about a dime. Here's how we made this special: pour the peanuts into the Co-Cola, which makes both taste better. This was long before Barbara Mandrell sang about this little pleasure. There was nothing more pleasurable after a fun afternoon of sandlot baseball.

Of course, there were other treats if you had enough pocket change. One of the boys said he knew what those bars of candy were saying, "Oh, Henry, call Dr. Pepper. I think I'm going to have a Baby Ruth."

You might be wondering why I didn't prefer a moon pie and RC Cola. When I first heard of the supposed delicacy, it was just an expression rather than something kids actually enjoyed and bought. The truth is that many white people imitated the black dialect in jokes and phrases, and the mimic always got a laugh. It was a way of reminding ourselves that at least black people deserved to be in last place, below us, partly because of their ignorance of correct pronunciation. In Black English, the R was pronounced *ar-ra*. So the RC Cola became Ar-ra C Cola. The "moon pie" was one of the original wrapped cakes to be bought, which also had a funny-sounding name. Slowly, the myth grew and was consistent with cultural values of the time. Eventually, the combination became ingrained in the language except over time, it became just the "moon pie and RC Cola" so to not sound racist. I've read of professional conferences in the South advertising that refreshments would consist of moon pies and RC Cola as if this had always been a unique Southern tradition. Have you ever tasted the combination? I did once and discovered there was nothing in the taste that made it in any way special. Well, at least this is my theory of how it started.

REPLICATION OF AFTERNOON RITUALS OF ENGLISH GENTRY

The last vestiges of Old South rituals of proper social interaction were only occasionally seen. Only a few organizations of Southern ladies ever referred to them anymore:

> Gentlemen on being introduced to a lady were expected to stiffen the body, bow from the hips down with the body and limbs forming a right-angle triangle. The lady acknowledged the introduction by dropping a "curtsey"—the depth of the curtsey being commensurate with the importance of the gentleman introduced.

At age eleven, I was flattered that the daughters of some of the large businesses and landowners invited me to various social events. My main concern was that I was not familiar with their afternoon rituals in which they wanted me to participate. After an invitation, my mother attempted to teach me what little she knew about the occasion. "Be nice, polite, and respectful." She always said that if you were mannerly, nothing else ultimately mattered. I was still afraid and uncomfortable but dared not refuse the invitation from these families. After all, it was me and not other boys who got this privilege.

I knew absolutely nothing about croquet. We had not played this game out on Route 3. Subsequently, I learned that it developed in nineteenth-century England and was quite popular among the gilded class. I can still picture all those hoops and large balls we hit with mallets in the backyard at the Alfred Bryant home. What was surprising to me, though, was that the game was so viciously competitive. When I violated some rule, those young ladies would place their ball next to mine and knock it to kingdom come. At the time, I didn't think that was very nice of them. But when the game was over, the dainty refreshments served on the sun porch seemed to make us forget the fierce competition. Going home, I felt quite proud, having increased my knowledge and skills of these games, not usually played by the common folk.

In later years, these experiences were advantageous when people learned that I was originally from a small town in Mississippi, and I saw in their facial expression the thought that I must be an uncultured, country hick. Often, some comments confirmed their false ideas about my upbringing. Given my level of self-confidence, I usually reacted by saying something like this:

Well, I don't know what your experience was, but I tell you, nothing was lovelier than a leisurely summer afternoon in Mississippi playing a game of croquet on the freshly mown lawn with two beautiful young Southern belles. Of course, I got croqueted a few times, but all was well when we retired to the sun porch for cheese straws, sweet *pate a choux*, and traditional fruit punch. And if you've never seen and experienced the elegance of the Peabody Hotel in Memphis, you have no idea what you have missed. And if you ever need a place for a banquet or ball, you must try the exquisite Centennial Ballroom at the Peabody. Afterward, to make the evening complete, a riverboat cruise is the perfect ending for an unforgettable day. Ah, how fortunate we were to have such privileges! Now where did you say you were from?

If this little show of panache didn't surprise or impress them, and just for the heck of it, I fulfilled their prophecy by launching into a graphic description of how we used to skin and gut a squirrel or possum. They usually said that this was enough when I explained how to hold up the tail and cut across its anal area.

GRANDMOTHER'S SMORGASBORD

My grandmother never had a public job as was the case with many women of her generation. Rather, she majored on preparing meals, preserving food, cleaning and washing, helping Granddaddy in the fields, and keeping the children in line (and not just her own). Even as Grandmother aged and was living in Coffeeville, she continued to cook big meals every day for dinner (before it was called lunch). Her cooking reputation spread far and wide. Many of our family and acquaintances knew about her daily spread and invited themselves to just happen by around dinnertime. Besides her and Granddaddy, the usual crowd involved Uncle Noffy and Evie, Uncle Clarence, sometimes Elizabeth or Joanne, my mother occasionally, others, and myself. You selected from whatever was on the table, which always included a vast array of vegetables and various meats with her regular sweet tea, along with banana pudding. It was a mile or more to walk to town, but she did two to three times a week buying groceries and walking home with the sacks in her arms. Indeed, it was a time when the "women were strong."

Regrettably, it was also a time before tipping became the norm. The men seemed to feel that their praise for the good meal was enough. How nice it would have been if we had created that value and practice on our own. I never heard her complain; I guess her satisfaction came from knowing that we all enjoyed her meal—a style that is seldom comprehended today.

FREQUENT FLOWING OF STRONG DRINK

Later in life, I was amazed to learn how shielded I had been growing up. My mother never wanted me exposed to societal evils. When grown, I discovered that during those innocent years, the liquor flowed more freely than I ever thought in our legally dry state. Oh, I knew about home brew by listening to others talk about it. Once, my father got drunk from drinking too much "rot gut whiskey" and threw up down at the Legion Hut one Saturday night. Joanne was summoned to go down there and lead him to Grandmother's house just up the street. I insisted that I go along. Once there, I could tell my father did not want me to see him in this condition. So we led him up the street with him stopping several times to vomit. My father, after he married and had a son, couldn't handle the vices of the flesh very well. I think it was because Ray and Harold Hughes, his boyhood friends, were not there. You see, when they were all together when they were growing up, they could set and impose limits on one another's behavior.

My cousin, Gerald Fly, told me about a fellow who worked in the clothing and shoe side of the department store. For the money, he would put a bottle of whiskey in the new pair of shoes you were buying. Gerald said some men bought shoes every week! One could hear someone say, "You know, I think I need a new pair of shoes. I think I'll go get me a new pair." Everyone knew their intentions.

Then there was a place just south of town known for the availability of strong drink. Some white entrepreneurs made a lot of money selling to black people up on "the hill." Another way to get alcohol was from the backstreet alleyway next to one of the two-story buildings. A rope hung down to the street from the upper window. You just pulled on the rope, sent your money up, and the whiskey was lowered to you. The wealthy elite had theirs as well, but they were able to get it from more respectable sources.

While a kid, I always suspected there must have been some unsavory places of business that were off-limits to some women and children. On Saturdays, after Mother had looked at clothing at Benoists, she would go down to Bailey's Store at the end of Front Street. I noticed that when we passed by Rena's Café, next to Bailey's, she took my hand and walked swiftly. Of course, I wondered what I must have been missing. The only thing I could pick up was loud music and laughter. Sounded like someone was having a really good time.

Some people sold bootleg whiskey out in the county. Some even paid state taxes on the unlicensed liquor. Probably, the most well-known place was called Shady Springs, just north of town. My mother wouldn't even let me look at the place when we passed by. The owner used part of his house for parties and kept the strong stuff in various places so the sheriff could never find it, though many of these sellers also paid the sheriff off each week to leave them alone. For years, the sheriff's wife would make the rounds on Monday morning, collecting their part from the proceeds. Most people knew why the sheriff could have a comfortable retirement.

The whiskey issue raged in political, social, and religious circles for many years. Politicians hated having to offer an opinion on the issue, knowing the emotions on both sides and needing their votes. It was during this time in 1952 that State Rep. Soggy Sweat of Alcorn County gave his legendary whiskey speech before a social group in Jackson:

My friends, I had not intended to discuss this controversial subject at this particular time. However, I want you to know that I do not shun controversy. On the contrary, I will take a stand on any issue at any time, regardless of how fraught with controversy it might be. You have asked me how I feel about whiskey. All right, here is how I feel about whiskey:

If when you say whiskey you mean the devil's brew, the poison scourge, the bloody monster, that defiles innocence, dethrones reason, destroys the home, creates misery and poverty, yeah, literally takes the bread from the mouths of little children; if you mean the evil drink that topples the Christian man and woman from the pinnacle of righteous, gracious living into the bottomless pit of degradation, and despair, and shame and helplessness, and hopelessness, then certainly, I am against it.

But if when you say whiskey you mean the oil of conversation, the philosophic wine, the ale that is consumed when good fellows get together, that puts a song in their hearts and laughter on their lips, and the warm glow of contentment in their eyes; if you mean Christmas cheer; if you mean the stimulating drink that puts the spring in the old gentleman's step on a frosty, crispy morning; if you mean the drink which enables a man to magnify his joy, and his happiness, and to forget, if only for a little while, life's great tragedies, and heartaches, and sorrows; if you mean that drink, the sale of which pours into our treasuries untold millions of dollars, which are used to provide tender care for our little crippled children, our blind, our deaf, our dumb, our pitiful aged and infirm; to build highways and hospitals and schools, then certainly, I am for it.

This is my stand. I will not retreat from it. I will not compromise.

It was during World War II that Mississippi started collecting black market taxes on the illegal sale of bonded whiskey. The state had liquor prohibition until 1966, at which time, they gave counties the option. The state tax collector's job was to collect the tax, and his salary was a percentage of the collection. In 1964, *Life Magazine* determined that the collector at that time, William F. Winter, was the highest-paid public official in the United States. To his credit, Winter recommended that the office be abolished.

Winter later held many statewide offices, including governor, from 1980 to 1984. After an illustrious career and the recipient of numerous awards, in 2008, he was given the Profile in Courage Award by the *John F. Kennedy Presidential Library and Museum* for his work advancing public education and racial reconciliation.

EVERY PARENT'S WORST FEAR

Parents in the first half of the twentieth century lived in constant fear of a dreaded disease called polio. They were terrified that the disease might leave their children unable to walk or might even have to spend the rest of their life in an iron lung. The disease affected mostly children and caused paralysis and death for much of human history. Around 1910, there was a dramatic increase in polio cases. The disease even crippled Franklin D. Roosevelt, who later became one of our truly great presidents. The devastating consequences of this terrible disease that struck so much fear led to the great race toward finding an effective vaccine. The eventual discovery of that vaccine by Jewish Americans, Jonas Salk and Albert Sabin, led to its virtual eradication.

But before that happened, polio struck our family. Aunt Jane and Uncle Howard Armstrong's little eight-year-old only son, Dickie, was a fine young man, a very lovable child. In July 1952, he was taken to the Charleston Hospital, where tests determined he had polio. This was the peak year in the United States when twenty-one thousand cases were reported. They sent him on to the Grenada Hospital, where Dickie was diagnosed with bulbar polio. In such cases, the virus invades and destroys nerves within the bulbar region of the brain stem. The symptoms include weakened muscles and difficulty breathing, speaking, and swallowing.

Jane and Howard admitted Dickie into the hospital on a Thursday in Grenada, and he would not go home alive. The disease ravaged his little body, and he couldn't respond. He held on till Sunday, when he died with all his loved ones by his bed, where they had begged and prayed for his life. Mother and Dad and I went to see the family during this time. What I remember was that no one spoke words, just a lot of crying, hugging, and holding hands.

The child casket was taken to their house, where throngs of people came to express their sympathy. When we arrived, there was a crowd of people standing around outside the house. To this day, I can feel and see the sadness that filled the atmosphere. Drops of grief were everywhere. A terrible disease had taken their only child. Within a short time afterward, Aunt Janie would bear twin boys.

LEGENDS OF MEN AND HOUNDS

In the golden age of coon hunting (1940s and 1950s), none were any better than two men from Coffeeville—Jake Sides (who owned a John Deere business) and George Schmitz (a local blacksmith). After finding a couple of trained bluetick hounds and learning the value and demand for these dogs, Sides started the Blue Pilot Coon Hound Kennel. Coon hunters from across the country came to purchase his special breed. In coon hunting lore across the country, the legends of Ol' Curley, Flora, Mourner, and Bouncer live on as the best bluetick hounds ever to run those marshy, dense, bottoms near Scuna River and Yalobusha River.

According to Sides, his legendary dogs and his friendship with the renowned coon hunter in Coffeeville, George Schmitz, would change his life forever. Thus began friendships with both man and hound that would lead them into unforgettable odysseys—coon hunting in the Mississippi river bottoms.

George Schmitz was a colorful character (philosopher, sage, theologian, skilled craftsman, and otherwise Southern good ol' boy) who owned a blacksmith shop on the backstreet of town. His work was hot, sweaty, and hard. No telling the number of farmers and many others who needed his blacksmith services from time to time. He enjoyed his work, especially when men came around to hear some of his cooning tales.

Schmitz started writing an occasional story of a memorable coon hunt for the local weekly, the *Coffeeville Courier*. Shortly, they became a big hit in the community. When the news was out that George had a coon hunting story in the paper, we would get a copy someway, usually by borrowing someone else's. All of us gathered around, my grandparents, Joanne and Elizabeth, myself, Dad, while Mother read the story by the light of a coal oil lamp.

George's style of writing was all his own, and he often compared the sound of the truck motor and the long lonesome howling sound of the hounds to the melody of some gospel song such as when George said, "As that quartet topped the hill in the southwest, chasing old Grayface, they were all harmonizing, 'When the roll is called up yonder, I'll be there.'" These men were more than just hunters though; one could just sense the joy they derived from the event and the cordial and respectful relationship with friends and the beloved dogs. Their descriptions of the hunt absorbed the imagination and allowed you to see each story unfold and to visualize the trails, hills, hollows, dogs, river, trees, and of course, raccoons.

The coon hunter had a special relationship with his dogs. Even some wives often made the comment, "You care more about them dogs than you do me." A hunter just couldn't share all those special moments when they saw firsthand what their dogs would do for them and not have a fond affinity with them. The dogs would find the coon and alert its owner where he was and, if the coon was running, which direction to follow. Once treed, the dog even climbed part of the way. Nothing received more respect than a good lead dog that could literally coordinate the other dogs on a successful run. The dogs would stay and keep the coon treed until the hunters arrived. They admired a dog that could tell when the coon had tried to deceive its path. A well-trained coon dog would go to the water's edge and determine that the critter had jumped in the water either to cross the river or to come back on shore a short distance farther on. The episode was not over until the owner had the coon in a sack, and the dogs were rewarded for a great run.

In my judgment, the whole coon hunting scene constituted a subculture, which had its own rules of behavior for both the dogs and the hunters. Standards for keeping the sport alive and well were maintained. If you were around a coon hunter long, you realized they had their own unique terms that distinguished them from the general population. They wanted a coon dog that would "ball on the track" and "chop on the tree," meaning that they would have one bark while on the "track" (the scent trail) and a different bark when they "treed." This trait is sometimes called a change-over bark. Dogs with this skill were in high demand. Some dogs might have a "loose bark," meaning that they barked at most anything, and others barked at "trash" (meaning unwanted game such as a possum). A "cold nose dog" was desirable because they could run a track that was two to three hours cold. Once a coon was treed, the hunter might do a little "squalling," which imitated a coon in distress and helped locate the coon while "shining" a tree (shining a light up into the tree).

Another coon dog contest involved an expert "dragger," taking a fresh coon hide and dragging it through dirt and grass and around the banks of a large lake. These events were called drag races. The trail might stretch for several miles, involving a few detours into some wooded areas. At some point, the hide was left for the dogs to find, usually hanging from a tree. At the starting point, a cast of four dogs got a whiff of the hide, started barking, and then at a certain time, let loose to chase the scent of the hide until it was found first by the winning dog. Afterward, another cast would run until every coon dog had competed. Eventually, a championship round determined the winning dog and its owner.

They had local, state, and national organizations, contests, events, conventions, and literature. For many, the experience became addicting and began to occupy a good portion of a person's thoughts and activities. Their feeling was that a man deserved to have some small personal pleasure before he crossed the chilly waters of Jordan. What a secret joy they created for themselves!

Hunters enjoyed telling about the night someone fell into a sinkhole, got lost for a while, had to chop the tree down, or maybe stepped on a snake. Stories included tales of poking the coon out of the tree so it would have the option of whupping all them dogs and walking off if he wanted to as country comedian Jerry Clower claimed. At least they would have a sporting chance!

Bluetick coonhounds were the preferred breed because their eyesight was especially good at night. One could always tell the males from the females because the male was usually fifteen pounds heavier and a little longer. The bluetick is distinguished by an interesting color combination on its body. The background is a mottled gray and bluish ticking with larger spots of black or dark blue on the head and body. They are gentle and good-natured as hunting dogs that can also serve as a good watchdog. They don't like being left alone for long periods and can actually suffer from separation anxiety. Thoughtful coon hunters will pay them some attention every day.

In the fall of the year around three o'clock in the afternoon, that old bug started on George. He would take a good look at the sky to determine what the weather would be like that night. You sure didn't want to be caught in a thunderstorm. The more the evening wore on, the more the excitement grew, and the more he anticipated a good hunt. He moseyed on down to Jake Sides's place of business after work, and Mr. Jake would be in the same mood. Miss Mary had George's supper on the table when he came home. She got where she could predict pretty well when George had decided to go hunting that night.

I always thought that the legend of George Schmitz and his coon hunting stories was just a local phenomenon. It appeared to me that locals were merely amused at his outgoing personality and his jovial manner. Nothing important was ever expected from him other than his entertaining stories of coon hunting. After all, he was a simple man with not many outward symbols of material success. He and his good wife lived on a dirt road across town in a shotgun-type house. I don't think he even had any transportation for most of his short life. He walked to and from work.

I've heard it said that to enjoy your later life, you should have created some special memories along the way and stored them in the back of your mind. Don't you know those coon hunting trips and all their crazy happenings with good friends, hot coffee, and fine dogs served them well when the twilight years crept upon them?

I don't suppose some folks in that community gave George Schmitz credit for teaching us anything worthwhile. But as I travel though this pilgrim land, I beg to differ. Men like him teach us the value of enjoying the moment rather than living life many years ahead. My memory of his life reminds me that it is not a sin to have an enjoyable hobby and to take the time to nourish and relish cordial relationships with friends of similar interests. Some of us need to unbind and be set free from the shackles of constant seriousness. Even when life has only brought us disappointment and deprivation, we should not drink from the bitter cup every day. Even the Good Book says, "So I recommend having fun, because there is nothing better for people to do in this world than to eat, drink, and enjoy live." –Ecclesiastes 8:15 (NLT)

After Schmitz's untimely death (victim of a falling tree while fishing), the *1966 Historical Blue Book Annual*, published by the Coon Hunters Association of America, was dedicated to his memory and contained some of his stories.

During this era, there was another popular holiday activity called coon on the log contest. Usually, it was held at someone's pond, where there was a large area with fairly shallow water. People brought their picnic lunch or bought their food. Occasionally, there was live music and games. The big event, however, was the time for all the coon hunters to enter their coon dog in the contest. The sponsors already had a supply of logs in the water and some raccoons previously trapped. A raccoon was placed on one of these logs and pushed out from the bank. A cast of several coon dogs at a time were let loose at a given signal to go after the coon on the log. The first dog that could subdue the coon and get it back to the bank without the dog being drowned or the coon being drowned was the winner.

This contest was an opportunity for all the coon hunters who had been bragging that their dogs were the best to show it. Spectators picked a dog as their favorite and cheered for its success. I'm sure there was more than a few money bets placed on these dogs. The winners from the trials were narrowed down until there was a championship run when the winner and its owner was recognized and pictures taken for the paper.

"Coon on the log" events, however, were short-lived. People began to observe that occasionally, dogs and coons would be killed or drowned in the struggle. When a raccoon was cornered or threatened, their strike and bite could be vicious. If one ever got the coon dog by the throat, they could take the expensive dog into the water and drown it. Some evidently saw it as a blood sport and too cruel to animals. Thereafter, the contests were outlawed.

Throughout the South are coon dog cemeteries where owners may lay their beloved hounds to rest with profound respect. The inscriptions on gravestones are quite moving: "Here lies my body. It died. But my soul waits for you on the other side, and until that faithful day, it's in your hearts and memories that I hope to stay." Often, the "Coon Dog Eulogy" by William W. Ramsey is read: "Let not your hearts be troubled, for in his master's swamp are many den trees. If it were not so, I would have told you. He has gone to prepare a place for you and where he has gone, (dog's name) will also go . . ."

◄o►

WORKING FOR THE MAN

Looking back, we were really blessed in our growing-up years to have a theater in Coffeeville showing all the latest Hollywood movies. Spearman McRee was the owner and was also the town mayor. I especially enjoyed the shows on Saturday, and occasionally, I saw Mr. McRee during the week since we only lived about a block away. One day he offered me a job taking up tickets in the balcony of his theater where black people sat. I discussed this opportunity with my parents, knowing that my mother would give me about a dozen reminders. For taking up the tickets, I earned a dollar and a half and could see the movie when I wasn't occupied doing my work.

For an eleven-year-old, I took my job seriously. Several times, the black guys teased me and tried to get me to lighten up a bit. It never crossed my mind that one of them would have been glad to have this job. I never had one problem, and I felt proud I was helping my parents out a little by making my own spending money.

BREAD AND ROSES

After World War II, there was an influx of factories, mostly textile plants, from the Midwest to the South because the owners were told of surplus laborers ready and willing to work for whatever they paid. In the late 1940s, one such plant, Rice Stix, a dry goods wholesaler, headquartered in St. Louis, built a textile mill in Water Valley. More than four hundred women were employed to sew pants and shirts under production, meaning that their job depended on their ability to produce so many dozens of pants in a specified period. Supervisors stood over the women, driving them to "reach production." Large fans stirred the air filled with cloth fibers that were inhaled and lodged on the lining of the lungs. The work had to be done with precision, fast and furious.

After a year of sharecropping on the Old Leonard Place, my parents knew they would have to find some public work. My mother was one of those four hundred women who was hired, and for most of them, it was their first public job. She made fifty-six cents an hour in wage slavery with no retirement, no health care benefits, and few holidays. She was supposed to be grateful for a job, which was more than she had previously. And the women were grateful but couldn't understand how their industrious qualities were not recognized in kind.

In 1952, the women were afraid to talk with the union organizers when they came, thinking they might lose their jobs. The men had ways to communicate the workers' rights that alleviated fears. Gradually, momentum began to increase. I remember the day the women walked out to strike for better working conditions, improved wages, some holidays off, a paid vacation, and overtime pay. I'm proud to say that my aunt Elizabeth and my mother were some of the first ones to make this bold move to stand for a better life for their families and especially their children.

During a strike in Boston, James Oppenheimer was inspired to write the poem "Bread and Roses" after hearing speeches and seeing placards held by striking women. In 1911, he wrote, "Our lives shall not be sweated from birth until life closes; hearts starve as well as bodies; give us bread but give us roses." In other words, we need fair wages and dignified working conditions. "The worker must have bread, but we want roses too." These women, whether in Boston or in Mississippi, wanted the same things for their children.

Again, I experienced one of those moments of truth about many people's attitudes toward the working class. All of a sudden, some people I had known, including some business owners in town, were aggressively opposed to the union. Others in opposition were the banks, the local newspaper, and the courts. They began to call us derogatory names. What was perplexing to me was the thought that if these women made more wages, they would spend it, thus benefiting these very people in opposition. I soon learned that many folks were selfish. If they already had a good and comfortable life, they didn't want others to have the success they had. They didn't mind grinding the faces of the poor into the ground. Even at an early age, I thought that there had to be some spiritual issue they had missed in church. But on second thought, such injustices had not been discussed in my church either.

The full force of the union movement had to be used to gain a victory in 1952 Mississippi. This involved the picket line and the spies who stayed on the job to report to the union organizers what management was doing on the inside. Feelings, emotions, and violence escalated to the point that the anti-union governor Hugh White declared martial law and called out the National Guard, which intensified the feelings. It seemed there was a grand conspiracy among local businesses, law enforcement, and state government to bust up the union effort. I had never seen such hatred of the common workers only seeking decent wages and protesting unfair practices by the owners (mainly for their children's future). The guard set up machine gun nests near the textile plant, ready, I suppose, to mow down the strikers. These lowly women and some male strikers were wrestling against principalities, powers, and might. Their thought was *If all hell assails us, we shall not be moved.*

One ally emerged in Sheriff Lloyd Farmer and his deputy, Henry Forsyth. The governor's national guardsmen, with drawn bayonets, began to arrest the strikers on frivolous charges. Farmer and Forsyth knew these people as friends and neighbors, not criminals, and released them out the back door of the jail. Local union opposition conspired to get Sheriff Farmer impeached for his actions but to no avail.

The strikers were disappointed to see such opposition from the owners where they did business. One grocery store in town, however, Jones Supermarket, agreed to give credit to the strikers with the promise by the union that all just debts would be paid.

During this period in the late 1940s and early 1950s, more than four hundred thousand textile workers went on strike in seven Southern states. More than fifteen thousand Natural Guard troops were mobilized during the union's simple effort to help these workers get a fair wage from these companies making huge profits off their cheap labor. Twelve strikers were killed and one deputy sheriff.

"DADDY, WHAT IS A COMMUNIST?"

Hanging out at the Union Hall in Water Valley allowed me to overhear a lot of conversation about what was going on with the striking workers. There were speeches by various union organizers from other locations as well as the local men. I was very pleased one day when my uncle Jimmie Price from Memphis came by and was invited to speak because of his work at Firestone Tire, which had a union. He thoroughly understood what the strikers had to do to achieve some improvements in the working conditions at the textile plant. I went around the hall telling everyone that he was my uncle.

One day some men were talking nearby about what all they were being called in the community. One of the negative labels was that the strikers were all communists. In 1952, I think I had heard the word but wasn't sure what it was. My father never minded me asking questions, so I inquired about what that word meant. His response was that many people who already had a comfortable living didn't want working people to have much, so they would call them communists to stir up resentment. But what was a communist? He said he thought it was where the government owned all the industry. The government was run by the Communist Party, and communists were people who were members of that party. I thought about that for a while but never could understand why American workers were called that when they only wanted a fair wage.

In John Steinbeck's *Grapes of Wrath*, the Joad family heard their adversaries call them *reds*, when they were simply looking for work, trying to survive the Great Depression. They wondered what on earth that meant. To them, their plight was easy to understand, and their quest was noble in that they were only doing what any family would do to provide food for the family. These examples of such negative and unfair labeling of workers have been persistent in American culture. For me, it was a lesson I have never quite understood. Why would others want to keep you down economically? Afraid you might get ahead of them? Is greed and selfishness that ingrained in our culture and psyche? Where is the application of Christian principles in all this? Didn't Jesus say, "Those who work deserve their pay" (Luke 10:7 NLT)?

—◄○►—

"WE SHALL NOT BE MOVED"

It appeared to me that the turning point in the local effort to unionize the shirt factory was when the organizers called for a mass meeting at the local gymnasium, located downtown right across the railroad tracks. The whole town was invited, and strikers and their families were urged to be in attendance. That was the largest crowd I had ever seen at that point in my young life. If there were any in opposition, they never spoke up. They passed out booklets for everyone containing union songs. To this day, I can see the grit in the faces of these strong and courageous women with their spouses and children. They sang with great fervor and feeling:

> We're fighting for our children; we shall not be moved;
> Just like a tree planted by the water; we shall not be moved.

By the time they had finished this rousing message of will, they concluded with an old standard union anthem, "Solidarity Forever."

> When the Union's inspiration, Through the workers'
> blood shall run,
> There can be no power greater anywhere beneath
> the sun.

Another song sung at these labor rallies was "We Shall Overcome," which later was adapted to become the civil rights anthem for African Americans seeking justice under the law.

Finally, the union movement prevailed in Water Valley. Today the children of those strikers have life a little better because of their parents' grit and courage.

THE LAST PICTURE SHOW

There was a mystique surrounding the last picture show, which ended well after midnight. Knowing that I had been forbidden about ever even thinking about going, and being the inquisitive little fellow that I was, I wanted to know what the allurement was all about.

Seemingly, it was mainly for courting couples. I had an older cousin who went with his girlfriend in town. One thing I overheard was that there was a race to get inside first so you could get a back seat. I thought that was odd, sitting in the back with all those people in front of you so you couldn't see the movie.

WALTZING INTO HELL

In an agrarian culture, for many, Saturday was the only chance to go to town, spend a little money, and experience a little entertainment after a long week of work. Stores stayed open till ten or eleven o'clock for that last dime anyone had to spend, attempting to make up for all the lost business earlier in the week. As the day wore on, more and more revelers seemed to be in a jovial and mellow mood after imbibing some illegal spirits. No one even thought about what they would then hear on Sunday morning at church.

Preachers often weighed in calling Saturday the "devil's night," which focused on working-class people mainly. They had to have been engaged in some kind of devilment. I don't recall them ever daring to be critical of employers or business schemes to defraud the vulnerable out of land, money, or few resources. It was the powerless, hardworking who were not spared their wrath, people who only sought some respite from the labors of their hands and backs that produced the wealth for someone else to enjoy.

It was amazing how we could put an aura of sacredness over many issues that were otherwise purely secular or at least a matter of opinion. We had to learn all these sacred points, which was not hard to do given that this was a vital part of our socialization into a proper human being that Mama and Papa could be proud of. The numerous expectations involved what to wear or not to wear, words we could and could not use, what we could do and not do on Sunday, and places we could go or not go. It always seemed to me that the list changed from community to community and even from family to family. What confused me was that preachers kept adding to the list.

At least one of these sins could be mentioned in most any sermon. Engaging in an activity they called mixed bathing would surely bring spiritual ruin. The devil has gone and got you now if this occurred. Actually, it took me a while to figure out that he was talking about boys and girls swimming together. Preachers were the only ones I ever heard call it mixed bathing. I didn't even know of any swimming pools in Coffeeville other than a water hole in a bar ditch by the railroad track. Of course, there were the creeks, but it took a brave soul to go in where all those cottonmouths were.

The next favorite sin for preachers to condemn was "dancing." Oh, the degradation that would surely come if a boy danced with a girl. "I'd rather lope like a cow into heaven than to waltz gracefully into hell," they ranted. The schools didn't sponsor many dances, but one had to refrain as a Christian. The question arose as to whether one could even attend. The conclusion was that it was best not to because one would surely be tempted. So several of us took our girlfriends out to the backwaters of Enid Reservoir, found a good parking place, and enjoyed the thrill of smooching. I felt those preachers were not nearly in the know as they thought they were. Although they occasionally condemned something called petting, I didn't mind that because I wasn't prone to petting a girl anyway.

The other great sin that received an overabundance of pulpit time was boys who wore long hair. Even though it was a relative term, the preachers seemed to know for sure what constituted long hair. Even the slightest variation from the styles of the recent past got curious looks from the watchdogs of tradition. A lot of the condemnation related to effeminacy, but honestly, slow dancing with girls in the eighth grade did more to create a heterosexual feeling in me than anything I think I ever did or learned. It would be many years later before I fully realized that we are defined far more by what's in our hearts than what's on our head.

SQUARE KNOTS VERSUS GRANNY KNOTS

One of the positive influences in my life was joining the Boy Scouts. I began in Coffeeville with Russell Bailey as our scoutmaster. To this very day, I remember the difference between tying a square knot and avoiding the infamous granny knot. There was something about the experience that taught me how to be a real man, a good person with character, and always "be prepared," which had many applications in life, I discovered.

Camping trips out north of Coffeeville involved stories to tell for life. One night near the Durden Creek bottom, two of us were sleeping in a hammock when some dogs began chasing a bobcat, all of which ran under us, turning the hammock upside down. On another occasion, the five guys under the tent competed in an, shall we say, expelling gas contest. The fumes inside the tent made it impossible to sleep there, so we learned the joy of sleeping under the stars by the directions of the aggravated camping guide.

A dramatic change in my interests came when our Boy Scout troop was invited by Ole Miss to serve as ushers at their three home football games in the fall of 1952. This would be my first exposure to college sports and seeing such a large crowd of excited fans. Being anxious a bit, I took in all the instructions on how to do my job well, which included being able to interpret a ticket, direct people to their proper seats, and give directions. That was pretty special to have all these dressed-up people (men wore suits and ties, and women wore dresses) coming up to me and asking for information. I saw Ole Miss beat LSU, Maryland, and Mississippi State that fall, having no idea that the Maryland game (undefeated and ranked third in the country) would be talked about for at least the next seventy years and would turn out to be the game that elevated the Ole Miss football program to a higher level.

Beside the games, the one incident with fans that I have never forgotten was when two spectators offered me a drink of whiskey. I told them I was in uniform, only eleven years old, and probably shouldn't at that time.

Soon after moving to Water Valley, I went with the Coffeeville troop to Camp Yacona (Yacona Area Council of the Chickasaw District) for a week near Toccopola, Mississippi. I was already a second class with ambitions of becoming first class. I'd never been away from home that long before. As I recall, my required letter back home was something like this: "Dear Mom, There are 150 boys at camp; I wish there were 149. Love, Alvin." I eventually dropped out of scouting when I reached the age where there were more attractive activities in which to engage.

—◆o▶—

GOOD OL' GIRLS AND GOOD OL' BOYS

The South's subcultural differences have been exploited, exaggerated, and dramatized in literature, movies, and common perceptions. Along the way, we developed some delightful, colorful, and unique personality types (sometimes obnoxious). We can identify them mainly through the language of the people. In that part of Mississippi where I grew up, these were the types that I remember:

Good Ol' Girls. They were younger women who were somewhat tomboyish, athletic, and possessed some valuable manly skills and were proud of it. They knew how to pump gasoline, change a tire, shoot a gun, shoot pool, cuss, and drink. They frequented places in town that were off-limits to nice girls such as service stations and pool halls. Their behavior was often viewed as shameful by the upstanding ladies in town who were quite upset that their gossip about them didn't seem to be much of a controlling factor. The GOGS couldn't have cared less what these socialites thought about them.

They were the forerunners of many archetypes that developed later in television, movies, and song. Remember the waitress in the TV sitcom *Alice* named Flo ("Kiss my grits")? Roseanne Barr in *Roseanne*? Daisy Duke on *Dukes of Hazzard*? Sally Field in *Smokey and the Bandit*?

Nice Girls. "Now you be a nice girl, you hear!" Every Southern girl knew exactly what her mama was talking about.

There is no question that the archetype for the nice girl image was the character in *Gone with the Wind* named Melanie Wilkes—sweet, lovable, adorable Melanie. "Oh, if my daughter could only grow up to be like Melanie Wilkes." So mothers set about early on training, instructing, cautioning, and reminding their daughters of the virtues of being a nice girl.

Most of the do's and don'ts had to do with language, places you were seen, appearance, and sexual behavior. "Honey, speak with expression." Heaven forbid that any profane language ever proceeded from their mouth. They were to always be neat and clean, always wearing appropriate clothing for the occasion. Specific instructions described how far she could go on a date. "My sweet little darling, you must always remember who you are."

The image of the nice girl didn't stop there. Her long-term goals included the expectation that she would "marry well," meaning someone with ambition, refinement, and who dressed neatly. At other times, she was reminded that she could marry whoever provided "they are a Southerner and think like you." In her relationship with men, she had to remember never to act too intelligently, lest she presented herself as too superior. In other words, she was to be sweet and a little empty-headed all at the same time.

Southern Ladies. Their primary purpose in life was to be keepers of the past and pursue the exclusive nature of high culture— an interest in refined tastes in music, art, and literature. Knowledge and participation in these types of activities kept them separated from the vulgar masses and provided them with opportunities not open to common people. Usually, they were older, wealthier, and true women of the Old South.

They were the centerpiece of organizations such as the Garden Club, University Club, Pentagon Club, Twentieth Century Club, Bon Tres Club, Bridge Clubs, Daughters of the American Revolution, and the United Daughters of the Confederacy. Such groups allowed for the social reenactment of rituals that reminded them of the way things used to be. In some Southern towns, they had an old antebellum home where they met in the mornings to drink their mint juleps and discuss issues of past importance. The emphasis was on money, investments, travel, family and Southern heritage, Southern history, etiquette, and the rare, vintage, and expensive antiques of past generations. And when they spoke of "the war-ar" (two syllables), everyone knew which war-ar—the Civil War (although many preferred an alternate term—the War of Northern Aggression or the War for Southern Independence).

Good Ol' Boys. They were kind (to in-group members), mean (to out-group members), daring, possessing a devil-may-care approach to life, Southern, a man's man, comrade, white (never refer to an African American as a good ol' boy mainly because of the historical negative connotation associated with the term "boy"), and affable. A good ol' boy was not a sissy, overachiever, pompous, formal, urban, or urbane.

Their dress was casual while they drove their pickup trucks. Their favorite sports were stock car racing, *wrassling* (not wrestling), hunting, fishing, tractor pulls, and football. Their music was undoubtedly country. They talked a lot about outsiders, the South, dogs, good ol' girls, ostentatious living, and raising hell on Saturday night.

It has been stated that the original good ol' boy was Junior Johnson, who is credited with a form of car racing that led eventually to NASCAR. In his early days, he ran moonshine through the North Carolina hills, eluding law enforcement with his skillful driving. Such driving success made him an outlaw legend in those parts, and he soon was portrayed as "the Last American Hero." Having only been arrested once, he went on to win fifty NASCAR races in the 1950s and 1960s. It was his "Aw shucks" manner and down-home lifestyle that elevated him as the archetypal good ol' boy.

This early good ol' boy type, developed in the 1950s, led to the pop culture glorification of the characters in the Dukes of Hazzard, early Burt Reynolds roles in movies, most all NASCAR drivers,

Jerry Reed, First Brother Billy Carter, Moonie Lynn, and Larry, the cable guy. The Jeff Foxworthy redneck jokes actually describe the historical good ol' boy rather than the genuine and original redneck.

Rednecks. Remember the "squeal like a pig" guy in James Dickey's *Deliverance?* Now that is your typical redneck! An illiterate racist, involving a life of extreme daring, hatred, and violence. If you are seeking to qualify, you must have been put in jail at least once. They were often recruited by political interests to do their dirty work. They were attracted to sporadic and temporary manual labor jobs.

There is no consensus on the origin of the term. Some believe it applied strictly to rural types who often wore that traditional red bandana as a sweatband around the neck or forehead. Others believe that it referred to a literal red neck from being in the sun for so long. At any rate, it was a negative term and a fighting word. Men took great offense at being called one. If you entered one of those roadside beer joints and yelled, "All of you are nothing but a bunch of rednecks!" I assure you the fight would be on. Outside the South, the meaning of the word is obscured. I believe the character type described above is uniquely Southern.

Country Gentlemen. This was not just a brand name for smoking tobacco but also a character type in the South from the late 1940s to the 1970s. These gentlemen were older landowners who benefited from the post–World War II economic boom in the country. Their two-hundred-plus acres were sufficient to create wealth from expanding markets for their crops. It was primarily a combination of cheap labor and mechanized farming that increased their economic well-being.

Even though the character and lifestyle would eventually fade, they displayed a discernible social type for a generation. In the mornings, they made sure all the work was organized for the day by the cheap labor. Then they drove to town in their new truck to pick up any needed supplies with a farmhand riding in the bed. Their dress was obvious with cowboy boots, khaki pants, often a cowboy hat, and an expensive leather coat. That image is still vivid in my mind. "There goes Mr. Walker to town. Wonder how many trips he will make today."

This type was the descendant of the old image of the idealized Southern gentleman glamorized in the literature and culture of earlier times. The normative role involved a man independently wealthy, who never worked himself, was polite to women, and who protected Southern womanhood. The role of Ashley Wilkes in *Gone with the Wind* (and to some lesser extent, the character of Rhett Butler, who also had no moral scruples when it came to womanizing and gambling) reflected the social construct.

Today, Southerners often feel they must neatly fit into one of these male or female character types. That is impossible because these are ideal, pure types, describing a particular person in the white South. Most Southerners do not fit into one of these categories. That does not diminish the fact that these unique types really did exist. Though the original image may have been somewhat overgeneralized, I would argue that remnants of the pure types still exist.

"NOW WHO DID YOU SAY YOUR DADDY WAS?"

In the Deep South during this era, socioeconomic class was the sociological variable par excellence in that it could be used to explain much of our politics, religion, lifestyles, values, associations, income levels, occupations, educational levels, and life chances. The indices generally used to determine one's class were income, occupational status, and education. Your social class determined the quality of your health care, what schools you will attend, whether you go to college, your job opportunities and your access to the avenues of wealth and power.

A five-layer class system had its roots in the South following the economic explosion after World War II. I could see this emergence in my youth and early on began to realize some very harsh realities about my own class and the unfair perceptions others had of us. The stereotypes and myths became culturally ingrained. Terms such as social credentials and family pedigree became important in affecting whether doors of opportunity were opened to you. When applying for a loan at the bank, it was not uncommon for the loan officer at some point to ask, "Now, who did you say your daddy was?" Even churches that were supposedly committed to the principle of "neither Jew nor Greek, bond or free, male or female," allowed great social significance to be attached to gender, class, and ethnicity differences that superseded the biblical description.

Lower Class. This status usually involved some degree of dependence due to illness, disability, lack of skills and opportunity, discrimination, and old age. The jobs at Rice Stix in those early years were for white people only. Women could not borrow money in only their name. Social Security was still attempting to get off the ground at a time when many women did not have a record of public working (lack of public jobs for women). Others lived in areas of high unemployment, lacked transportation or an address, or a victim of the "culture of poverty" (learning how to survive in poverty).

Poverty was not even considered a social problem until 1962 and out of the recognized need to do so, one of president Lyndon Johnson's Great Society programs, called Headstart, came to Mississippi. One of our church members got a job there but had to keep it a secret because other members argued that it was a communist plot. The rationale for the program was simple: poor children who start first grade should not be at a disadvantage in learning compared to other children. Our sister shared with us how some of her children had never seen themselves in a mirror. Now, many years later, we know how much this program has benefited poor children.

I was always bothered by the treatment of the children of poverty in school and the reactions of other students. Some boys whose parents couldn't afford haircuts had what was called a bowl cut. A large bowl was placed over the child's head, and scissors were used to cut the hair around the edges of the bowl. These kids were obviously embarrassed, and some insensitive kids made belittling remarks. Their clothes were not adequate and required school expenses were an issue. One of the worst things I saw was boys hitting these kids hard on their empty stomachs, knowing how much this would hurt since they had not eaten breakfast. These kids would sometimes cry, though trying not to, in the midst of despair and loneliness.

Working Class. Their work was often temporary, or they were vulnerable to lay-offs. The expression "last hired, first fired" applied. Unless it was a union job, fringe benefits were few or none at all (paid in cash). By the time all the bills were paid and groceries were bought, there was not much left. Serious health issues and other unexpected expenses created a crisis for the working poor. It seemed that no matter how hard they tried, they could never "get ahead" or out of debt.

These blue-collar workers took pride in the knowledge that their work provided the means and products by which other people could enjoy life. The thing that bothered them the most was that those who benefited the most from their cheap labor failed to recognize the value of their hard work. Their mantra was "wake me up early, be good to my dogs, and teach my children to pray," as sung by John Anderson.

These were the workers with strong backs and willing hands that literally built this country. Wherever you are, look around at the material objects in your space that make your living and work possible, and realize that they were made by people willing to work long hours in dirty conditions, and at the bottom of the wage scale. When northern factories heard about all the available cheap labor, the textile mills sprang up in numerous towns across the South. As more of these jobs became available after World War II, it hastened the migration of people to the towns and cities and away from their rural lifestyle. My parents were a part of that transition as we moved first to Coffeeville and then to Water Valley, chasing the dream of something better on the horizon.

In my grandfather's later years, he enjoyed hearing the anthem for the working class, "Sixteen Tons," sung by Tennessee Ernie Ford:

> You load sixteen tons, and what do you get? Another day older and deeper in debt. St. Peter don't you call me cause I can't go; I owe my soul to the company store.

Even then, the working class encountered the same old themes of low wages, poor housing, and disrespect for their worth as human beings. Yet when the country needed young men to fight their wars, it was these children mostly that went half way around the world to fight and to die.

Our family was working class since we were just getting by. We were living from paycheck to paycheck, which meant starting over every Monday. With a little more expendable income though, our first jump into these new consumption patterns was to purchase on credit a brand new electric stove for my mother when we rented a two-room apartment in town. I heard her say many times that preparing meals was so much easier with that new stove at age thirty-seven. My parents would be in their late fifties before they moved up to the old middle class by buying a house of their own and getting it paid for before they walked through the valley of the shadow.

Old Middle Class. Our economic system called capitalism in the United States began to show flexibility that allowed more upward social mobility and thus become a little more humanized. This was the result of Roosevelt's New Deal programs and the government allowing labor and management to negotiate for better working conditions and fairer wages to form unions plus the GI Bill that made possible returning war veterans to go to college. With the GI Bill, the percentage of those college educated rose from six percent to twenty percent. And those families were able to send their children to college. Higher education became the common route to take them into a higher socio-economic class. The result was our largest and expanding class, the middle class, which became the backbone of the nation. This was not easily achieved because of strong opposition from those who wanted to maintain class exclusiveness, afraid that others might have as much as they did. They called the programs allowing this upward mobility socialism. Our allowance for greater opportunity and better incomes thus creating another class was something not predicted by Karl Marx in *Das Kapital*.

I saw the sense of accomplishment by workers able for the first time to open up a checking account at the bank, maybe buy a car for transportation, even buy a home, or own a little piece of land. They became the local citizens with the modest homes with manicured lawns, a garage or carport, and the children bribed for bringing home good grades. I remember people bragging about every one of these steps of progress.

The middle class was divided between the old middle class and the new middle class. Their incomes were about the same, but their values and lifestyles often varied.

The old middle class placed value on education and a modest life. Many were churchgoers with their conservative values based on the Judaeo-Christian tradition. Their favorite verse was "let all things be done in moderation." This included spend wisely, live within your means, save now to buy something bigger later on, don't get in debt over your heads, and get out of debt as soon as you can. Older people worried that they might die before the church debt was retired or before their own debt was paid. Many regarded it a gross negative reflection on them to leave their church or their family in debt.

Though happy to achieve middle class status, moving further up the class ladder was not considered vital. If, through some good fortune, they did become quite financially successful, then, of course, this would be okay.

New Middle Class. Right before our eyes we also saw a new class developing, distinguished from the old middle class, though their incomes were similar. It was in their values and lifestyles where they differed. They were social climbers, and their dream was to someday move into the upper middle class. Being upwardly mobile meant they were constantly figuring out the ways and means of achieving a higher status. Usually, they were college educated and occupied new job categories in finance, insurance, and business management. As recent graduates of Ole Miss, Mississippi State, and Northwest Community College, they were now ready for the new, good paying jobs wherever they could be found. Job promotion was extremely significant so they sought to be socially "correct," and to present themselves in favorable light. These other-directed types tried to increase their social networking in order to "be in the right place at the right time."

One interesting observation about these younger professionals was that they sought way too early to possess the images of success long before they could afford them. So they bought the car that best portrayed them as achievers with good taste, which was too expensive for them at their current income. Again, they carried a mortgage on an impressive house but too expensive for them at their current income. Everything they bought had to be state-of-the-art, meaning that soon they had overextended themselves financially.

Part of their efforts to move on up was to join community organizations that brought them into contact with the types they were attempting to impress. When the Country Club was built in Water Valley, it became a place where these eager beavers (later called "yuppies"–young urban professionals) could network and make his or her mark.

Upper Middle Class. These professionals were formerly in the new middle class but moved on up through hard work, possessing rare skills achieved through higher education, business success, privilege, or just pure luck. Often they were workaholics, having known the necessity of commitment, time, and effort. Along the way they learned how to be good organizers and to be disciplined so they could get a lot of work done in a short period of time. Often possessing a drive to succeed, they developed a Type A Personality, which meant they measured their success by the volume of work performed. This also meant they would develop over time some health related problems due to excessive stress.

These class-conscious folks were called "winners," a term I despised because it implied that other people were "losers." Not really knowing what this meant, they often left the impression that it was because of Social Darwinism (the survival of the fittest) that they made it. The strong won out and the weak fell by the wayside as in nature. And they were among the strong. Some of them mistakenly believed they achieved their high position strictly because of their own efforts, without realizing other built-in advantages they had. This might have included inherited wealth, rare opportunities, more life chances, family pedigree or other ascribed statuses such as gender and ethnicity. They are often invited to speak on their "keys to success." The conclusion was nearly always the same: just follow these steps and you will succeed too. I have never yet heard one ascribe the reason as one of "white privilege." They were oblivious to those other variables affecting their status.

The upper middle class included professionals such as doctors, lawyers, engineers, business owners, and politicians. The rest of the community often saw these as the "movers and shakers," the opinion makers, and the ones who could get things done. Colleagues who were slow and inefficient really got on their nerves. They valued efficiency and risk taking because they had learned this from experience.

New Upper Class. This booming economy also produced another social class. A few were able to really reap the benefits of their own risk taking and business savvy and created a new upper class. They possessed as much money as the old upper class, but had a different set of lifestyle values. Flaunting their money was their way of showing the old upper class that they had arrived to claim their share of the prestige of the upper class. They built bigger estates, drove more expensive cars, and indulged themselves with whatever images of upper class status they wanted to demonstrate to their wealthy neighbors. Their divorces and lavish spending sprees became the talk of the town. The old upper class was appalled at how they spent their money—in such nontraditional ways. "What a shame to have that much money and not know how to spend it well." The extravagant lifestyle resulted in drawing a lot of attention to themselves, which was just the opposite of the old upper class who wanted privacy from public scrutiny.

Old Upper Class. There was a saying, "Old money sure is a lot better than new money." This is true because people who had wealth for generations have accumulated more than money such as power, influence, and politicians. Often they sat on local bank boards meaning that they controlled the flow of money in the county. They determined who got the loans and what business flourished. These were people who had money for so long that they had forgotten all the ways they got it.

Sometimes, the money was simply inherited wealth. And even though the sons and daughters may not have reflected the work habits of their forebears, they shared their upper class status nonetheless. Literature is replete with terms describing their status such as the planter class, patricians, blue bloods, and the gilded class. Manual labor was beneath their dignity and their "help" included an assortment if specialists who drove, prepared meals, cleaned house, did yard work, oversaw the finances, and tended to the young.

Their pedigree indicated an interest in rare, vintage, and expensive symbols of class. The key word operating in their lives was "exclusive." They prided themselves in knowing what designer labels were appropriate for their lifestyle and that they knew the difference between quality and quantity. "Spending money well described the gracious living, the hallmark of their existence."

Privacy and secrecy were emphasized or demanded in their dealings. Their estates sat off the main roads farther than others.

Privacy gates and high shrubs sometimes separated them from the eyes of the general public. Recreational activities were also private such as tennis courts in their backyard. There were examples of extended family members all living in the same compound. Their children were taught the expectations that would most likely ensure the continuation of their wealth and power. Endogamous marriages were likely achieved by sending them to exclusive colleges where they would meet other children of the old upper class.

Preferred churches were those where one could be a member in good standing without much participation. This was usually achieved by making liberal contributions on special occasions. The church pretty much allowed these upper class families to live their lifestyle without bothering them. Old-line denominations, well respected, dignified, and formal usually met the criteria.

They seldom ran for political office, though they greatly influenced the process without a lot of people knowing it. This is the way it often worked: A young college educated professional moves to town, is well liked, and has effectively articulated their ideas. One day in the bank, someone tells him or her the bank president would like a word with them. The conversation went something such as this:

"I've been noticing that you are well-liked in this community. You impress people with your ability to speak and be persuasive. I think you have a lot of promise here. Have your thought about running for political office."

"Well, sir, I've not really thought about it much. I know that to run an effective and competitive campaign, one would have to have a lot of financial resources.

"Oh, let's forget about the cost for a minute. If the money were there, would you consider it?"

So the person runs as a candidate of the people, gets elected without the citizens knowing that in reality they are bought, owned or rented by wealthy interests. Should they ever change their benefactors by voting the wrong way on certain legislation, they would be completely destroyed.

Where I grew up, there seemed to be more old-monied people who were business owners and who operated large farming operations with many hired hands working for cheap labor. Through their influence, they were able to keep some industry away thinking that their hands might be attracted to better jobs. Because of this practice, many small towns in Mississippi eventually became ghost towns as many of their citizens moved away to find work.

UNFORGETTABLE

All the people I have mentioned were, in a sense, unforgettable. One of the more colorful ones was a black man who lived in the "poor house" in Coffeeville who bore the nickname "Nig."

I never knew how Nig got his nickname, and frankly, I didn't want to know. Poorhouses, or some variation of them, existed for hundreds of years. Formerly called almshouses and old men's homes, they later evolved into "rest homes." Usually, some town official served as the overseer of the tax-supported home. They were effectively and negatively used as strong motivation to care and provide for yourself and to develop independent resources in old age. I remember my dad driving by the one in Coffeeville and seeing the residents sitting on the porch or working in the yard or garden. Neither my parents nor I ever said a word; we just stared in silence with a sense of foreboding and empathy.

Nig was often seen walking to downtown Coffeeville. Having been given clothes over the years, it appeared that he put them all on each day, especially on days he walked to town, which was almost every day. Nig was probably mentally challenged. Local residents and business people came to know him and were friendly with him. "There goes Nig. Wonder where he's going today. Hey, Nig! What are you up to today?" He picked up trash along the streets as he walked by. Sometimes my grandfather sat on his front porch, and Nig would stop and talk with him. Basically, he was the object of amusement, tolerated, and enjoyed because he responded with something funny or unusual.

Once, while I was getting a haircut in Chester Pate's barbershop, Nig came in to sit and talk. The men were discussing which cars were the best. Nig stated he thought the red cars were best; others argued that another color was best. Nig always had some amusing response to which all the men would laugh. He had fairly good health, probably because of his walking so much every day. His colorful demeanor and presence added a lot of flavor to an otherwise dull morning or afternoon. I heard that old Dr. Criss, a local medical doctor, took care of him in his declining years.

VI

GROWING PAINS (1953–1959)

Young man, it's wonderful to be young! Enjoy every
minute of it.
Do everything you want to do; take it all in . . . so
banish grief and pain, but remember that youth, with
a whole life before it is still transitory.
—Ecclesiastes 11:9–10 (NLT)

WHEN WE MOVED to Water Valley in 1953, the first thing I
heard was that it was the "Watermelon Capital of the World." Some
years, more than five hundred acres were devoted to this crop in the
area. It was mostly a "side crop," in that the profit and pleasure was
in addition to the other crops grown. Its reputation had spread far and
wide. Some trains left Water Valley with thousands of watermelons
headed as far north as Chicago. One local family visited and dined in
a New York restaurant and discovered "Water Valley watermelons"

on the menu. (New York City!) They also had a special market in the Mississippi Delta. One could carry a truckload to a Delta town and advertise "Water Valley watermelons," and it would not be long until they were all sold. This crop and the resulting success in selling them added much to the local economy.

My father had a fine crop one year, and when it came to be gathering time, several of my aunts and cousins helped load them onto the old truck. After I dropped one and busted it all over the ground, I was thanked for my effort and promptly relieved of my duties. When Dad returned from the Delta, he revealed what turned out to be virtually the end of the local watermelon success. He said that people came into the Delta from everywhere else advertising "Water Valley watermelons," and their melons were not nearly as good. After a while, people couldn't tell where those melons were grown. Sometime during and after World War II, the lore of the early watermelon success was pretty much a memory. Like all rural Mississippi boys, I learned how to determine when watermelons were ripe by looking at the stem and the belly and by the proverbial thumping. Through the years, I've impressed a lot of people with that skill. In later years, the city revived the spirit of those times with a huge annual watermelon festival.

THE BELLS TOLL FOR THEE

No, this is not a reference to a line from a John Donne poem: "Therefore, send not to know for whom the bell tolls, / It tolls for thee." Donne said this is a reference to the fact that all of us will someday die. Somber thought indeed!

My experience with church bells was far different. My bedroom window was only about three hundred yards straight from the steeple of the First Baptist Church, which had large church bells in its tower. Every Sunday morning at eight o'clock sharp, those bells sent out the music of gospel hymns so loudly that the entire town could hear them. The nonverbal message was "Okay, it's time to get up and get ready for Sunday School," because there was no way you could sleep through the thundering, ear-piercing sounds of the heavenly highway hymns.

My father liked the church songs because they occasionally played one of his favorite old folk hymns, "Life Is Like a Mountain Railroad."

> Life is like a mountain railroad
> With an engineer that's brave.
> We must make the run successful
> From the cradle to the grave.
> Watch the curves, the hills, the tunnels;
> Never falter, never fail.
> Keep your hand upon the throttle
> And your eye upon the rail.

One day some of my friends were talking about how this music interrupted their sleeping in on Sunday morning. We surmised that the church had some kind of mechanism with a timer that played hymns from those plastic albums. We thought how funny it would be if someone changed the first album to one by Elvis Presley. We all agreed that the appropriate song would be "You ain't nothin' but a hound dog . . ." We all swore that none of us would ever tell if that actually happened. I've often wondered if it did, and if it didn't, it should have. If they really wanted to wake up the town, now that would have done it!

You know that is a fairly accurate spiritual thought. "For we have all sinned and fallen short of the glory of God." In other words, we're just hound dogs with no renowned pedigree, sort of like what John the Baptist told some folks who were boasting how they should be automatically accepted because they were "of Abraham's seed." We all have to take our place at the foot of the cross, where the ground is all level.

In Water Valley, we didn't need an alarm clock during the workweek. Every morning at six o'clock, the Stave Mill whistle blew to awaken their workers (and the entire town) to let them know it was time to get up and get to work on time. The whistle blew again at quittin' time in the late afternoon. So during the week and on Sunday, we heard the sounds to let us know the time of day and what we should be doing.

DEPOT GIRLS

The towns of Oakland, Coffeeville, and Water Valley were on main railroad lines, which contributed greatly to their early growth and development. Representatives of various companies traveled these lines, stopping off at towns to find customers for their products. Others were in town to find new business opportunities. Often, these traveling men, called drummers (attempting to "drum" up business for their wares), had to stay overnight, and to accommodate this need, hotels sprang up near the railroad depot. In fact, there was so much demand in those days Water Valley had two hotels—the Herring and Trusty hotels. They had the Hamlett Hotel in

Coffeeville and the Gaines Hotel in Oakland, where a passenger train stopped every hour.

The original term "depot girls" referred to the women who worked at the depot, many of whom met and married their husbands through these social contacts. The presence of dressed-up men, possessing a business future, also did not go unnoticed by local single women aspiring to find a man with ambition and potential.

Historical lore surrounding the railroads, the depot, and the hotels in those early days abounded, and no doubt, the stories were embellished a bit. I heard some older men tell a story that involved four female friends who developed a plan to find their man by frequenting the depot just at the time the promising prospects were unloading.

Their competition was to see which one could capture the most handsome and richest among the unsuspecting travelers. One man turned out to be a womanizing paramour who had dalliances with women at every stop on his railway journeys. Another man looked promising, was a good dresser with persuasive qualities, but it was all a sham. He had no money or property. The man chosen by the third woman was a fine partier with a happy-go-lucky approach to life, a lot of fun to be with, but completely unreliable and couldn't keep a job. The shiest and most comely looking of the four just didn't have the aggressive social skills to get the attention of any of the prospective male visitors.

One day a traveler, one who didn't draw much attention, started to cross the dirt street in Water Valley to check into the old Herring Hotel but accidentally dropped his briefcase in the mud created after a rain. The shy female was standing nearby, picked up the man's briefcase, and proceeded to clean it. The man, a widower, was quite impressed and insisted on buying her dinner that evening. In the weeks and months following, these two met every time he was in town. They wrote letters, fell in love, married, and whereupon she discovered that he was an extremely wealthy man living in a mansion in New Orleans. To use an old literary cliché, they lived happily ever after. I'm sure there is a moral somewhere in this story, one that has many plot motivators—rivalry, the chase, ambition, disappointment, discovery, betrayal, and love-hate. No doubt the adventures of the depot girls could fill volumes.

Other towns in the area, not on a railroad line, were jealous of the growth and progress of places like Water Valley and Coffeeville on the Illinois Central Railroad tracks heading north and south. In nearby Calhoun County, a newspaper promoted settlement in Calhoun City by pointing out their city's advantages. One of their ads stated, "Your daughters will be safe here because we have no railroad." This implied that having one meant a lot of people traveling through, and with all these people came trouble. Protecting Southern womanhood has always been given great emphasis.

The depot girls were putting into practice the theory of propinquity, which stated that people tend to marry others they get to know. That may sound simplistic, but actually, it is rather profound. Many prospective brides and grooms feel that they will somehow select from among all the eligible people in the world. Not so! Only those you get to know. Therefore, these girls figured out that they must put themselves in a social setting where they were most likely to meet a promising prospect. And in those days, it was at the depot where the trains stopped to unload its traveling men.

DRIVING MISS MAME

Earlier, I mentioned that we lived in the old Redwine house apartment in Water Valley for about a year and a half before moving back to the Old Leonard Place near Coffeeville. Next door lived an older couple in a fine upscale house named James and Mame Terry. It was fairly common in Southern small towns to have a formerly nice house that had over time been divided into apartments that might stand beside an old aristocratic house still occupied by the wealthy. It was an example of caste (usually doomed to just getting by) and class (experiencing upward social mobility) side by side.

The two-story apartment house was in disrepair, and the owner was mainly interested in his monthly rent he collected from families needing a cheap place to live and work. My father and Mr. Terry often talked across the fence while they were working in the backyards and helping each other out in some way. I usually strolled up to listen to grown people's conversation, and Mr. Terry always flattered me with some compliment. He was quite likable, and I wasn't afraid or intimidated by his presence.

One day he called me over to the fence where a plank could be removed, and he said he had something he wanted to give me. I timidly walked over, and he said he wanted me to have this little pocketknife. He stated that he thought I would be careful with it and would enjoy whittling. I was only about eight years old, but that small act changed the course of my family. It has always been amazing how sometimes one simple word, one gesture, one act can have lifelong consequences.

What I said was "Thank you, Mr. Terry!" He was quite impressed that a child my age would be thankful for a gift and say so. He bragged on me to my parents and everyone he saw, and this small gesture resulted in him making a major decision about the future of his wife and us after his death. It was like a concept found in popular culture called the *butterfly effect*, which is a metaphor stating that a small change at one place in a social system can produce large effects elsewhere. One small variable like a butterfly flapping its wings could make a difference in outcomes in other areas. Similarly, there is a law in physics called *morphic resonance*, which describes how even the smallest actions affect the future. Much of creation can be altered by even the smallest acts of kindness. The lesson to be learned here is that we should never forget the power in a smile, a handshake, a good deed, or an encouraging word.

From my earliest memories, I had been taught traditional Southern manners. Practicing these was not supposed to be taken lightly. You were rewarded or scolded based on how well you performed these mannerly rituals. It was "Yes, ma'am," "No, ma'am," "Yes, sir," "No, sir," "Thank you. That's awfully kind of you to say that," "Maybe this will help you a little," "You call me anytime you need help," "I'll be over to help," and "Let me carry that for you." Then there were things you actually did such as opening the door for women, give up your seat to a woman or the elderly, treating your dogs and animals right, being nice and friendly, and respecting your elders. The approved manners involved both saying and doing. If one possessed a good heart, they were usually mannerly.

However, there was another type of behavior by which some people judged your worth and value as a human being. That had to do with various forms of etiquette, which involved knowledge of protocol and custom. Some social classes prided themselves in knowing these rules, while others did not. These rules included knowing which fork to use with certain dishes, how and when to use the napkin, when to shake hands or not, and numerous other little rules that tended to be the exclusive domain of certain socioeconomic classes. What I always despised was people who put one in a situation and deliberately embarrassed them, which I never thought was very mannerly. It may be nice to know both manners and etiquette, but I think I prefer manners over etiquette any day.

We didn't know it at the time, but Mr. Terry and his wife, Mame, had a strange relationship. It seemed that each of them had their own separate lives. She was always dressing up and going to Oxford, Grenada, or Memphis to shop with her socialite friends. And these elite, fluty women hosted bridge parties about twice a week that they seemed to enjoy more than anything else in life.

Mr. Terry had a profitable career working for a large railroad company. They had no children of their own, with only some distant relatives of hers living in Atlanta. It was years later before I knew this, but Mrs. Terry never let him have any intimacy with her. In fact, she was the most asexual woman I think I had ever known. Her preoccupation with high society evidently didn't even allow him to sleep in the same bed with her. There was a category of women who thought sex was dirty and could never overcome that image even after marriage. Only dirty old men would focus any attention at all on such an activity.

So as the story goes, Mr. Terry had a mistress across the tracks where he spent much of his time when he was off work a few days. It appeared that the townspeople didn't blame him for this, knowing something about the prudishness of his wife.

Mr. Terry was saddened when we decided to move back to the Old Leonard Place, west of Coffeeville. Both Mother and Dad continued to work in Water Valley. After moving into Coffeeville, we heard that Mr. Terry had died. We didn't know this until later, but Mr. Terry knew he was going to die and leave his wife alone.

Being the good-hearted and chivalrous man that he was, he set out to make arrangements for her to live safely in her house.

The facts were a little sketchy, but the best we could tell was that he instructed her to contact us, wherever we were living, and encourage us to come and live on one side of the house, which had three rooms, a bathroom, and an outside entrance. The only conditions were that we take care of the yard, make repairs, and look after her welfare until her death. And since there were no close family members, she was to leave the house to us.

She did invite us to come live in her house, but she had some added conditions on her own. Instead of having three rooms, she gave us only two. She used the front bedroom for guests (which she never had). We shared the kitchen, with each having places for our own kitchenware. No going to the kitchen after 10:00 p.m. We could use her dining room only on rare special occasions. Before she sold her car, Dad was responsible for taking her places. The phone was off-limits and could be used only in emergencies. When her bridge party friends were over, there was absolutely not to be any interruptions. In fact, we were supposed to stay out of sight so she and her friends could perform their usual social games within an atmosphere of exclusionary sophistication.

One instruction applied to me specifically—I was never to slam the back door. Well, I didn't slam doors anyway, but this screen door had the tightest spring on it that I ever had seen. Why, it didn't take but about two inches of space for it to make a loud slam. Occasionally, I forgot to close it by hand all the way, and it would slam. Immediately, she would come to scold me, making it seem that I did it on purpose, had no manners, no thoughtfulness, or no civil upbringing. I always showed her deference for fear it might harm my parents if I didn't. I would say, "Well, I'll try not to let it happen again."

And for the privilege of living in her spacious house, taking care of her needs and wants, and under these conditions, we would have to pay this dowager a monthly rent! Mom and Dad didn't like the added conditions but felt they could endure these indignities if, in the end, they inherited the house. There is an old saying in the South that the surest way to live a long life is to leave an inheritance to some worthy cause or person.

Mrs. Terry regarded us as the "unwashed" and in need of rehabilitation. We weren't even the hired help since we had all these responsibilities while paying for this precious and rare opportunity to live in servitude that close to wealth. But again, my dear mother and father could walk to town and to work, and I suspect it was still about me. I was at an age when they wanted me to live in a nice house like my classmates. I stood on her front porch wrapped around half the house upon a hill overlooking the town, hoping that this move meant that someday my parents would actually own a nice house. We endured the indignities with grace because we naively believed and trusted that someday it would be ours.

There is a historical parallel found in the Middle Ages when lords and nobles required peasants, called serfs, to perform labor in return for certain rights. In such a feudal society, serfs were to spend three days a week on the noble's land, and if they paid dues or taxes, they could use part of the land for themselves. That is what we were to Mrs. Terry—serfs living in the midst of high culture. She seldom introduced us to any of her company. Mainly, we were to stay out of sight. The sad part of all was that she really thought this was a moral and generous arrangement. Mr. Terry would have turned over in his grave had he known what she had done. But the worst was yet to come.

In the early summer of 1953, we moved into the two rooms on the back side of her house on Clay Street in Water Valley. She went over the rules several times until we assured her that we knew the boundaries. Since she and my mother were to use the same kitchen, she made sure the divisions were clear. The large corner cupboard had designated places for our few dishes, tableware, and glasses. We were never to use hers. There were rules surrounding the sink and how it was to be left once we were done. There were rules around the cookstove and how it was to be left. Once, my mother was reprimanded because Mrs. Terry found some unexplained grease on the stove. She also didn't like for us to be back in the kitchen once we had completed supper. Dad and I sometimes became hungry later on in the evening. My mother would tiptoe into the kitchen, trying not to disturb her. But there were times when she did hear us in the kitchen, and she would shout, "Christine, is that you?" My parents swallowed their pride and endured the shame.

Mrs. Terry had her own car when we first arrived at our new living quarters on Clay Street. She had reached a point, however, where she was too afraid to drive herself. So Dad became the perfect one for driving Miss Mame. We didn't know about her little secret competition with her lady friends over who could demonstrate the greater style of Southern gentility. The one devastating blow to her fellow gentry class was for her to have a driver when the others did not. To help her image, the socialite had my father drive her across town to be seen as she rode in the back seat. Sometimes she had him pull up to the house of one of these ladies and say, "Now just wait here in the car, and I won't be gone long." She stayed just long enough to say "Well, I don't need to keep my driver waiting any longer. I must be running along." At that moment, she had scored big and, in effect, was saying, "In your face! Now look who has their own driver." We were somewhat amused at the social games these ladies seemed to enjoy so much.

When we first moved in, she had an elderly black man mowing her yard. Even though my father was there, she decided on letting "Old Jim" continue since he had been their yardman for many, many years. She required him to use her push lawn mower, the old-fashioned push mower, not gasoline-powered. She knew that he kept the blades sharpened. Old Jim was so old that Daddy sometimes helped him complete the yard, front and back. She derived some amount of perverted satisfaction in that she would occasionally give him some of the "scraps that fell from her table" and some other secondhand items she no longer wanted. Old Jim thanked her and went on his way.

One day Old Jim's grandson came over to report to Mrs. Terry that he could no longer tend to her yard. Evidently, she had been planning for this day and reminded my father that he promised to do "whatever else" needed to be done around the house. So my dad inherited Old Jim's job except she just added that onto the list of expected work and for which she did not have to pay him anything. Her sense of financial management just saw this as good business dealing. Behavior like this was strange to us. We wondered if all rich folks acted like that.

After a long day's work, Dad came home to use her push mower. The front yard had a steep bank, probably ten feet down to the sidewalk and street. One had to stand on the sidewalk and push the mower sideways across that bank. One day while Dad was attempting to do this, one of the Shearer boys who lived up the street came by with a friend. After walking by and seeing how Dad was struggling, they returned and asked if they could help mow that steep bank. That was a refreshing incident of someone being neighborly and considerate.

Our move into two rooms of her house brought other changes for Mrs. Terry. On special occasions when she had invited guests such as local lady friends and some distant relatives from Atlanta, she had a black lady to come and be her "help" preparing and serving just for that event. Having help like this was also a sign to the guests that she was in the privileged class. But now with Mother there, she was given the privilege of also being her help. This was yet another way for Miss Mame to save her money at our expense. To her, we were her vassals and thralls, available house servants to provide recompense for her supposed generosity.

Helping Mrs. Terry took many turns Mother never expected. She was on call at any time of day or night to assist her with bodily functions or when she had messed up her bed, reaching something, finding something, going to town to buy her things. The list was long and varied.

Some months later, she discovered that we actually had friends, were popular in town, even dressed up for church on Sunday, and Daddy wore a tie. Realizing that we were civil people trying to make an honest living, she began to think that we actually had potential and that she could teach and train us in the norms and behaviors of high society. She began to see us as a project to be rehabilitated at least to a point that we would not embarrass her before her friends. She bragged about all Buddy (my father) had done to the house or yard and that Christine (my mother) kept the kitchen real clean. I always thought that her motive was to gain the admiration from her friends that she had found some ideal live-in help and that they would be jealous of her. She didn't appreciate the fact that she had most of what the old plantation owners had in the Old South to help keep up her place. To her, my parents were mere common chattel to be available at her beck and call. My mother was her cook, maid, nurse, handmaiden, companion (when needed), and the one to communicate her wishes to my dad and me. My father was her driver, yardman, field hand, garbage collector, repairman, and advisor on manly matters. I'm not sure what my role was in all this delegation of responsibility except I did know what the don'ts were.

She corrected my mother on word pronunciations and stated that she was just polishing her speech that other people would admire. One word I distinctly remember was *again*. She taught mother to say "a-gain (long A)" instead of "a-gen." Mrs. Terry said pronouncing it that way made the person sound so educated and sophisticated. "A-gain and a-gain. All the proper families in the South pronounced it like this," she said. This particular pronunciation used in British English was a regional variation that was used in the South to signify social status.

My instruction session was thirty minutes before supper. I was to go into her room, knocking on the door first, where she had written down her notes, especially for me. She was determined to smooth my rough edges and give me some cultural refinement, all according to her superior, upper-class values. The first thing she did was to change my name from Alvin to Al. She explained how having an appropriate nickname enhanced a person's popularity. Like Alvin H. (Al) Price looked better if I ever ran for political office. Al never caught on in Water Valley among my friends. It was not until I entered college and introduced myself as Al that it stuck. The main thing she taught me was proper etiquette. I listened patiently and thanked her for her time.

After giving me personal instructions on proper ways to present myself, she decided that I could enhance my social standing by having me take piano lessons. The retired lady across the street, Mrs. Bennett, had given piano lessons most of her life. Mrs. Terry informed her that I needed to be taught this desirable skill. Since I was a work in progress, these two ladies decided, I suppose, that I was fixable. That we did not have a piano on which to practice did not deter Mrs. Terry's determination to improve my social status. Of course, if all this occurred, it would reflect well on her efforts to mold a nobody into a somebody.

I balked at first, but Mother encouraged me. "Little Buddy, go ahead and try it. You might even like it." At that point in junior high school, I didn't view playing a piano as being cool and something that would definitely not impress my peers. Heaven forbid that they should even find out. The lessons came to a rather abrupt halt soon after beginning. Eventually, my obvious impertinence was overshadowed by my obvious lack of even a lick of musical ability. However, I must admit that through the years, I have impressed others by my knowledge of the location of middle C. Then it happened! One day it became clear what her intentions were all along. She had been preparing us for introductions in her church, which would put her in the good graces of her pastor, who thought she could volunteer more in the church's women organizations. Like we would be grateful to have the opportunity to be among some of the more educated, refined people of the city. Besides, the polity was considered to be much more High Church than the simple church services we attended. And she would be given more recognition for having brought this working-class family up in the world, even to the extent that she would not be embarrassed to say that we were living with her as caretakers rather than referring to us anymore as the help.

In her mind, I was to continue to learn the social graces, language, and style that would prepare me for a formal education at Millsaps College in the heart of the state's capital, Jackson, Mississippi. She kept saying that it was a private college with a selective undergraduate education program. She didn't use words such as *expensive, elitist, and exclusive*, but they were implied.

To get us used to the idea, we needed to attend one of her church services. We explained that we would be willing to go to church with her some Sunday night. This was okay with her, so we set a date. That night, we first had to pass inspection. Of course, that was not how she described it. We were invited to meet her in the living room, which was rather unusual. This is where she looked us over to determine if we were dressed appropriately.

I noticed at the service that not many children were there. The service was about what I would have considered normal religious ritual. After the service was over, Mrs. Terry said she wanted us to meet the minister and that we would have to go down to the front of the sanctuary to get the privilege. What I thought was that this would surely not work where we went to church because our preacher had to go to the back of the auditorium, where everyone had to pass by him to speak and to tell him what a great sermon he preached. Evidently, in the Methodist church, members had to go down front to see him. In our church, if that happened, the preacher would be a lonely man, just standing there.

We were complimentary and told her how much we enjoyed the service. Later, when we told her that we were satisfied with our church and would not consider changing, I could tell that she was disappointed. Now that she had refined us to such an extent, she thought she would be honored for bringing in some new members. Looking back, she never really recovered from her disappointment.

Her bridge parties, held twice a week, were going on in full swing. I knew that when those other three women arrived, it was time for me to go elsewhere, be quiet, and stay out of sight while they played out their social games. Well, being the curious boy that I was, observing this new way of living, I had to know more about the ways of the upper class, sometimes called the leisure class. The old upper class usually lived off inherited wealth and therefore had a great deal of leisure time to pursue their interests. In the case of Mrs. Terry, her greatest pleasure was in socializing with her elderly women friends in a bridge club, taking turns to meet in each of their homes.

I could access that front bedroom that she kept for herself through a door from our bedroom. The bridge party was conducted in the living room, which meant that I could quietly sneak into that front room, look through the keyhole, and hear every word spoken.

I must say I was absolutely amazed at what I saw and heard. I assumed that these ladies enjoyed their game just as much as we also did when we played rook. We always lightened up a lot, and no one took himself or herself too seriously. For us, there was a lot of laughing, joking, kidding, smoking, drinking coffee, and eating whatever was left over from supper. I don't recall anyone ever having hard feelings after a game. No one thought it was the end of the world when they lost.

But what I heard from these old ladies' bridge party took me by surprise. I didn't know how serious the upper class took their competition. When all the pleasantries ended, the game was on, and each put on their game face. The pace was fast and the competition fierce. Each gave directions to the other as to what they should or should not be doing. Each carefully calculated where they were in relation to other players.

If, at some point in the course of a game, someone felt that another had taken an unfair advantage, an aggressive form of backbiting began. I was reminded of hens eating their grain from a feed bin. If one hen got too close to another or wandered out of their own territory and started pecking grain that belonged to another, the victim hen would flutter their feathers and peck at the offending hen. That's pretty much what I imagined as I watched their serious contest that involved occasional ruffled feathers. Indeed, this was an old hen party; that's what I thought.

After a specified amount of time playing bridge, there was a break in the action to enjoy refreshments. Now at this point, a different set of behaviors prevailed. First, the hostess excused herself to go and prepare the dessert delicacy to serve, while the other three ladies wondered out loud what surprises lay ahead on that day. The goal of the hostess was to serve something so exotic that it would overshadow what the others had served at their place. Competitive forces were still operating, but public etiquette required that they pay compliments regardless. But gossip also ruled the discussion as they were enjoying their dessert:

> Well, I guess you all heard . . . I would never have believed . . . Well, I heard . . . You all know Mattie Jane, and she said . . . Why, if I were that woman . . . Did you notice that outfit that Evalena had on last Sunday? . . . I think if I hear that preacher preach another sermon on tithing, I'm going to just get up and leave . . . You are so lucky to have such a good yardman. I know, well, good help is hard to find these days. It would be a lot better if the cost of labor weren't so high . . . Well, I want to know what you all think. I voted for Ike, but he

seems to be hell-bent on enforcing that blamed Supreme Court ruling in Little Rock . . . I call Lura Lou every Monday morning, and she knows about everything that's happened over the weekend . . . Betsy Ann should be wearing a girdle, don't you think? Yes, it would help . . . Why, Mame, this dessert is most delightful. Now why don't you break down and tell us where you got the recipe? . . . You know Bessie Mae tries real hard. Bless her heart.

When they returned to playing a few more bridge hands, one would think that they might be in a more cordial and congenial mood with one another after enjoying their dessert together. Not so! When it came to competition, it was dog eat dog. They created a small amount of amusement by always saying when cutting the cards after someone had shuffled, "Cut deep and win a heap." Seemingly, they never tired of saying this every time. I reached the point where I could predict when it was coming, and I would mouth the words and say it too.

I was amazed that I could learn so much about the upper class just by listening to their conversation through that bedroom keyhole. Never before in my life had I witnessed such a display of ostentatious behavior. It made me wonder why so many people wanted to get into that social class. However, I think there was a difference as to whether it was inherited or achieved wealth. If I had to guess, this group of ladies had *inherited* wealth called *old money.*

Eventually, these women grew older and decrepit, some of them died, and there were fewer occasions for bridge. This social activity was about the only joy for Mrs. Terry because it meant an opportunity to impress and engage in more class ritual. Later, she became somewhat depressed, bitter, and short-spoken as the ravages of time crept upon her.

But during the heyday of the bridge parties, something really amusing happened. The local Methodist church had gotten a new minister, which happened almost every two to three years. They have this system whereby the conference bishop appoints preachers to move on to another congregation after a short time. I always liked the system because it was well organized, everyone expected it, and the preacher's financial and housing needs were provided, including retirement benefits. That was indeed a considerate gift to those who had given their lives to the ministry.

The new preacher noticed that very few women were volunteering for activities in the Women's Society of Christian Service (WSCS), one of the organizations for women to serve various mission and benevolent needs. The group was primarily for the older women like Mrs. Terry. The problem was that some of the women who normally volunteered for this group had an enormous conflict. You see, it interfered with their bridge club activities. The lack of participation was a matter of discussion, and the issue even reached the preacher. Even though there were a good number of these women in the pool of qualified members, very few showed up for actual service to foreign missions and to the poor.

Well, as I understood it, and as I recall all those events many years ago, the minister was one of those Peter Marshall types. Marshall was the well-known Scottish Presbyterian preacher who was called to preach for the New York Avenue Church in Washington, D. C. He was so popular that he became the chaplain to the U. S. Senate.

Some years after his sudden death, his wife, Catherine Marshall, wrote a book about his life titled *A Man Called Peter: The Story of Peter Marshall*. It was subsequently made into an acclaimed movie. Marshall understood the message of Jesus and the prophets much better than most of the preachers of that day (and today).

The new preacher in Water Valley didn't hesitate to call out these available women who could be serving in the WSCS. His sermon on service one morning shocked these ladies. No previous preacher had the courage to address the lack of participation in good works by certain upper-class segments of the church. How dare this new preacher who needed to incur their favor to embarrass them in such a way! Why, some of these women had an impressive spiritual pedigree with this church. Some had connections back to charter members and, over the years, had even made liberal donations to various causes sponsored by the church.

Of course, we were not present because we were attending our usual church. But we heard about this preacher and his sermon for weeks from Mrs. Terry. She, along with the rest of that leisure class, was so humiliated and embarrassed that only intense anger could help them cope. Her face glowed fiery red every time I saw her during this period of distress, which was the way she always appeared when angry. These bridge club ladies conducted a vindictive campaign for about two weeks, attempting to get the preacher fired or replaced. She was on the phone most of the day. They called every influential person in the local church and in the conference about this egregious transgression by their minister. It was fairly easy for the recipients of their wrath to figure out what was going on. Simply put, their bridge parties meant more to them than WSCS activities. The matter was not completely resolved until the Conference Bishop decided to move the preacher to some other town and church. Finally, we didn't have to listen to all her venomous attacks, to which we could only listen and make believe that we concurred with her anger.

The passing of the years only intensified Mrs. Terry's disappointment that we did not conform to her societal designs for our lives, even though we went beyond the ordinary expectations to please her by keeping the house and yard repaired, cleaned, and pruned. We drove her to Holly Springs occasionally so she could get a train to Atlanta to visit with distant relatives for a short time. Because of Mr. Jim Terry's railroad career, she had this pass that allowed her free trips. It seemed as if she always came home earlier than she planned.

Her few friends in Water Valley were frequently telling her how fortunate she was to have us living with her. They knew us to be hard workers, paid our bills, went to church regularly, and were mannerly, friendly, and nice. These traits always incurred favor and greatly improved one's public reputation. But when I graduated from high school and revealed my plans to attend an unknown junior college in Tennessee, she offered this fake smile, but that was all. She always had her way in most things, and at one point, she had decided I would attend some prestigious Methodist college, and I would become a professional in one of the more highly respected fields.

I left home for college, and the usual routines continued for my parents. When I was home, I always attempted to impress her with news of some of my accomplishments, but I never felt she was genuinely impressed. She could have helped us pay some college tuition bills, but she never offered, and we never expected her to do so. Savings from my working in local grocery stores since age fourteen helped defray some of the expenses.

When my uncle Thomas died at Kennedy Veterans Hospital in Memphis from tuberculosis, contracted during World War II, he left each of his sisters a small inheritance. Since we were the only ones not to own a television set, he left Mother with this black-and-white set that made us feel as if we were moving up in the world. Mother's part of the money was $600. She could have used that money to buy better furniture, a better car, some new clothes, jewelry, or a hundred other things. Instead, it was used to pay for my first year of college.

Their son was going to attend college and get a degree and, hopefully, have a better life than they had. I had a job in college that required the use of a car, so they gave me their car to drive to my work. By living close to town, my mother and father walked to work every day. And to church! They also took the job of cleaning up the church building, which paid very little. One day at college, I received a letter from them with two $1 bills in it. A note said, "We know this is not much, but we love you, and we want you to get a college education more than anything. We will work till we drop or whatever it takes." As the hymn says, "If that isn't love the ocean is dry, there's no stars in the sky, and the sparrows can't fly." This is also called grit, characteristic of so many working-class parents of their generation. For them, it was always about the children and their future.

Mrs. Terry had a sister, Mrs. Greer, who lived on the corner of North Main and Market Street. The house was unique in Water Valley, a finely built Victorian-style dwelling with an English turret at each end of the front porch. It had embellished exterior latticework around each turret and across upper and lower portions of the porch. Beautiful stained glass adorned the windows across the front. The house was constructed at a time in the South when there was competition between the wealthy families to build a mansion bigger and more ornate than anyone else, similar to the competition that abounded in Natchez before the Civil War.

I often wondered if this was the reason why Mrs. Terry and Mrs. Greer never had any meaningful relationship, even though they had no other family there. They never talked, called, or visited. Maybe Mrs. Greer's house was fancier than Mrs. Terry's, and this evoked jealousy. I never knew, but they lived their lives as if the other did not exist. This was really strange to me at my age. I thought that wealthy people would also have a wealth of friends and at least cared for their kin. I could not imagine living like that when in truth they needed each other.

The day came when the aging Mrs. Greer became quite sick and needed some nursing assistance. Going to a home of some type was beneath her dignity and would be an embarrassment to her status and past reputation. Mrs. Terry asked my mother to go down to her sister's house to see what she could do. *She* certainly wasn't going! Other ladies were present by volunteering to help, though they didn't feel compelled to give her the care she really needed if she were to stay at home.

On one occasion, as Mrs. Greer neared death, she became extremely nauseated and began to regurgitate all over herself and the bed. At the same time, she lost control of bodily functions. Her gown, the bedclothes, and sheets were drenched with fluids and stench from bodily excrements. The other women fled the room. It was more than they could tolerate through their volunteer services.

My mother saw this situation as needing an automatic benevolent response. Forget about the messiness and the unpleasantness. That was part of her experience from being the eldest of six girls and given the responsibility by my grandmother to help her with the rest of the family. Many times, she had held a damp cloth over the forehead of her brothers and sisters (and me) while they vomited. This is what empathetic human beings do for each other. It was built into her character, and she could not imagine neglecting a person at such a moment. Where I was reared, this was the kind of grit I witnessed and experienced from loved ones. In fact, that was the ingrained cultural expectation that some people outside the South never quite understood about us.

My mother rolled up her sleeves, took some towels and pans of water, and cleaned up this woman who may or may not have appreciated what was done for her. But this kind of humanity shown by my mother didn't require recognition or reward. That is why it was so mystifying to us that some wealthy, upper-class people couldn't bring themselves to get personally involved in caring for someone. If anything at all was done, it was done by proxy—paying someone else to do the actual work. I doubt that Mother was ever paid a penny for what she did.

For folks like these two alienated sisters, money was sparingly spent on paying others for their personal services. At Christmastime, Mrs. Terry gave my mother a pair of stockings and my father some handkerchiefs. We were supposed to be grateful for any expression of her attention.

After my parents served this woman for eighteen years in addition to laboring hard in a textile mill and a dry cleaning shop, Mrs. Terry began to decline in health. But we continued to serve her needs because she promised us that we would inherit her house and furnishings when she died, something she reminded us many times. I still tried to impress her with my accomplishments. What folly on my part! Some years before, at twenty-three years of age, I shared with her that I had been chosen to be the pulpit minister of a church with 220 families in Jackson, Mississippi, almost in the shadow of the capitol. As I recall, the response was a mechanical show of pleasure to hear this. But no real feeling of congratulations or best wishes!

So now she had come to the end of her life as an embittered, disappointed woman with no close friends or family. And then came the most devastating act of shattered dreams. My parents began to suspect something was different with Mrs. Terry, who became indifferent to them totally, not saying a word. They knew her attorney really well and had his respect. Mr. Horan probably violated attorney–client privilege, but he couldn't stand to see us treated unfairly. He revealed to my parents that she had changed her will after our caring for her all those years, even paying rent. Against the wishes of her late husband, she made some distant relative in Georgia the beneficiary.

When I heard about it, I was as angry as I had ever been. Equal to my anger was a profound sense of empathy for my parents for the long years of hard work and having something like this dashed into their faces. To see my father experience yet another great disappointment in life was tough to witness—a man who taught me so much good by his own heart and who started every prayer every evening at the supper table "Our gracious heavenly Father . . ." My mother asked me not to call Mrs. Terry, but I did write her a letter expressing my dismay over her duplicity. Except I might not have been that polite.

Looking back, I now believe this was her plan. We didn't deserve her house and furnishings, even though she had promised her deceased husband it would be ours for taking care of her till her death. To this scheming Jezebel, we had no socially redeeming value. She reached a point when she knew she would not live much longer, and she had the will changed, thinking that my parents would never know. We would continue to care for her right to her dying breath. And then only to discover we didn't get the house after all. Only some depraved minion of hell could possibly devise such a scheme.

I heard that on her deathbed while treading the verge of Jordan, she cried out, "Christine, Christine, where are you, Christine?" It is absolutely beyond my comprehension how another person could be that cold and deceptive. How could someone treat a family like that? Take from them for eighteen years under false pretenses. That is what a preoccupation with money, status, social class, and ritual games of the blue bloods did to a person. Exploiting the poor for monetary gain is a skill learned early as well as doing so without a twinge of the conscience. I have to believe there is a judgment day in which people like that will have to account for such calloused behavior with hearts of stone.

After sacrificing all those years and with only a bed, a couch, a rocking chair, and a chest of drawers, my parents moved to another apartment in town. They were now having to start all over again late in life. But starting over was nothing new for them. More than the few material items they possessed, they knew that they still had their honor.

I encouraged them to sue her estate after she died, claiming payment for services rendered and a promise not kept. Taking some dramatic legal action like that in a small town scared them. Their feelings were similar to an African American filing charges against a white person for some crime committed, knowing that they would be violating the old Southern moré that they were not to act uppity as if they thought they had equal rights. Some working class and poor whites had that same beat-down fear that something even worse might happen.

I was in graduate school in Knoxville at the University of Tennessee at the time. I could only endure six years of full-time church ministry, so I decided to return to graduate school to pursue a degree in another field. I scoured the yard sales and salvage lots and was able to accumulate a U-Haul trailer full of furniture and accessories. Mother and Dad went into debt to acquire several appliances. Here they were in their fifties and still had not quite reached the middle class. But that changed as they neared their sixties, when they purchased their first house on Blackmur Drive and paid it out before retirement.

I've often wondered how my parents could accept this injustice as calmly as they did. Then I remembered how they had setbacks before and had to experience the uncertainty of not knowing whether they would find another work opportunity. It was like when Mom Bea lost her husband in 1928 with five children and no public jobs for women. The rational explanation heard so many times was that they would just have to "go savin'." I think my dad experienced so many disappointments, brick walls, closed doors, and lost chances in his life that he somehow expected he would always drink the bitter cup. They were strong, willing workers, and they would just have to make-do with what little they had and build on it what they could. That was the remarkable strength of that working-class generation, generally unappreciated by society in general.

I was from another generation that knew our rights and demanded them. We knew the law, and we expected equal justice under the law. We wouldn't stand for rich people exploiting the poor for their own advantage (at least white people had some legal rights in this regard). After Mrs. Terry died in 1972, and while visiting my parents, I left the house by myself and went to Oakhill Cemetery, looking for her grave. My plan was to spit on it! That was the most revengeful thing I knew to do. (Isn't it revealing how some people will be more critical of that remark than what this woman did to my parents?) As it turned out, I couldn't find the grave to my disappointment. The act would have been cathartic in that possibly I could have walked away from the total experience at that point.

--◄O►--

REACTING TO CLASS PREJUDICE

On Halloween, Joe Ross Wright, a classmate and friend, invited me to go trick-or-treating with him on Panola Street, where they lived. Some of the residents only gave treats to kids they knew. I was new to that part of town, so Joe Ross had to introduce me. Then once they were reassured that I wasn't an evil young man, I got a treat. One couple wasn't too sure whether I deserved the same prepared special treat his wife had made. Joe Ross tried to reassure by stating that my father worked at Happy's Cleaners. Well, that was sufficient for them to treat me differently and not in a good way. The man gave me a few pieces of store-bought candy instead of the real homemade treat he gave to the others they knew. The obvious denigration bothered me, and when they closed the door, I just stood there as the others left. Impulsively, I reached over and took their mailbox off the wall and threw it in the shrubs (which is a federal offense). My behavior fulfilled their prophecy that I was no good. They had brought out the worst in me, something I would not normally do. I went back and apologized the next day. But their behavior cut to the heart because I was old enough to figure out what they unfairly and unjustly thought of people like us. The anger was not so much what happened to me but the implications about my mother and father.

DEVOURING WIDOWS' HOUSES

I was privileged to have relatives on both sides of my family who had a strong sense of integrity. My aunt Alice McAllister, who lived on the Oakland–Coffeeville road, told me about an African American neighbor of hers, an elderly lady living alone on large acreage. She didn't have much, just surviving, but she became the target of jealousy by others because she owned this land. One day a white man arbitrarily built a fence across her property, taking in a large portion for himself. He knew the woman was timid and good-hearted in the sense that she didn't want to cause anyone any trouble. He also knew that she probably didn't have the courage or the money to legally challenge his actions and that authority figures would not do anything except to recommend her hiring an attorney, which was expensive. The widow mentioned what had happened to several of her neighbors, but in the end, nothing was done. She just allowed the unscrupulous person to have her land without any further protest.

This was long before free legal services for oppressed victims came to North Mississippi. Even after that, their offices and staffs were eliminated or cut sharply because of the influence of those who commonly exploited others for personal gain. This bothered my aunt Alice greatly, but she felt helpless herself because of her own limitations. I couldn't help but remember Jesus's statement of condemnation of those who "devoured widows' houses" and then went into the synagogue to deliver "long prayers" (Matthew 23:14 KJV). Most of the time, these people could do such heinous acts and go to church on Sunday, knowing the probability that they would never hear employers, large landowners, or businessmen called into any kind of spiritual questioning.

The exploited would never hear of any recognition of wrongdoing by those who perpetrated the crimes or from those who were silent. Instead, they would hear white people say that this was history, and we should not bring up such stories and stir up more trouble. I've often wondered if white people would feel this way if they were the victims of such injustices. The ones I know sure like to talk about the injustices done to their forebears during and after the Civil War.

MURDER OF EMMETT TILL

My uncle sat on the twelve-white-men jury in the trial of Roy Bryant and J. W. Milam in 1955 for the brutal murder of the fourteen-year-old black teenager from Chicago visiting relatives in Money, Mississippi, in Tallahatchie County. Allegedly, Till referred to Bryant's wife as "baby" as he bought some bubblegum in their store and later wolf-whistled at her outside the store. That night, Bryant and his brother took Till from his grandfather's house, savagely beat him, shot him in the head, tied his body to a gin pulley with barbed wire, and pushed him into the muddy waters of the Tallahatchie River. No one I knew thought any Mississippi state court would find a white man guilty when charged with a crime against a black person. The fear I heard expressed was that "Up in Chicago, they are chanting, 'March, march.'"

The national news and attention just served to reinforce the South's determination to prevent interference into a way of life most sought to preserve. The alleged behavior of Emmett Till was the very violation of an old Southern moré that could not be tolerated, lest the South lose control of preserving Jim Crow. Even though Mose Wright, the grandfather, identified the body and the men who took his grandson, the two men were found not guilty. The course, unflattering, graved side of our culture was on public display.

Amazingly, with double jeopardy protection, Bryant and Milam sold their story for $4,000 in which they admitted to the murder in an interview with William Bradley Huie for *Look Magazine*. The jurors were incensed and felt betrayed by the proverbial "thirty pieces of silver." I believe the men took what is called the death vow, meaning they agreed not to talk about it to reporters and take what they knew to their graves. A New York newsman offered my uncle $500 a minute if he would speak to him about the trial and jury deliberations. My uncle refused his offer. After the trial and verdict, family members wanted him to talk about the verdict, but my uncle was reluctant to say anything. He did say, "I think if you were to ask any of the other jurors, they would say the same thing. We didn't believe the state proved beyond a shadow of a doubt that the body was Till." It appeared to me then and now that the jury agreed what they would say and what they would not say.

In later years, I've had opportunity to talk with my aunt about the case and what her late husband confided to her. Uncle Howard had never served on this type jury before. It appeared that jurors were carefully selected to ensure they were the proverbial country boy types. The whole process and especially the antics of the attorneys were new to him. They appealed to Southern suspiciousness and Southern stubbornness by referring to how smart Southerners were and that people from Chicago could not come down here and make us out to be a bunch of fools, thus stirring resentment toward "outsiders." In Richard Rubin's article (2005), "The Ghosts of Emmett Till," he wrote that one of the defense attorney's told the jury:

> There are people in the United States who want to destroy the way of life of Southern people . . . There are people . . . who will go as far as necessary to commit any crime known to man to widen the gap between the white and colored people of the United

States. They would not be above putting a rotting, stinking body in the river in the hope it would be identified as Emmett Till.

The aggressive tactics of the defense somewhat bedazzled the jury with their use of the examining doctor's testimony that the body could not have been that of a fourteen-year-old boy, with such large genitals, hair on his chest, and the overall size of the body. In my uncle's mind, the defense was partly to blame for using these men knowing that, in the end, the jury would bear the consequences.

Also, my uncle verified that there was one juror who wanted to convict and held onto that feeling for two polls, but in the end, he went along with the other eleven. One interviewer wanted Uncle Howard to admit that he was that juror, but he denied it and even told his wife that he was not the one. He never revealed who it was.

After their verdict, jury members were often teased by locals and asked, "How much money did you get for your verdict?" Through the years, he received calls requesting an interview. School children, writing a paper on the case, wanted an interview. Uncle Howard often told them to check the records at the courthouse. In some of the interviews he agreed to do, he would say just the opposite of what they wanted him to say such as regretting his decision. Rubin (2005) wrote that he could "perceive a certain defensiveness in his words, an urge to keep the conversation short and narrow."

But in the privacy of his home with his wife, he spoke the truth. "If I had it to do over, I would have voted to convict. If I had figured out what the defense attorneys were doing to us, it would have been different." He never wavered in what he confided to his wife, even just a few weeks after the trial on to the end of his life when both of his legs were amputated because of his diabetes.

Timothy Tyson, a Duke University researcher, has published a new book on the case, *The Blood of Emmett Till* (2017), in which he reveals that Carolyn Bryant, the wife of one of the accused murderers, admitted in 2007 that she fabricated the most damaging part of her testimony during the trial.

Most historians believe it was the Till incident that sparked the Civil Rights Movement from 1955 to 1966 and successfully led to the Civil Rights Act of 1964 and the Voting Rights Act of 1965, the end of unlawful lynching, the end of Jim Crow laws, and many other injustices.

The Till case was several months before Rosa Parks refused to go to the back of the bus. She stated many years later, "I thought of Emmett Till, and I just couldn't go back." The sordid details of the murder and the subsequent acquittal of the murderers left American citizens across the country outraged. Fifty-three years later in 2007, Tallahatchie County issued a formal apology to Till's family. It read:

> We the citizens of Tallahatchie County recognize that the Emmett Till case was a terrible miscarriage of justice. We state candidly and with deep regret the failure to effectively pursue justice. We wish to say to the family of Emmett Till that we are profoundly sorry for what was done in this community to your loved one.

Considering the viciousness of this heinous crime against the fourteen-year-old, Mamie Till-Mobley's son, she refused to allow hate to rule her life. In an interview, she was asked, "Don't you harbor any bitterness toward the two men—toward whites, for that matter? It would be unnatural not to." This was her response:

It certainly would be unnatural not to, yet I'd have to say I'm unnatural. From the very beginning, that's the question that has always been raised: "What would you do to Milam and Bryant if you had the opportunity?" I came to the realization that I would do nothing. What they had done was not for me to punish and it was not for me to go around hugging hate to myself because hate would destroy me. It wouldn't hurt them.

The Lord gave me a shield. I don't know how to describe it myself. It was as if he put me in a neutral zone where I had no feeling whatsoever toward Milam and Bryant. I did not wish them dead. I did not wish them in jail. If I had to, I could take their four little children—they each had two—and I could raise those children as if they were my own, and I could have loved them.

Now that is a strange thing to say, but I haven't spent one night hating those people. I have not looked at a white person and saw an enemy. I look at people, and I see people.

KILLING AN "UPPITY" BLACK MAN IN JAIL

Word spread in the summer of 1958 when I was seventeen years old that Sheriff Buster Treloar "had beat a N— to death while he was in jail" at Water Valley. When the identity of the victim was reported,

Woodrow Wilson Daniels, a man I knew who was employed just down the street from where my father worked, was quickly described as an "uppity N— that deserved what he got." He had been charged with reckless driving, drunkenness, and possession of whiskey. Two witnesses later testified that the sheriff repeatedly assaulted him while he was incarcerated for not going to the Negro cells. His wife bailed him out of jail and took him to a Memphis hospital, where he died of a stroke on July 1. The autopsy revealed he had suffered severe head injuries.

Locals were quite surprised when the grand jury indicted the sheriff on manslaughter charges. The historical precedence was that seldom did a white person get charged for a crime against a black person, and if they did, the acquittal was an automatic expectation. Remembering all the bad publicity during and after the Emmett Till case over in Tallahatchie County three years earlier, local white people convinced the victim's family not to get a NAACP attorney involved. They collected money to pay for a white attorney to assist the district attorney in the case.

The trial received widespread publicity and was covered in the Memphis Commercial Appeal and in national magazines.

The sheriff's defense attorney was our neighbor and good friend, Ben Horan. He and his wife were well respected, and we knew them as really good people. A few years later, when I was away in another state going to college and sick, they let my father and mother borrow their car to come and drive me back home. The Horans knew they could call on my mother and father anytime for any help they needed around their house. As an attorney, you defend the people you are hired to represent.

The courtroom was filled with whites sitting on the main floor and blacks in the balcony. Being an inquisitive young man, I was present in the courtroom to see how this system worked. Attorney Horan was a master in appealing to the sentiment of the all-white male jury. He was certainly no backwoods Southern lawyer, but he possessed that flair for courtroom drama when he sought to drive home his point. I recall him taking a huge Mississippi law book and reading from it to the jury. His argument was that if in a fight, one of the participants happens to fall and hits his head against a blunt object and dies, the other person cannot be found guilty of a crime. The jury deliberated twenty-eight minutes before finding the sheriff not guilty.

When the trial was over, Daniels's wife, Annie Margaret, moved away. She was quoted as saying, "I'm hurt, and I'm scared. I don't know how I'm ever going to pay Wilson's medical and funeral expenses and take care of our five children."

As an impressionable teenager, knowledge of these two cases of injustice and the observed sensitivities I saw in my parents in various other incidents, some mental incongruence began to develop deep within my conscience. However, groupthink pressures prevented me from outwardly raising any questions regarding the morality of this behavior. Seeing first hand this gravel side of our culture, though, would eventually lead me to a moral and spiritual plane I never imagined.

QUICK JUSTICE

I well remember the event where I learned what quick justice was. Gradually but surely, my innocent view of the world began to be shattered. There is evil in the world and injustice and unfairness;

many of the people I knew didn't seem to care. Was I to become calloused too and not care?

Once my family came upon a wreck in which a young black man had driven in front of a car driven by a white man, who was quite vocal about his displeasure over what had happened. The law was present, taking notes and talking to witnesses. The youth was obviously scared, and it appeared that no one wanted to talk with him to get his account. Suddenly, an older black man came up, surveyed the scene, and started talking to the young man. He became very animated and was shouting to the youth, "Do not run! You stay right here! Do not move! Wait and see what they want from you!" At the time, I didn't quite understand what was going on. Later, I was told that the law sometimes turned their back to the accused in hopes that they would try to snatch their gun or run. Those who ran were summarily shot and killed. The rationale involved satisfaction that a lot of time and money were saved, and justice was not delayed.

CAR DATES, THE RADIO, AND JAMES DEAN

Frankly, I didn't like having to be the driver on a date. As a maturing, coming-of-age-teenager, I wanted the back seat occasionally. Tom Cox and I doubled dated some, and we swapped around being the driver. Each of us knew how to drive slowly, which roads to take, and where the best places to park were. There was not much nightlife in Water Valley or Coffeeville, so usually, the only people out were the cruisers and those with dates. Often, we dated Coffeeville girls, about thirteen miles away to the south. There were certain implied rules, and one cool thing to do was to have the radio dial set on WLAC out of Nashville.

Now that is a great side story in itself and a cultural phenomenon among teenagers about which most parents never knew. The Clear Channel station was legendary in the South, Northeast, Midwest, and points beyond. "John R." played those rhythm and blues songs that white kids were not allowed to listen to by parents who warned about the dangers of listening to that "N— music." It is true that the intended audience by the station was black American listeners in the Deep South, but white kids were just itching to listen to some music that would soothe the soul and allow some of those repressed feelings to be set free. Jimmy Dorsey and Glenn Miller just didn't seem relevant to this new generation or even capable of addressing these issues.

Movies of the time starring James Dean helped excite this new desire for individual freedom and expression. *Rebel without a Cause*, *East of Eden*, and *Giant* gave young people a face to associate with their newfound fascinations. Guys at the time tried to look and act like him because they knew this was what the chicks swooned over.

My ultimate dating experience was to have the back seat on a moonlit night and a Johnny Mathis song to come on that provided romantic magic. When he sang "Chances Are," it was so easy to slide your arm around the shoulders of your date. I'll bet a lot of good memories abound around that moment. In truth, it was this white generational interest in this music that laid the foundation for the rock and roll phenomenon of the middle 1950s.

Ah, the lore surrounding courtship in those days and discovering ourselves in the midst of adolescent changes. Speaking of an awkward experience! Many of the rituals were learned socially by overhearing the older boys exaggerate their dating adventures and conquests. The younger ones of us carefully listened for some bit of insight and skill into the anticipated process. Then, parents generally didn't address such matters with their teenagers for whatever reason. You had to learn in huddles of guys embellishing their exploits in front of their younger peers, often giving unhealthy and ignorant advice and counsel.

Once you were allowed to drive the family car and to date, you had to act skilled in all aspects of the dating art. We called it being cool, smooth, and suave. One important aspect was reaching the point when you were ready to *park*, which entailed the issue of just *where* you would do this. Often, it depended on what part of the county you lived. Water Valley had the traditional lover's lane with many cars parked side by side. I never liked that situation for some reason. Besides, I had better, more secluded spots next to the backwaters of Enid Reservoir. I discovered these places when fishing with my father on Wednesday afternoons. (Workers in town received Wednesday afternoons off from work, and we would nearly always go fishing.) In fact, I was always on the lookout for such amorous locations without ever mentioning that this was part of my mission.

Coffeeville was a different story. Lacking a designated lover's lane, couples had to find more convenient places for their parking pleasures. Rising to the top of preferences were church parking lots and cemeteries. The implicit rule about the use of church parking lots was that you should not use the one where you attended church. Something about not feeling comfortable on Sundays having to sing "Almost Persuaded." Cemeteries provided isolation and quietness. However, the law would sometimes drive by and run you off. I never understood why because we were certainly not disturbing the peace.

◄○►

SERENDIPITY IN THE CEMETERY

Cemeteries in our community were places of curiosity, respect, and opportunity. Yes, we visited to see family plots and to view the newest graves. I've even attended family reunions at the cemetery. One just never knew what unexpected surprises waited in visiting the cemetery and those resting there in anticipation of eternity when the darkest night will turn to day. I even met one of my high school girlfriends at the Coffeeville City Cemetery, who was there with some of her friends. I followed that up by asking her out for a date, and to my surprise, she accepted. I suppose the thought was that any young man visiting the cemetery with his mother couldn't be a bad person. If I ever asked my grandson if he had thought about picking up some dates while visiting the cemetery, he would have this quizzical look on his face, shake his head, and decide that I really was a dinosaur.

Usually, while my mother viewed the family plot, I moseyed over to see the famous grave of the person who requested to be buried standing up on his feet, and the community accommodated him. The details are somewhat unclear, but a construction worker from Alabama came over to help with the erection of the county courthouse in 1859. Upon completing his task, he fell and broke his neck or back and would not survive. His last request was "Bury me standing up because I've been standing up all my life working. I don't want to lie down now." As you would guess, the rather unusual grave attracted many a curious visitor. I suppose "Standing on the Promises" took on a special meaning for him. And on that great gettin' up morning, when the Lord returns to resurrect the dead, he won't even have to rise.

One of the things my mother taught me by her example was the need to go back to the family cemeteries to pay respects to the memories of those who had joined that happy angel band. When I could drive our car in my high school years, she would request a trip to the Coffeeville City Cemetery. Her father and brother had died a few years earlier and another brother before that. She took a few flowers to put on their graves, and we stood there solemnly in the silent city, thinking about dust to dust. I didn't know it at the time because I was too cool to be seen with my mother in a cemetery, but the significance of moments like that stayed with me throughout my life.

As one stood there in the midst of the stones, you realized that you were looking at a solemn prophecy of your own ultimate destiny. It was like being in the somber silence and serenity of a sacred sanctuary. To this day, I like to read the inscriptions on the grave stones, some ancient in design that keep alive a memory of one whose life was well-lived. Collections of strange inscriptions have been published. The one that always brought a smile was "I told you I was sick!"

Something rather strange happened on those visits. Each time that I remember, when we got back in the car to leave, the pop music station to which the radio was tuned would be playing Ferlin Husky's song titled "Gone." I don't know how to explain that. After several occurrences of this, my mother became nervous and afraid. We didn't visit as often after that.

Having reached that time when I am more aware of my mortality, I must admit the thought comes to me: will my children ever want to visit my grave and reflect on the good and the pleasant memories? I don't know, but I like to think that they will. One fellow said he had figured out how to ensure visitation after he was gone. He said he wanted to be cremated and his ashes scattered at the front door of the beauty shop. That way, he knew his wife would come to see him.

COMING OF AGE AND TABOO TOPICS

I never even knew the proper word for the physical phenomenon besetting every normal and healthy young man at the onset of puberty. Parents never addressed it, preachers or Sunday school teachers didn't dare discuss it, and no kid would ask an older adult about it. Some health classes in school didn't mention it. It just seemed that every few days (or less), I had this strong, overpowering urge for "release." Since no one said anything about it, I assumed that it indicated that I was abnormal, was seriously flawed in character someway, and was bound to hell. I kept hearing at church about "keeping ourselves pure" and about lust and many other sexual sins. These "sins of the flesh" seemed to take precedence over "sins of the heart." As a young Christian, naturally, I wondered whether this was a moral matter. No one, it seemed, was aware of this most disconcerting and uncomfortable topic. In dealing with the internal fears, guilt, and anxiety, I listened and searched for some written information on this absolutely embarrassing dilemma.

Gradually, more and more insight came to light. My first exposure to anything written was from a rather unlikely source. For some reason, we started receiving *The Plain Truth* magazine, published by Garner Ted Armstrong, who constantly talked about signs of the end of the world on his *The World Tomorrow* radio program. There it was in an article in black and white! One of the signs of the apocalypse was young men engaging in the M-word.

That article revealed things I had never considered. For example, God would take care of this by making sure we occasionally had "wet dreams." This was supposedly the natural way to gain release. I had never heard that term before, but I knew what he was talking about. I would take the matted and sticky underwear, put them in a paper sack, and place in the bottom of the garbage can, afraid my parents might see this mess for which I was responsible. My mother said, "Little Buddy, I don't know what is happening to your underwear. I'm having to buy more every three months." The guilt and stress were increasing. I had to find some answers someplace.

A small gang of four early teens got to talking about it as a result of one boy bragging that he could perform three times a day. The discussion evolved into questions we felt comfortable raising in this little group of peer confidants. Numerous questions were raised: Is this wrong? Why is this feeling so overwhelming? Do other boys have this problem? Wonder what the consequences will be to us physically? Everyone agreed that the wet dreams didn't come often enough. So we decided that each of us would do our best to ask around and try to find some explanations and meet again to discuss. Several weeks later, we came together to review our findings, which included an assortment of conflicting data. One guy said he had heard that it caused blindness and acne. There was silence as we just stared at him while an array of thoughts rambled through our heads. "Man, I know a lot of kids with acne, even some girls." Another said he heard Coach Rogers say in health class that research had found that 95 percent of boys admitted to it and that it was also found that the other 5 percent were liars. Then the other boy said that he heard this story where a boy went to his preacher and told him when he went out on a date, he got so bent out of shape that it was embarrassing and tempting. The preacher told him that the solution was to jerk off just before the date, and he wouldn't have this problem. Now we were as confused as ever.

I said, "Okay, let's see what we've found so far: First, this activity could lead to the second coming of Jesus. Second, blindness and acne might occur. Third, all the guys our age do it. Fourth, at least one preacher said it was okay before a date in order to preserve self-control."

Several observations ensued:

"What I don't understand is if it is a sin, why doesn't the preacher preach against it? He is constantly finding more sins to condemn, but he never mentions this."

"Maybe he doesn't because my preacher said the other Sunday, there were some things that should cause us to blush. Maybe this is one of those things you're not supposed to talk about, just blush about it."

"I can't talk with the doctor about it because every time I have to go, my mother is right there in the room."

"All I know is that afterwards, I feel like crap. I immediately get down on my knees and beg God to forgive me, and I promise that I will never do it again. And after a couple of days, here comes that ol' feeling again. And it just repeats itself over and over. And sometimes I think I'm just going crazy. I don't know what to think." Well, we did not solve the dilemma or come to any final conclusion.

The social setting most often feared in dealing with these anatomical anomalies was our biology class. It couldn't have been the ugly frogs in those pictures. And it sure wasn't because of the attractiveness of the teacher. Really, she looked more like an offensive guard on the football team. We avoided altogether any courtship with the girls in class. We wouldn't even sit close to them. I suppose it was because the teacher was from that old school that had students to stand up when she asked you a question. There was plenty of prayer in the public schools that year, praying that the member with its own brain wouldn't decide to perk up and look around. If she did call on you to stand up or go to the chalkboard, the first thing you did was to try to smooth out the front of your pants. I had nightmares imagining her making me stand at just the wrong time and then shaming me for such a disgraceful show of adolescent misconduct.

STEALING WATERMELONS

Rites of passage are rituals, ceremonies, and celebrations that mark the transition of a person's life from one stage to another. In mainstream American society, we do not have elaborate rituals and ceremonies recognizing one's entry into adulthood such as those found in some African cultures, among Native Americans, or in Orthodox Judaism. However, where I grew up, we did have a rite of passage into manhood, and it was called stealing watermelons. Yes, that's right; being able to tell your watermelon-stealing story put you in the respected class. One day at recess at Water Valley High School, my friend Joe Ross Wright and some other buddies approached me. They said, "Well, Alvin, it's time. We have all reached that age in our lives when we have to show ourselves a man. And you know what that means." All of them had already gone through the ritual, and it was now my turn.

Of course, I knew the routine; I had to drive our car downtown to Benny's Place, a teenage hangout in front of the bus stop. Only Joe Ross and I would go on the venture. A carload was risky as it could draw way too much attention. He knew the place alongside Highway 315 and would drive my car while I jumped out to get the watermelon. He just slowed down enough for me to get out of the car, and he drove on down the road. I was to get the watermelon from the patch and wait for him in the ditch below the road. Everything was going according to plan except in my haste to place the melon on the back floorboard, it busted open, allowing watermelon juice to run all over my daddy's back seat.

We parked the car and took everything we could find in attempting to wipe up that watermelon juice. We got it fairly dry before I went home. I parked the car at its usual place out on the street in front of our house and rolled all the windows down, hoping that would get rid of some of the smell. The next afternoon, my dad asked me about that smell in the car.

I said, "You know, I noticed that too. Maybe we could take some baking soda and sprinkle on it. Maybe that would help."

He just looked at me and said, "Well, be careful."

I always wondered if he really knew. My guess is that he did because he could well remember when he and Harold Hughes did the same thing. For two weeks, I continued to find watermelon seeds in the back seat. The next day at school, Joe Ross announced to the group what I had done the night before and gave me passing marks. The guys all came around, agreeing and patting me on the back. Man, I could feel the glory! It was like I had gone from the door of an orphanage to the house of the king. My rite of passage was now complete.

OUR LAST RIDE

As juniors and seniors in high school, life had become quite confusing. We were told that we had reached a point when we needed to enjoy being young and "have a good time." They said, "You're only young once." When we heeded that advice eventually, someone would say, "Now you've reached the age when you need to get serious about life and responsibility. You need to stop all that giggling and realize that you are growing up and show yourself to be a man." These mixed signals indeed complicated life even more. We had no idea how to address such conflicting expectations.

One day one of the guys said, "You know what we should do? Let's meet early in the morning on our bikes downtown. Forget about the cars, and let's just ride our bikes the two miles to the high school." Nothing else was said about it, but we all thought that was a cool idea. Besides someone saying how much fun it would be, we didn't actually articulate the real meaning behind this unusual behavior.

So about twenty of us gathered in town as planned, got in the right lane of traffic, slowing down the early morning commuters while waving and smiling at all the curious onlookers. When we arrived at the high school, one would have thought we had just completed the Tour de France. Other students were clapping and cheering while the teachers and administrators looked sternly upon this spectacle never before seen in Water Valley. Should the law be called to put down this break with protocol? It appeared they were assessing the seriousness of this outbreak of rebellion because we had dared to upset the daily routine.

In all the days of our years, we looked back at that glorious moment when we said, "Screw the routine, the dull and boring, living as predictable little robots with no spontaneity." I mean, we had already seen all the James Dean movies, and there were parts of this growing-up business we didn't like. We were saying that life with all its unfairness and complexity could wait at least one more day. "Hey, life! Things are happening too fast. Let's slow down a bit. There's more to life than constant seriousness." There were some parental and societal values we didn't particularly admire. This symbolic gesture was our way of expressing our individual rights and freedom. And thus it has been with every generation, I suppose.

That morning on those old bikes, long since stored away but now had reappeared for one last hurrah, we concluded our last ride with glory and class.

◄O►

SCHOOL FOLLIES

There is nothing more enjoyable than telling those wild and crazy antics of high school students such as the time when the basketball team had their school picture made. Our dressing room was a vacant classroom at the end of the hall. While most everyone was buck-naked, Billy Beck called Billy Jack Davis over and pushed him out into the hall and locked the door. At that same moment, the bell rang for classes to change. Billy Jack was pleading to get back in, but we were just laughing on the floor. Our math teacher, a Baptist preacher, was the first to let out his class, which had to line up and march out. When he saw the naked student at the end of the hall, he just pushed all his students back into the room to prevent them witnessing this sordid, ungodly scene. After the basketball coach was summoned to investigate this horrifying and unspeakable incident, Horace Ashford came down to resolve the matter. He opened the door, led Billy Jack back into the room, and said something about us behaving. But as he left, we noticed a little smile on his face. After all, he knew it was not the end of the world.

Most of our high school basketball team ate in the lunchroom at the grammar school about three miles away. At 12:00 p.m., we ran to our cars in the parking lot and sped out the driveway onto North Main Street at breakneck speed. Carloads of students drag-raced down the street to make sure we were first in line. We thought this added to our sense of self-worth to beat the school bus carrying other students who didn't have a ride. Why, if you were not first in line, you might have to wait maybe two to three more minutes before getting to eat.

Evidently, some citizen reported this three-car racing side by side down North Main Street to Old Man Barber, the chief of police, who stationed himself right in the middle of the street, and who waved us down. No one slowed down any. When he realized that no one was going to stop, he froze in that one spot as cars zipped by on both sides of the lawman, LaDerl Adams on one side and Bobby Miller on the other.

BENNY'S PLACE

Every town had one in the late 1950s—the place where teenagers hung out and acted like we knew more about the world than we actually did. We just talked about stuff—girls, cars, Elvis, and the music. Benny Appleton had a jukebox and served sandwiches and drinks. Couldn't ask for anything more. White kids used the front part and the space on Main Street, while the black kids used the back entrance for "coloreds." It was also the bus stop, which allowed us to see who was coming into town and going out of town and those cruising the streets. It was our Mel's Drive-In and where we acted out roles that gained peer acceptance.

WHEN ELVIS WAS CALLED DELVIS

I don't think we knew at the time that we were witnessing a transformational moment in musical history. Almost overnight, everyone wanted to be a "cool cat" with the collar turned up under a "duck tail" wearing rolled-up blue jeans, white socks, and sneakers. A little curl of hair hanging down on the forehead added greatly to the coolness factor. Your ride needed to look somewhat like a jet airplane, low in the rear and with fins. Some guys put heavy sand stones in the trunk to lower the rear. The hood ornament and fender skirts added a special touch of class. Cruising town with the radio playing rock and roll on WHBQ/560 out of Memphis on the AM dial was the ultimate thrill on Blueberry Hill.

In the late 1950s, the disc jockey at WHBQ in Memphis was Dewey Phillips (no relation to Sam Phillips of Sun Records fame) who had a TV show in which Dewey, known as "Daddy-O," and some studio buddies clowned around while the music played. This program was quite popular in the late afternoons after school. Phillips referred to Elvis Presley as "Delvis," and we thought that was so cool. He played both black and white music, defying the cultural expectations of the parent generation.

Youth of that generation had found their avenue of rebellion as every generation of young people had done for years. Preachers and parents felt they had lost control and warned of dire consequences from such behavior and preferences for what they called the devil's music. I think they actually thought we would just prefer big band songs as they had. The tension increased so high that we were interrogated by the older generation. "Who is your favorite singer?" they would ask suspiciously. We learned to answer "Pat Boone," and they seemed to be reassured that we had not gone down the path of moral degeneration. But when free from the oversight, it was rock and roll time all the way.

POP CULTURE

I don't think we knew we were living in a new golden age with a new form of music, movies, fashion, and television. We were oblivious to injustices, and all our newfound success made many resent any social change that would spread that wealth and opportunity to more people. When Mrs. Terry finished her Memphis Commercial Appeal, she put it out on her dining room table for us to read. We could keep up with the pop culture of the "hoi polloi," such as the adventures of Snuffy Smith, the cantankerous mountaineer moonshiner suspicious of outsiders. We learned about men of steel and velvet such as Will Kane in the movie *High Noon*, played by Gary Cooper. The television shows often portrayed unrealistic, stereotypical families, overlooking large categories of people and failed to address some of the serious issues of the day. However, at the end of those shows, we knew that good people win, and we were not perplexed over what was right or wrong.

NO LITTLE ROCK IN MISSISSIPPI

In 1957, I was a sophomore in high school when all the news in the fall was about the desegregation of Central High School in Little Rock, Arkansas.

We always had a lot of clever people who could come up with poems, songs, stories, and jokes that reinforced our resistance to everyone having equal justice under the law. One day in English class, our teacher, who was a product of her culture, had received a poem from a relative that addressed the situation in Little Rock, and she read it to my class.

'Twas the first of September
And all through the South
Not a sound could be heard
From anybody's mouth.
The kids were all ready
For school the next day
When all hell broke loose
Down Arkansas way.
Old Ike had ordered to
Mix up the schools, but
Faubus said, "Hold it,
We ain't no fools."
If you know what's good
You'll stand back and listen
Cause we ain't gonna stand
For this N— mixing.
He hollowed an order heard
Around the nation:
He'd call out the Guard
To halt integration.
The Guard came running
To take their stand
And uphold the rights

Of our dear Southland.
Ike didn't like this
So he ran to his phone
And called up Faubus
At his Arkansas home.
He said, "Meet me in Newport
Tomorrow night
Cause the N— and white folks
Is fixing to fight."
Faubus agreed, so he
Hopped in his plane
And took off for Newport
In a blinding rain.
They talked for hours
And everything seemed
Okay in this
Land of ours.
Faubus returned, but he
Stuck to his rule
Ain't no N– going
To this here school.
Ike called on his troops
And said, "Make ready to fight,
Be in Little Rock, Arkansas
Tomorrow night."
So on came the troops in
Numbers bigger and bigger
To make the white folks go to
School with the N—
Faubus was brave and

Made a gallant stand,
But he had to abide by the
Law of the land.
Old Ike had won
And felt mighty nippy,
But bless their souls
When they try it in
MISSISSIPPI!

When she ended, yells went up from all over the class. You know, a high school English teacher is a fairly influential person in the socialization process of us developing a value system. As students, we thought she was an authority figure who knew what was right, and she was just passing her view of right on to us. The message she sent was that this is a cultural value we should all believe in as true Southerners. And we did!

MOVIEMAKING IN OXFORD

In my senior year of high school in Water Valley, fascination developed among the students over a movie being made in Oxford, *Home from the Hill.* We heard that you could go and watch the filming right there on the Square. Sometimes the directors would select someone from the crowd to be in a scene. All this aroused our curiosity, and several students went up to Oxford to witness this rare event right there in our own back yard.

Ten years earlier, my parents drove into Coffeeville to see a movie based on a novel by William Faulkner, *Intruder in the Dust.* What made the movie more attractive was that it was made in and around Oxford. A really amusing story came out of that experience that circulated throughout those parts. In preparing scenes for the movie, the directors needed an old country store. They found the perfect dilapidated store with drink and gas signs everywhere, a few dogs, a gas pump, and a screen door almost off its hinges. They approached the owner to get his permission to use in the movie, and he proudly agreed to let them use his store. The movie people stated they would be back in three weeks to film.

After they left, he began to fully realize that his store was going to be in a Hollywood movie and be seen around the country. So wanting his store to look well kept, he had it newly painted, repaired the door and signs, cleaned up all the junk around the place, and waited for their return. Upon returning, the set directors were disappointed to see an almost brand-new store, which was now inappropriate for their scene. They kindly explained that they couldn't use his store and left to find another. We heard that the old man never understood why they were disappointed after he went to all that extra expense to get his store looking so nice.

Locals who saw the movie had a hard time seeing and understanding the subtle emphasis on common human frailties and ineffective ways of dealing with them.

WAY TO DETERMINE WHETHER THEY WERE FROM AROUND HERE

In the movie *Home from the Hill*, there is a reference to snipe hunting. We all knew how to embarrass a kid from up North visiting the South for the first time. They were told that in the South, you had to prove yourself by going snipe hunting with the other boys. Of course, they wanted to know what a snipe looked like. Well, the answer to that varied considerably, but our description was that they were no good little critters running around in the woods. All they had to do was to go out there by themselves and catch the snipe in a sack and bring them back to the truck where we were. These gullible boys went out in the dark night, deep into the woods, only to report back apologetically that they didn't see any. After an extended period of laughter, the ruse was over, and the kid had passed his initiation into the fraternity of Southern foolishness.

EARLY ENTREPRENEURS

While Uncle Bo and Aunt Earline Fly, along with their children, were living with Nora Kemp, the widow of Old Dr. Fughball Smith, some of the children showed early signs of thoroughly understanding the nature of our economic system of supply and demand. Highway 330 was still gravel, and after a heavy rain, muddy places were made where one could easily get stuck. One such place was in front of the Smith house.

Several cars came along only to mire up, needing some assistance in getting out. There was an old tractor on the place, and the kids came up with a brilliant idea. They parked that tractor down by the road and waited. When the next car came along and got stuck, the driver saw the tractor and the kids playing in the yard. The driver usually tried several things to get out but ultimately failed. He then approached the kids about pulling him out of the mudhole with their tractor for a fee. They were making some serious money from their little enterprise. It was to their benefit that the mudhole stayed a mudhole. There was a spring branch nearby, but they denied that they kept the place well-watered.

This little venture was no different than what was portrayed in a novel by William Faulkner, *The Reivers*, and dramatized in a movie with Steve McQueen. Boon Hogganbeck (handyman played by McQueen) borrowed the new 1905 Winton Flyer owned by young Lucius's grandfather when he was away, and along with a wily black guy (Ned) on the place, they drove to Memphis from rural Mississippi. They were to visit Boon's girlfriend, who worked at a bordello.

Along the way to Memphis, they had to cross a spring branch dammed up by the landowner, sitting on the porch, just waiting for people to come along and get stuck. After attempting to get the car out and failing, they had to pay the man to pull them out with his mules. Yes, a rather ingenious way to make a little money on the side, but he didn't have anything on my cousins.

In the movie when they reached the bordello, no one was home, and they couldn't figure out where the girls were. Twelve-year-old Lucius said, "It is Wednesday evening, so maybe they have gone to prayer meeting." Ned replied, "Well now, no, sir. I really don't think so."

MY BAPTISM INTO CHRIST

After my parents were restored to faithfulness in the church when I was ten, I was also taken to Bible school and preaching. As I became older, I became aware of the need to decide about my spiritual well-being. The character qualities I had been taught helped me understand what was involved in living a Christian life such as feeling a sense of responsibility for others and myself, a feeling of empathy, being remorseful for my mistakes, and being grateful for what others did for me. I was taught the need to make a confession of my faith and to be baptized, which would put me into Christ.

My parents were great encouragers by putting some old clothes in the car and telling me that when I thought I was ready, the baptismal garments were in the car and ready to be used. The church in Water Valley had not yet obtained any clothing for baptisms. The Sunday night I went forward at age thirteen to make my confession and to be baptized is a memory I have to this day. Our church believes in total immersion in water, and I do mean total. I remember the preacher looking back as he took me under to make sure my elbows, knees, and toes were all under the water at the same time. I remember the feeling in my heart, that the water was cold, what members said to me afterward, and the letters of encouragement I received. 'Tis done; the great transaction done! Since that time, I have spent much time and effort in increasing my understanding of spirituality as it was demonstrated in the life and ministry of Christ.

My spiritual growth has taken me where I never dreamed because in those early years, I was also a product of my intolerant culture. Now I know that a major theme in both the Old Testament and the New Testament is justice and God's displeasure with injustice back then, today, and on the Day of Judgment. God says that a sense of justice and the practice of justice is "the measuring line" (Isaiah 28:17). When Jesus referred to "weightier matters of the law," justice and mercy were listed first and second. The disappointing thing was that not many people I knew shared that spiritual conviction and insight.

◄O►

FIRST BIRTHDAY PARTY

In the growth of a child, birthday parties are now important milestones. But country kids just didn't have access to such celebratory events. My mother always wanted more for me than she and my father could afford. She was so proud when I had my first birthday party when I was in junior high school. Mame Terry agreed to allow us to have the living room and dining room. It was great except with all the neighbor houses nearby, we couldn't enjoy as much our favorite party game, "Let's Go Walking." Mother kept asking what that game was and how we played it, but it was never explained to her in understandable terms. (A girl sits in a chair and raises both index fingers and closes her eyes. Two guys take hold of her index fingers, and she pulls her hand down from one. The other guy still holding on gets to "go walking" with her. We even figured out a way to determine how we could kiss her one, two, or three times while walking.)

Mother felt rewarded for the success of the birthday party. She possessed traits of a histrionic personality, which meant she had very high expectations of me, some of which were unrealistic. This often made me feel that I was never measuring up, never quite being successful enough to gain her approval. Before I learned how to love her anyway and appreciate her sacrifices, I found myself always seeking her approval. Finally, I concluded that it was a part of that whole syndrome of her strong determination to make sure her son had experienced all the celebratory events in every child's life.

◄O►

SACKING GROCERIES = WANTING A COLLEGE DEGREE

When I was around fourteen years of age, I decided it was time for me to public work and help out the family. That would take some pressure off my parents, I thought. My father asked George Surratt, the owner of Jitney Jungle grocery store, if I could sack groceries for him. George told my dad to get me to come by some afternoon after school. I was hired to work from three thirty on Friday till closing time and all day on Saturday for a salary of $4.75 for those two days. To me, this was high living. Mr. Surratt taught me some basics about how to interact with customers, principles that have stayed with me for life.

A rather embarrassing thing happened the first weekend I worked. I accidently broke a gallon jug of molasses on the floor of one of the aisles. Of all the things to break, that was absolutely the worst. Mr. Surratt told me he would clean up all that sticky mess. It left a spot on the floor to remind me to be more careful. I even offered to let him take the expense out of my pay, but he wouldn't do that. The work was so repetitive for such a long period that when I went to sleep that night, I rose out of bed and started sacking groceries all during the night.

This chain of grocery stores with the strange name started in Jackson, Mississippi, in 1919 and was in existence till 2005. It seems that a "jitney" can refer to a nickel. The idea was that customers could save a "jitney" in the midst of a "jungle of bargains." The grocery chain is mentioned in popular culture about the South during this era, including *To Kill A Mockingbird* by Harper Lee. In Kathryn Stockett's *The Help*, the whites shopped at Jitney Jungle, whereas the black maids shopped at Piggly Wiggly.

I became a pretty good stocker and sacker and actually worked in grocery stores throughout high school until the summer before

I left for college. I moved on to Liberty Cash and then to People's Wholesale working for E. L. McVey, who paid me $5 for the weekend. The first thing I bought with my money was a Bible the size I liked and a Zebco fishing rod and reel. I thought that combination of items reflected a fairly balanced approach to life. Later, I was able to save some money for my college education. Being from the working class and just getting by from week to week made it difficult for my parents to pay for college. I always thought that if a kid needed some motivation to go to college, he should try sacking groceries for a living. You never get caught up in a grocery store.

When George Surratt opened another grocery store down the street, I moved there, which is where I met the new manager, Elmo Baggley. Elmo had been in the navy in World War II, traveled everywhere, and knew the ways of the world better than anyone I had met. Well, I had been to Memphis and the zoo, but Elmo described places in the world hard for me to imagine. He always had an adventure to tell about some large cities, exotic islands, and base camps, which always involved women one way or another and far removed from fighting a war. I must say that Elmo contributed mightily to my learning all the things a man should know. Of all his unforgettable stories, one stands out: all I can say is that it involved some remote island and a roach in an inconspicuous location, which did not deter Elmo. I was never sure when Elmo was being real or just trying to get us to lighten up a bit.

The meat cutter was James Pierce, whom I helped on weekends. We had contests on who could cut up a chicken to be wrapped the fastest. My fastest time was seventeen seconds. His knives were always so sharp that I cut my pinkie, a scar that remains with me to this day.

One of the other workers there had a drinking problem. One day after work, he offered me a ride home, but on the way, he detoured to the bootlegger's house on Panola Street Extended. While he told the man how much whiskey he wanted, Sheriff Buster Treloar drove up behind us in the driveway. There was no way for my fellow worker to escape, but he did crank his car as if leaving. The sheriff verbally reprimanded him for being there. Before he left, he leaned down to see that I was sitting there on the front seat beside the driver. At this point, I was no longer breathing. My fellow worker did explain that he was only taking me home right after his little detour. Later, the sheriff told my father about seeing me with this guy at the bootlegger's house. I already had the fear of God instilled into me after seeing that sheriff's car. All sorts of images came to my mind. I could see the headlines in the paper, the jail, and the prison at Parchman. My father understood what had happened, but I always walked home from work after that.

VII

MY DAMASCUS ROAD (1959–1965)

Then he started home down a different road.
—1 Kings 13:10 (CEV)

It WAS AUGUST 1959, the year I went away. It was time for me
to carry out my plans to enter college by leaving all the crappie in
Grenada, Enid, and Sardis reservoirs and attempt to find other joys in
other places. This was a solemn point because I had not been that way
heretofore. It was a day that my parents had dreamed about ever since
I was born. While college was an automatic given in some families,
there was some uncertainty in mine. They had sweated blood to get
to this day. With the money I had saved sacking groceries, and the
inheritance money my mother received upon Uncle Thomas Eldon's
death, we had enough to pay for one year at a Tennessee Christian
junior college. I knew not what lay ahead, and secretly, I had doubts
and fears. I did not know what unknown waves around me rolled.

New experiences in new places can be frightening. My parents drove me, and the few things I owned, to enroll in college out of state. It could not have been more like the military to me in that I faithfully followed every instruction with the precision of a private scared of his drill sergeant. Untold numbers of freshmen students have no doubt experienced the same uncertainties. I'll bet my parents said many a prayer as they returned home, feeling both sad and happy at the same time. Theirs was a faithful love that would never let go. There are depths of love that so many children could never know.

Yes, it was my existential leap into the unknown. I knew not what of good or ill might be reserved for me. And there was no turning back, no turning back. Knowing that this was a business proposition since hard-earned money was at stake, I could not blow the chance. In this new chapter of life, I took seriously my studies and had no time for dating or socializing. I would become a preacher, a great preacher, and with my savior complex, I would change the world that I knew was just waiting for me to show them the way. No wonder they often refer to these years in a young man's life as "the Salad Years" (as in green).

OLD VALUES REINFORCED

Earlier, I mentioned that I adopted the major values of my culture growing up, including racial attitudes, though my mother and father had taught me some things by example that would later help cleanse my life. I had my intolerant values reinforced when I enrolled in college in 1959.

One of my Bible professors occasionally started class with a joke, most often a racial joke. I distinctly remember one of them:

A black teenager dies and appears at the pearly gates. Peter says to him that before he can enter, he must tell of some good he did on Earth. The young man replies that he was the first black to desegregate the school district where he stayed. He related how he had marched for civil rights. Peter interrupts, "I need to know what good you have done in religion." So the young man thinks for a while and says, "Well, I went in one of those white churches and offered myself as a candidate for baptism, and they put me under the water too. And come to think about it, that was the last thing I remember."

Everyone laughed except some students from Michigan. I heard them say that they just could not understand why we, as Christians, could disparage other human beings in this way.

During a speech tournament, I represented my social club by giving a black preacher's sermon in black dialect I had learned from one of my great uncles growing up. It evoked much laughter, and I easily won first place. An announcement of my winning performance appeared in my hometown newspaper.

The annual black minstrel show provided students and faculty an hour of outlandish, crude, and purely stereotypical images of the black race with all speech spoken in black dialect. The white students, dressed shabbily with black face, presented the program. And I was silent on such matters and personally promoted an extreme form of conservative, racial politics.

Later, I heard the story of how the college earlier refused admittance to an African American student from Selmer, Tennessee, only twenty miles away. Calvin Bowers was an outstanding young man with excellent grades, from the same church that supported the college, and who logically wanted to attend a Christian college near his home. Although the college admitted Asian and Arab students, he was denied admission with the suggestion that he attend a Christian high school in Nashville, even though he had already graduated from high school. The only college associated with Churches of Christ that would accept black students was Pepperdine University in California. There, he earned two MA degrees and became a fully tenured professor. Dr. Bowers, in addition to his college administrative duties, preached for over fifty years at the Figeroa Church in Los Angeles. The policy of racial segregation did not change at the Tennessee college until it was considered safe to do so from a community perspective.

A legendary African American preacher was given the privilege of giving the last speech at the Annual Bible Lectureship in February each year. It was on Friday morning at ten thirty chapel. Large crowds attended because he usually spoke on fundamentals of the faith with a lot of humor. Several local black families were allowed the opportunity to hear this well-known and respected preacher. Later, I found out that this time slot allowed him to drive from Nashville that morning and have time to return before dark on Friday afternoon. I was told this was arranged out of consideration for his safety.

These experiences in my formative years, in a setting I considered ideal, actually reinforced my own inclination to justify the South's intolerance and reluctance to change in certain areas of social relationships. From chapel speeches, I heard "Little Black Sambo" jokes. From Bible classes, I heard "darkie" jokes. In church bulletins, I read degrading racial jokes. I was told that the people influencing me in those years were "spiritual giants." The manipulation was a form of gaslighting in which one did not dare to question lest you be labeled "unsound" or, worse, "librul." It would be some years later in a state university before I was required to objectively look at these issues.

(In 2019, the president of the university apologized for the school's past discriminatory practices.)

TENT CITY

When I left for college, the newspapers were reporting that black plantation workers in Fayette County, Tennessee, had been evicted because they registered to vote in public elections and actually did so. They had no place to go except to some donated spot where army tents were provided for them to live in. Around 250 people, including 105 small children, moved what little furniture they had on a cold, dirt floor. The reported rumor was the landowners were going to starve them to death. Nightriders shot through the tents, hitting a father as he sought to protect his baby. They sought treatment for him in Memphis, fearing local help. When newspapers picked up this story, help in the form of food and other basic necessities began to arrive from other parts of the country, including a group of men who put down flooring in each tent. Students from Oberlin College in Ohio came to help in any way they could.

The college I attended was only two counties away, but this plight of injustice was never mentioned to my knowledge. The great moral issue facing the male students was whether our hair hung down too far on our foreheads. The dean of students put two fingers above a student's eyebrow, and if any hair touched, he was ordered to the barbershop. Attending chapel each day was required because this period would enhance our spiritual growth. While scores of families were sleeping on the cold dirt inside tents and being shot at during the night, we were able to hear a professor speak on "the sin of holding hands." While a category of citizens were not receiving equal justice in numerous areas of life and enforced with violence, we were to remain silent on such issues.

One of the marvels of American history has been the profound patience of ethnic minorities while enduring such deliberate harm being wrought upon them, with little to no protection from the law. I can say with some amount of certainty that if the tables were turned and someone was shooting at wives and children, white people I know would not be shooting out tires. We haven't seen violence as we would see then.

But most of the white churches in the South were products of the racist culture. They dared not speak publicly about the immorality of unequal justice. There were no prophets like Amos, Isaiah, Malachi, or Nahum to speak on the social and economic injustice. Most white church members were content with beliefs that minorities should "stay in their place" of subjugation.

The famous folk musician Pete Seeger took notice of the voting rights struggle in West Tennessee and recorded a song titled "Fayette County" with these lyrics:

> They kept us from voting for nearly a hundred years,
> And all because our color is not the same as theirs.
> But now we've gone and voted and we live in tents today.
> Our families cold and hungry but here is what we say:
> We were born in Fayette County here we will stay.
> It will take more than hunger to drive us away.

"MY VOTE SHOULD COUNT MORE THAN YOURS"

When graduation day came, all the junior college graduates were told to go by the administration building and pick up a free book the school was giving them. This gift was something special to me because I had already started to build my own personal library. It was a small book titled *Alpaca* by H. L. Hunt. It was not immediately obvious what it was about, so I laid it aside for several years. When I finally did read it, I discovered that the author was one of the richest men in the country, owning assets all around the world, living in a mansion in Dallas, Texas. The main thrust of his little book was that people like him controlled a lot of wealth and needed elected officials to give them special consideration. His contention was that he deserved more than just one vote in elections. Surely he was more valuable to society's welfare than some poor working-class person. Of all the books they could have given us, this was the one.

BAPTISM OF FIRE

After transferring and graduating from Abilene Christian College in 1963 in Texas, I married and moved to Northeast Mississippi to be the minister of a large rural church. With my eagerness to succeed, the next six years of full-time ministry, from age twenty-two to twenty-eight, would bring about a physical and emotional state never imagined. A doctor asked me to hold out my hands, which were quivering from attempting to bring unity to a divided church. After seeing that reuniting happen in 1964 at age twenty-three, I was invited to be the pulpit minister of the Capitol Street Church of Christ, a large urban church in Jackson, Mississippi. While succeeding there with a mix of young adults along with an old Southern aristocracy, the unexpected and unintended consequences again shook my emotions to the core. I evolved from idealism to the stark realization of our human frailties.

Reactions and observations about a turbulent time in race relations seemed to dominate the interests of most everyone I knew. The only other more overriding factor was so much silence from the church in the face of gross injustice. So what did we do? We developed an elaborate rationalization that supposedly justified the silence and relieved the cognitive dissonance. The church used group-think pressures to keep us all "sound in the faith." It was Pres. John Kennedy who defined providing equal rights to minorities as a moral issue and not the churches of my persuasion. When President Kennedy was assassinated, one Christian College student yelled to a black janitor, "Hey, N—, your president has been shot!" When four little African American girls were killed in Sunday School by a bomb planted by men associated with the KKK, I don't recall outrage in the spiritual circles of my life. When three civil rights workers were brutally murdered for helping to register black people to vote in public elections, one fellow preacher surmised that he thought this was a trick to make the South look bad and that the activists were hiding out in Cuba. When their bodies were pulled from an earthen dam, the preacher had nothing to say. The KKK, acting with seeming impunity, threw leaflets in yards where I lived at night stating that they were Klan members because they believed in Jesus Christ. After the 1965 "Bloody Sunday" incident in Selma, Alabama, one of the town's preachers came to Jackson to speak on how immoral the marchers to Montgomery were. So many Jewish synagogues and homes were being bombed that the FBI opened an office in Jackson in an effort to protect some categories of people who could not rely on local law enforcement. A few years later, a member called me to report the assassination of Dr. King, who "had it coming." Witnessing these injustices began to raise my own consciousness somewhat, but I still needed more movement in the area of recognizing sins against humanity.

In addition to these concerns, there was the daily responsibility of dealing with issues for which I was not trained: putting people in jail; getting people out of jail; getting restraining orders for a family's protection; committing alcoholics to dry-out farms; committing the unstable to a mental institution; finding people housing, jobs, and food; finding homes for homeless children; counseling prostitutes and drug addicts; finding people medical and dental care; being called to intervene in marital disputes; addressing suicide and even murder in the congregation. I even became a mark of organized crime because I was willing to help a woman held in white slavery against her will. None of this was covered in the college course titled "The Preacher and His Work." It would be many, many years later before I realized that my involvement with these type issues made me more like Jesus than the expected, formal participation in church bureaucracy and ritual. It was there when I first saw the light into what real Christianity was about.

While we had four foster children living with us, and with my wife expecting our first child, the church members insisted that we must hire some "help." The spiritual aristocracy thought that if we did not, this would not look favorably upon the church. They evidently thought that my salary of $135 per week with no benefits or any expenses paid would allow us to hire someone, even though, as they said, "Good help was hard to find." We secured an elderly

African American lady to come one day a week, who came highly recommended. We were not used to such privilege, and not wanting anyone to see an unkempt house, we cleaned and straightened before she arrived.

Occasional flashes of spiritual insight caused me to question some practices. At the beginning of my ministry there, I noticed two men standing at the back door for part of my sermon. I asked the elders why they did this. I could tell immediately that I had asked an embarrassing question. They explained that the city had some agitators who were trying to integrate the churches, and those men would redirect them to a local black congregation should they come to our building. The elders said, "They are not here to worship." I reminded them that we had people present every Sunday who were not there to worship such as wives or husbands of members who just came to accompany their spouses. We advertised "Everyone Welcome." After preaching on several neglected texts, those elders reversed the discriminatory course against the will of the aristocrats.

DISCOVERY OF SOCIOLOGY

After serving three congregations in six years, I decided to return to graduate school and study the field of sociology. I wanted to understand why and how the variables of socioeconomic class, race, gender, and impact of culture determined so much about values, beliefs, and behavior. For example, church leaders were chosen on the basis of a background as a professional, businessman, or large landowner. I ended up at the University of Tennessee (Knoxville). Courses in "race and ethnic studies" challenged many of my previously held views and values. I discovered that when my values were put on the public altar for analysis and scrutiny, they didn't hold up. It was at a state school that I learned how to respect the dignity and worth of all people more and how to be intellectually honest and not to avoid contrary information.

THE MOMENT OF TRUTH

Upon completing my master's degree, I moved my wife and two small children to Winona, Mississippi, where I preached part time while pursuing my doctorate at Mississippi State University. Maybe this move was providential; I still had to take that final step in my evolution of thought, and God had to get my attention. I just didn't know he would symbolically allow me to be hit in the head with the proverbial sledgehammer.

Before arriving in Winona, an elderly black lady named Katie Pernell completed a Bible correspondence course she heard advertised on radio. She wanted to be baptized into Christ, so she called the only Church of Christ in town and made her request. At first, this put the men in a dilemma, knowing the consequences from members and the town if they did that. Eventually, they decided they would baptize her in the church baptistery, but she couldn't come to services. The men would bring the communion to her house and have a short service on Sunday afternoon. After her baptism, enough members left that they formed their own congregation by taking over the empty preacher's house. Some brother told me (and I don't know if he was joking or not) that the members who left felt the baptismal water had been contaminated. After three weeks, the men decided it was wrong for them to deny this lady the right to worship at the building with them. "Next Sunday, we will come by and pick you up and take you to church as our sister in Christ." When that happened, a few more left the congregation.

The split-off members spread the word in town, seeking to stir up resentment. Locals were encouraged to boycott the remaining members' businesses and engage in other acts of hostility toward what the church had done. From Knoxville, we packed up and left for this small town in Mississippi so I could work on my terminal degree. Some church members attempted to open up the house for us the night before but were driven away by men with guns. The next day we arrived with our small son and daughter and our family dog, but locks on the doors had to be changed before we started moving into the house occupied by dissident members for their Sunday services.

In moving a few items out of the house, I was struck by seeing the elements of the communion, the unleavened bread and the fruit of the vine. A church built on the foundation of refusing to accept a fellow Christian because of her race yet felt spiritual enough to engage in a communion celebrating the death, burial, and resurrection of Christ. Wow! This sort of symbolized the dichotomy that had long prevailed in the South, that is, reconciling a society built on race prejudice and race violence and, at the same time, somehow felt God was approving of them anyway.

As word spread to the other group that we were moving into the preacher's house they occupied, real anger built and then exploded. Suddenly, two men in a truck barreled onto the yard, dressed in cowboy boots and with cowboy hats with a gun rack in the truck. One of the men demanded to know what was going on when they approached. The fear and anger collided to such an extent that no one really understood what was being said or the answers given. All of a sudden, one man hit me across my jaw, knocking me to the ground. The men present helping us to unload the moving van pulled the attacker away.

This began a sequence of events one could only imagine in a movie script. I ran to a member's house a block away to call the police, who referred me to the mayor, who wanted me to meet him in his office. I went back to the house to make sure the family was safe and then went downtown to meet this mayor. He didn't seem to be concerned about what had happened in his town and talked in generalities. Finally, he said I could sign some John Doe warrants, stating that if we were hindered from moving in, I could call the police and have the protesters arrested. Upon that promise, I returned to the house to continue moving in but was prevented by members of the faction who stood in the doorways cussing and claiming they were right while condemning societal changes that included black people.

Something had to be done, so I called the police to come out and serve those warrants on those impeding our move. The chief of police came out by himself, announced to everyone that he did not know who belonged in the house and that we would have to decide the matter among ourselves, and left. The sheriff came and removed something that belonged to his wife out of the house and refused to help. At that moment, I fully realized that we were in real danger.

I called my father, who was about an hour away, and asked him to get his gun and come down to Winona and spend the night, which he did. At 6:00 a.m., a city employee came out to the house and turned off our water. At church, my jaw was so swollen I could hardly speak. To add to my fear, these brethren where I was preaching appeared to be afraid to do or say anything. After church, I asked them to meet to discuss the attack and to call the police and complain. They made me no promises. They probably never felt that the conflict would go this far. So my wife and I and our two small children were pretty much on our own.

That afternoon, I secretly called the nearest FBI office and reported the inaction of the mayor, police, and sheriff to protect us. They seemed to fully understand and revealed that similar events had occurred in other towns nearby. They came the very next day, meeting with the mayor, police, and sheriff, and warned that they had better enforce the law. That seemed to calm things at least for a while.

The nightmare continued for several months. The newspaper deliverer refused to bring us the daily paper. When the phone was installed, I began to get threats of various degrees of seriousness. We discovered that people who were once our friends were no longer friends because they preferred the position of the other side, including some area preachers. One person called and wanted to have a Bible study at an old abandoned gin about three miles south of town. I told him I would be there and for him to make sure he was also. I arranged for some men to arrive five minutes after I did. When I drove up, no one appeared, but I hollered, "Where are you? I'm ready for our Bible study! Come on out!" It was all a threat and scare tactic.

Anxieties over various things increased. I was attempting to complete graduate courses in Starkville, never knowing what was going on back home. Every time I heard a car coming down the gravel road, I wondered if our house was going to be firebombed. I was aware that some people living near our house had a German shepherd dog they pinned up because the dog was known to attack people. One day the dog escaped his pin (for whatever reason) and wandered into our backyard, where our five-year-old daughter was playing. Dixie, our mixed breed family dog named after our son's kindergarten teacher, sensed an imminent attack and jumped the German shepherd. Of course, Dixie didn't have a chance and was mutilated so badly that she escaped into the woods, probably to die. We heard the noise of the dogs, rushed out and swept up our daughter, and ran the dog off with a baseball bat. For days, we looked for Dixie to no avail. Late one afternoon, she wandered back to our joy and relief. She probably saved our daughter's life. The stress was present every day, but what made the experience a double burden was wondering whether the incident was intentional. Years later when Dixie died, we buried her in a box with a large sandstone to mark the place.

My Damascus Road

The primary consequence of this transformational period was what was going on inside my mind. I began to get a glimpse into what African Americans had been experiencing every day for centuries in this country. As the preacher of this church, I was the symbol of the change that hardly anyone wanted and thus became the target, "bearing on my body the marks" of their resentment. I went back to the New Testament and found Jesus encountering these same prejudices on almost every page. For the first time, I saw verses in their real context I had never really learned. I became angry with preachers, politicians, former friends, mentors, and myself. "Al, how could you have missed this in your studies?" I asked over and over. I had always earnestly tried to get things right in my belief system, but now I was developing a more spiritual and biblical perspective. I spent days walking up and down that old gravel road in front of our house in a daze, staggering in shame from side to side with regret and agonizing in prayer and repentance. How could I have made such a theological and spiritual slipup? I called it my Damascus Road experience because on that road, I began to have an insight into Christianity I never had before. I had been "woke," a moral and spiritual journey in which my eyes and ears were finally opened and transformed. I was like a bird from prison bars that had flown. My darkest night had turned to day. This was my moment of truth.

Spring Hill Church of Christ
Montgomery County, Mississippi

I began to feel as a lone voice crying in the wilderness, so disappointed that I could not find many sympathizers anywhere. But God provided just what I needed. There was an African American congregation called Spring Hill Church of Christ located somewhere between Grenada and Duck Hill, and they needed a preacher twice a month. The contact person said I could come and preach those two Sunday afternoons. I found a spirit and a fellowship I had never felt but desperately needed. I didn't know that Christianity and assembling could be that enjoyable. I even learned how to avoid the monotone style of most white preachers and use inflection and pauses that allowed a response from the audience. On eating Sunday, they brought lots of food in large suitcases. They gave me the entire contribution down to the last penny. It would have been an insult to refuse it. We stayed till late in the afternoon, and we didn't want to leave after a softball game or just story telling. Part of their prayers I had never heard before included "Lord, bless those men in prison falsely accused."

Every Sunday I was there, the song leader led an old spiritual titled "When Morning Comes," which was sung with much emotion and fervor. For the first time, I understood why when I considered the lyrics:

> Trials dark on every hand, and we cannot understand . . .
> Temptations, hidden snares often take us unawares
> And our hearts are made to bleed for some thoughtless
> word or deed;
> And we wonder why the test, when we try to do our
> best,
> But we'll understand it by and by.
> By and by, when the morning comes,

When the saints of God are gathered home,
We will tell the story we've overcome.
We'll understand it better by and by.

As we drove the thirty-minute drive back to town, it was like entering another culture and atmosphere filled with tension and fear. I don't know if the folks at Spring Hill ever knew how God used them to become my strength and my refuge during the darkest chapter of my life. I like to think they did. In later years, I wrote them a letter explaining how they had blessed my life. I hope to go back there some Sunday to visit.

After we moved from Winona and I began my college teaching career, one day my wife told me that the man who had assaulted me was on the phone. I refused to talk with him, even though I had no idea what he wanted to say.

Breaking news! Thirty-seven years later, I found the man's phone number and called him back and stated, "I want you to know that I was wrong for not taking your call thirty-seven years ago." The brother immediately began to tell me how sorry and how wrong he was. "In those days, I was full of hate, and I hated black people, and I am now trying to undo all the damage I did. I want you to forgive me. The churches have gotten back together. My son is the song leader, and my grandson is studying to be a preacher. We have several black families attending now. One of them wants to preach, and I'm trying to help him all I can."

I could not speak a word at first and finally requested to come see him. He liked that idea and said, "Come soon. I'm in my eighties, not in good health, and I would love for us to sit down and talk." We met at a restaurant on Highway 82 in Winona one Saturday morning. He repeated all the things he had said on the phone. We prayed together right there in the middle of that restaurant. I asked him, "Do you think that the change you have made is the result of making a spiritual application of the teachings of Jesus in your life?" He said yes, he did. I had to help him a little for him to walk to his truck. We call each other from time to time. Both of us had experienced redemption.

LASTING IMPRESSIONS

In my early years, some who influenced me were remarkably good people. They tended to fall into two categories: First were people such as my grandmother Price (Mom Bea), who possessed a sensitive heart and treated all people (both black and white) with respect and graciousness. Her wish was stated as "just wanting everyone to get along." Her home was always open to the midwives and black neighbors who came to see her and were treated as equals. She offered them whatever service she could when there was a sickness or trouble. But she was a powerless person, a quiet rural widowed mother who had no influence over the "principalities, powers and might" of the community and state. Second were those who limited their goodness and kindness mostly to others of the "in-group" and not so much to those of the "out-group." Their expressions of generosity and love to the "in-group" were often beyond description. Sometimes individual minorities were given recognition because they were known and respected for their honesty and hard work. But their group identity was most often denigrated and stereotyped. Overall, this latter category and the larger community institutions and culture were the most powerful forces that slowed the transformation of my own views. Perhaps I owe people such as "Mom Bea" more honor for giving me an early glimpse into what real humanity looked like.

Looking back, there were at least two events in my early socialization that helped eventually shape my attitudes toward the rights and dignity of black people. When I was five years old, my mother explained to me why it was a good thing to provide a meal for our friend and helper George. She taught me empathy by telling me how he must feel being all alone in the world, with no family, not knowing how to cook meals, making little money, just surviving, and working hard every day helping my dad on the Cress Place. That one small reminder of our humanity never left my memory through the many long years ahead.

As a teenager just starting to drive by myself, I had a little driving accident that was not my fault. It was a busy Saturday afternoon with many folks in town. I pulled up behind a car, waiting to drive onto Main Street by the Water Valley Bank. Suddenly, the car had to back up to prevent a collision with another car. When the elderly black gentleman backed up, he hit the front of our car. While the law was being summoned, I went a short way down the street to get Dad. The chief of police cussed out this black man and made him commit to getting our car repaired at a certain dealership. After the law left, my father told him that he knew a place where he could get the car repaired much cheaper to help him out a little. Dad said he knew that if he had not backed up, the wreck could have been a lot worse, even doing more damage to our car and to me. Though the years have been long since that afternoon, I never forgot what a real man my father was in his display of empathy and understanding. I don't think he ever knew what an impression that one incident made on me for eternity.

EPILOGUE

All is fleeting.
—Ecclesiastes 2:1 (The Voice)

Fifty years later, I have the time to look back and reflect on those early years that were the most formative. Some of those experiences and impressions are described in this book. Today I live in my Southern home with my Southern life. My wife of fifty-seven years and I are parents to a great son and daughter, are proud grandparents, and are giddy great-grandparents. I became a university professor for nearly forty years, influencing several thousand students to have a more inclusive and humane view of the world. I am an advocate for labor and minority rights and thus became a more spiritual human being. Having a vegetable garden is a moral priority. I never pee off the front porch and always wear nice underwear. My frugality in spending can be annoying to my loved ones. I never saw down a dogwood tree. I must admit, though, that my grandfather kept his gun, tools, and plows much cleaner and oiled than I ever did. I need to sit on the front porch more. If I could say something to my mother and father, I would say, "You did it! You did make a way for your son and your posterity, whose lives are far better today because you lived, worked, fought, endured, and 'saved.' It was never in vain. And I still weep over your graves."

To paraphrase Walt Whitman, "And so the powerful play goes on, and we each write a verse, and what will your verse be?" As common people, and perhaps even regarded by some as nobodies, nonetheless, my family contributed an extraordinary verse in the powerful play.

COME HOME BEFORE DARK

I can still hear her voice. She was so good at remembering last-minute pieces of advice to shout as I left the house. When I got a little older and more independent, made possible by my bicycle, friends down the road or up the street, or just roaming around with Big Puppy, my mother would say, "Now you be sure and come home before dark." Through the years, I've come to see that advice in a metaphorical sense. In many areas of our lives, we need to come home before dark. We need to get some things done and some things said before we live in regret.

THE WIND HAS PASSED OVER IT

Today, snakes and lizards crawl over the good earth where the old houses stood and where my family worked, prayed, laughed, cried, and sang their song. The mystical, nostalgic signs of life and living around the yard, the pasture, the barn, are no more. If the surrounding large red oaks, standing as statues to a past life, could speak, they would tell stories long since faded from public memory. Deep within the bark are the remnants of the sounds of my youth I wish I could hear again.

And what would those sounds be? The sound of clucking hens after laying their eggs. The sound of drawing water from that old sulfur well. The sound of grandmother frying chicken on the old wood cookstove. The sound of country music coming from the battery radio. The sound of Granddaddy yelling "gee" and "haw" to his old mules. The sound of Big Puppy barking at something. The sound of Joanne and Elizabeth and others on the porch singing "Do Lord." But time has passed over that place, and they are no more because we are after all but frail children of dust. As the Scripture says, "As for man, his days are like grass; as a flower of the field, so he flourishes. When the wind has passed over it, it is no more. And its place acknowledges it no longer." The memories and old home scenes fly across the lonely years.

Some sixty-three years later, I went back to find where the houses stood on the Cress Place at Oakland and the Old Leonard Place near Coffeeville. After seeing no signs of a house at the Cress Place, the owner said, "Well, I've noticed that every spring a row of daffodils bloom right there." And at the Old Leonard Place, I finally spotted the blooms of a row of crepe myrtles in the midst of undergrowth and where the well had been covered over. Small signs but a remnant of flowers still flourished. To me, they were saying, "We're hanging on after all these years, so you do the same. We're still blooming, so you can too." In the words of an old John Denver song, "This old place looks like a long-lost friend."

The last great obscenity is the ravaging, rampaging passage of time, ultimately leading to our own unceremonious demise. This is what makes us all equal. This is the one thing I wish I could slow down.

One of my favorite poems is by the Irish National Poet Thomas Moore (1779–1852), who knew and was friends of Byron and Shelley. It is titled "The Last Rose of Summer" and was written in 1805. The metaphoric poem about an aging person whose friends and family have all gone on recognizes that nothing lasts forever.

> Tis the last rose of summer left blooming alone;
> All her lovely companions are faded and gone.

My parents, grandparents, uncles and aunts have all walked in death's dark vale. Were the whole realm of nature mine, I cannot bring them back. I have no brothers or sisters. In a sense, I am similar to the last rose of summer. I also think of the song "Precious father, loving mother, fly across the lonely years, and old home scenes of my childhood, in fond memory appear." That is what I do have, those affectionate memories.

What a dance we have had in our short lives! Sometimes when I see my grandchildren growing and achieving, I wish my parents and grandparents could see what their lives produced in subsequent generations. I think of all those young family members who will grow up and have their own children and grandchildren whom I will never see. But you know what? I can write them a letter. That's right! I'll write my values and hopes for them, seal it, and give to the younger family to someday pass along. Maybe, just maybe, that message might be meaningful, even life-changing. Somewhere beyond the blue horizon, long after I am gone, I can still speak (and you too) to a new generation.

LESSONS LEARNED

Even though we were deprived of certain opportunities and advantages, we could still enjoy the beauty of the earth and make astute observations about what we saw every day at the Old Leonard Place. Sometimes my father or grandfather said something that sparked an insight. A light went on, and I thought of some lesson in living to be learned.

My grandfather put **blinders on his mules** to keep them from veering too far to the left or too far to the right. Those blinders kept them focused on the task ahead. I have often reminded my students that there are times in life when they have to put the blinders on and stay focused on the immediate goal such as becoming a college graduate. Delay gratification now to have something really special later on that no one can ever take away from you.

Those trees on the place, standing as expanding statues of grace and beauty, **shed their bark** to grow bigger and bigger with each passing year. To do that, they had to expand their boundaries. Our growth depends on our ability to soften, loosen, and shed boundaries we no longer need. Maybe we need to expand our circle of friends. Maybe we need to expand by realizing that we cannot run or control other people's lives. Maybe we need to soften up a bit by not being so judgmental. Maybe we need to learn new joys by being more generous. Maybe we need to get out of our ruts and expand our opportunities. In this process, we become metaphorically bigger people.

Our water came from a **sulfur well** in the backyard. After a while, one grew used to the smell. That well provided many a visitor a cold dipper of water on a hot day. That reminded me that we have all drunk from wells we did not dig. This reality should cause us to recognize those that have graciously given us opportunity and other valuable resources.

After my father died, I found a keg of **bent nails** in the outbuilding he constructed himself. He saved every nail, even the bent ones. When he was living, he reminded me that we are bent nails. All of us have experienced brokenness at some point. Our lives become twisted and turned and bent through the experience of living. But my father taught me that a bent nail still had some use. You could take a hammer and straighten it out, and it would have worth again. All was not lost; there was just a lot of straightening and overcoming to be done. Today I stand not as a smooth, straight, or polished nail but one that is making the effort to still be someone of value in the world where I live.

ANCESTRY OR SERVANTHOOD

I once heard a preacher say, "God has no grandchildren." You are either God's child or none of his. You cannot gain his favor on someone else's faith. You have to have your own personal faith if you succeed in the Christian life. But the tendency to think that ancestry and pedigree make one more credible is still with us. It mattered greatly in many of the organizations I heard about growing up. Membership was dependent upon proving some direct connection to famous causes or prominent relatives in your past. What mattered was our own individual initiative to work, provide, care, serve others, and develop our skills.

Our family never thought that these sacrifices made any difference in who we were. We always thought we would be judged by our own individual efforts and motives. Once, a Chicago banking firm wrote a Boston investment company for a letter of recommendation for a young Bostonian who was from a prominent English American family. They responded by pointing out that his mother was a member of the Lowell family, his father was a member of the Cabot family, and the rest of his relatives were members of other prominent New England families. The bank wrote back, thanking the company but noting this was not the type of recommendation they had in mind: "We were not contemplating using Mr. Smith for breeding purposes."

—◀○▶—

CAN ANY GOOD THING COME OUT OF NORTH MISSISSIPPI?

Once a guy asked, "Can any good thing come out of Nazareth?" I'm sure some folks doubted that any good thing could come out of North Mississippi for those living in my rural area back in the 1930s to the 1960s. But they often underestimate humankind's ability to endure and to prevail even when cultural barriers interfere and other life chances are nowhere in sight. At one time, William Faulkner (Union County), Oprah Winfrey (Attala County), Morgan Freeman (Tallahatchie and Leflore Counties), and Elvis Presley (Lee County) were just small children playing silly games in the yard, blending in with all the others. Three of the four had no inherited credentials ensuring that they even had a worthwhile future or signs that one day they would influence the whole world. Yet they grew up here, and they reached, risked, overcame, and used what they discovered within them not only to survive but also to achieve. Countless others from this little patch of Southern soil persevered to accomplish greatness by simply being a good human being. So when an unassuming child says to you, "I'm going to be somebody," be careful because you may be dealing with another Oprah, Elvis, Morgan, or William.

—◄○►—

THE REMNANT

A remnant in our beloved South continues to uphold intolerance of others who are different. Many are psychologically still fighting a war that was over 155 years ago. Some still hold onto all the old stereotypical images of ethnic minorities and poor people. Others project an "in your face" gesture of Jim Crow symbols and values.

Here is something many others in other parts of the country don't know. Among the people I knew was a side of our nature that exceeded common goodness and kindness and was willing to go the proverbial "extra mile." Many remain hopeful that this region would take that final positive step toward an ideal model of how people with diverse backgrounds could live in common respect and acceptance of one another. The possibility remains that the South could be a model for the whole world to observe.

Why haven't a few been unable to take that final step and become the ideal for the entire world? One reason is because of politicians who get elected by reigniting those old latent forms of intolerance and prejudice. They heighten fears and create an "us" versus "them" kind of mentality and have used issues of "race" and "welfare" successfully for years in Southern politics. Many other opinion-makers have adopted the same mind-set by thinking of some categories of people as "the other" or "less than."

We have not taken that final step because we don't have a term in the language of the South that describes it. If we don't have a word or term for an action needing to be taken, it is highly unlikely to be accomplished. Confucius said,

> The beginning of all wisdom is to call things by their proper names, for if things are not called by their proper names, then what is said is not what is meant, and if what is said is not what is meant, then that which ought to be done is left undone.

Below are some descriptive terms that clearly show where the breakdown has been on our journey toward greater humanitarian attitudes and behavior. Insight into these terms would help break down barriers between what people call the in-groups and the so-called out-groups.

The Spiritual Paradox. This was demonstrated by those moved to tears in a Sunday church service but on Monday used the most vile and degrading language imaginable describing their feelings toward people of color. There was an obvious lack of empathy and understanding of the concept of "white privilege." No spiritual applications were made in the face of prejudices, discriminatory behavior, or even atrocities. Churches and their pulpits were simply silent on such issues as sins against humanity. The prophet Hosea predicted the conformity of preachers to the values of the culture when he said, "And it will be, like people, like priest." Few voices were advocates for equality and justice.

The Cultural Curse. The most powerful force in our lives in the formation of values, beliefs, ideals, and behavioral norms is the impact of the unique culture into which we were born. Its persuasive forces were all around us and reflected in our family, our community, our schools, what we read and watch, and our culture-bound churches. When our social contacts, including most of our significant others, reflect the same values, it is predictable that we will adopt them as well.

An illustration of the cultural curse of Jim Crow was that I knew factually that Calhoun Street was paved only so far in Water Valley, and then it became a gravel street. It never occurred to me to notice or to question that the spot where it changed into a gravel street was where the black community began.

The moral opinion-makers in our community spoke the same cultural message as it related to race relations. The newspaper editorials (and what they didn't report), the harsh and fearful rhetoric of the politicians seeking our votes, the sermons (and what we didn't hear), and the everyday language we heard all reinforced our racist values as being right and reasonable. We saw hambone cartoons in the paper and heard racial jokes spoken in black dialect. Any white person who dared to question these values was negatively rebuked, ostracized, fired from a job, or labeled a "N–lover," which was supposed to deal a fatal blow to one's credibility.

The Tragic Flaw. I did not say "fatal flaw" because the flaw can be cast aside, abandoned, and become the motivation to live on a higher plane that includes tolerance, acceptance, and the joy of knowing how to interact with all people from every socioeconomic status and ethnicity. Every day growing up, I saw goodness, kindness, real love, hospitality, and a willingness to give the proverbial coat off their back. Just one flaw, though, our *hamartia*, ingrained into our psyche and character by a narrow, prejudiced, and corrupted culture on this one trait—to cast it aside, was all that was/is needed to become that model.

The Languishing Legacy. The consequences of our cultural insularity continue, weakening us every day. Many live in bitterness and fear, not really knowing or experiencing the freedom and joy that is so close to creating a new spirit for living. Sometimes it is plain old selfish pride that prevents the change. Sometimes it is a lingering fatal thought that maybe someday we will return to the Old South. Sometimes the hardened, closed-minded people who hold us back keep on repeating the same old race and welfare myths. Sometimes the hatred and resentment just won't go away because we don't take the initiative to think for ourselves. Sometimes we have concluded there is nothing to change that is important. Sometimes we believe that to accept change would mean the loss of face. The languishing legacy remains where people will often vote against their own self-interests and eventually die with way too many filthy rags in their hearts.

In my time, the barons of the Bible Belt baptized bigotry, benefiting from the bitter brand that beguiled believers into a bastion of backward, bull-headed blather and barbed bondage.

No region of this country, as it turns out, has a premium on racial and ethnic prejudice. Our history is replete with the mistreatment of native people by taking their land and driving them westward to live on reservations. For many years on the West Coast, nightriders harassed unwanted immigrants. Newspaper editorials such as the *San Francisco Chronicle* wrote inflammatory pieces on how the host culture was being invaded by Asian Americans who were negatively called Chinks and Japs. The Midwest made famous the stereotypical "Polack" jokes that depicted Polish Americans as ignorant and wanting only manual labor jobs. The Northeast treated the Irish (especially the Catholic Irish) and Italian Americans harshly with their discriminatory hiring practices and reinforced with the negative Pat and Mike and Guinea Wop jokes. In the Southwest, Mexican immigrants were viewed as "greasers" and "pepper bellies" prone to steal. It is amazing how these historical perceptions and realities in other parts of the country are often overlooked in any discussion of race and how the host culture reacted. I am aware of our flaws in Southern history as much as anyone; I just don't like hearing them from someone else.

Occasionally, even now, all parts of the country experience an upsurge in those feelings usually because of national political rhetoric. What is most distressing in the twenty-first century is the marriage between religious conservatism and political conservatism. The result has seen evangelicals conform to political policies based on exclusion and selfishness contrary to the teachings and example of Christ.

The states of the old Confederacy had their ideological leaders who wielded great power in the formulation of racial values and beliefs. South Carolina had Strom Thurmond, Alabama had George Wallace in his early years, and Mississippi had Zach George (a U.S. senator who was the architect of its Jim Crow laws) and governors such as Ross Barnett. But there is no question that a former two-term governor and U.S. senator (until the 1940s) Theodore B. Bilbo, an avowed white supremacist and Ku Klux Klan member, shaped the racial views of several generations in Mississippi.

Bilbo unified white people using the issue of race to convince them that they needed to fear the black race. He created that fear by using the concept of "last place avoidance." Otherwise, if given equal rights, they would take their jobs, their women, and their social and economic status. Northern liberals were going to create a mongrel race in the South and destroy "our way of life." His scandals in the senate were so outrageous that a resolution was passed calling him unfit to sit with honest, upright men in a respectable legislative body. His infamous legacy in the state remained throughout my early life in the mid-twentieth century.

In the fall of 1962, a black man by the name of James Meredith applied to the University of Mississippi graduate school for admission and was denied. The aftermath involved violence, mobs, fatalities, and the federalization of the National Guard to restore order and to ensure the enrollment of the student.

Usually, during a time of great injustice, if one looks hard enough, they will find some lone voice crying in the wilderness against it. One such person was Duncan Gray, rector of St. Peter's Episcopal Church in Oxford. On the day before Meredith was enrolled, Gray said in a sermon, "The seeds of anger and hatred, bitterness and prejudice, are already widely sown, and as Christians, we need to do our utmost to uproot and cast them out." One week later, he said,

> You and I didn't go out there and throw the bricks and the bottles. You and I didn't go out there and fire the guns. Yet you and I, along with every other Mississippian, are responsible in one degree or another for what happened. We are responsible for the moral and political climate in our state, which made such a tragedy possible . . . The decent, respectable and responsible people of Mississippi have failed when events like those of last Sunday night can take place within our state.

The university has traveled a journey similar to mine. Today there is a statue on campus to honor James Meredith for the courage he showed in simply wanting a better education. The mission now is to "create . . . an inclusive environment." One of the core values is to "require respect for all individuals and groups." Writer Susan Glisson states, "No University has done more to acknowledge its role in perpetuating segregation." Ole Miss stands today in defiance of symbols, policies, or practices that seek to divide rather than unify.

Yes, we have a stubborn remnant in the South, as in other parts of the country, that continues to hold on to Jim Crow ideologies, and under those banners, hatred and entrenched resistance to change have endured. For most of my life, I've believed we in the South only had to take one final step in acceptance of equality and opportunity (eliminate the gravel and maintain the grit) that would make our region a model of racial inclusiveness.

(Occasionally in history, a single precipitating event can bring people from different backgrounds together that results in more "liberty and justice for all." Additionally, in June of 2020, the Mississippi legislature decided to design a new state flag, thus eliminating the Confederate symbol on the old flag.)

A SOUTHERN BOY'S LAMENT

I miss my parents so much that I can't even think about them without getting a light feeling in my stomach. For me, it was truly a privilege to be the son of working-class parents who instilled the values of family, faith, work, frugality, and grit. On Mother's and Father's Day, if your parents are still living, wear a red rose on your shirt or lapel. The best roses are those grown in your yard that you can clip and pin. Now I wear a white rose. I've noticed that not many people do this anymore. I think men feel that doing this would indicate too much effeminacy. Nay, my friend, real men do this respectful gesture. It is so easy to spend so many years in vanity and pride. As I became preoccupied with my own family, career, producing, and achieving, my parents only grew old, and one day they died.

A DEBT OF LOVE I OWE

In 1959, when I left the nest, Mama said that wherever I went, always remember there was a lit candle in the window and that I would be all right as long as I remembered that the light was still on. I knew I had to move on to start my life. I reminded them not to worry, that I would be coming home and that I would not lose my way. But I never really came home after that. I was only as a visitor for short periods. That is what I did because time is filled with swift transition.

As I drove furiously to the Oxford hospital that night where my dad had been admitted in 1981, it was like I was rushing back home to make up for all the years I had been gone. Driving down that highway, I got the feeling I should have been home yesterday, yesterday. He was still alive, but really, I was too late for so many reasons. He was diagnosed with acute lymphoblastic leukemia. He died at Baptist Central Hospital in Memphis. He would not reach the proverbial three-score and ten.

"The man" had finally drained the last ounce of life from him after using him as cheap labor all his life. He was exposed to the chemical benzene for many years on two different jobs, a carcinogen causing leukemia when it gets into one's bloodstream. Finally, the chemotherapy killed off his white blood cells, and he had no defense against infection. His body was racked with strange diseases and pain. Around 2:00 a.m., he raised himself out of bed and said he wanted to put on his clothes and go home. While I held him on the bedside, he gave up his last breath. The specter in the night had arrived, and my heart was sore. We buried him in Oak Hill Cemetery overlooking Water Valley in Yalobusha County, where he had offered his labor and goodwill all his life.

Before the funeral, local people stopped by the house to express sympathy. Several were African American individuals who had come to know my father through the years. "Mr. Price was always a nice man." What a tribute in my mind! My faith and insight into minority issues were reinforced for the years ahead.

My mother lingered on for twenty-five more years. In her last days, she lived with us, often reliving the days of despair and hopelessness as well as joys remembered. Her retirement gave her a comfortable income, which she promptly spent on grandchildren. She was so afraid something would happen to take her little pension away. She didn't like direct deposit; she wanted to see and hold the government Social Security check in her hand.

Even though her hands and fingers were gnarled from arthritis, she made beautiful quilts for my grandchildren using the pattern of "Joseph's Coat of Many Colors." She hand-stitched every small piece mostly in a room by herself, feeling that someday those children would love that quilt and think of the vastness of her love for them. She told me about her favorite quilt patterns such as "Trip Around the World," "Windmill," "Turkey Tracks," and "Geese in Flight." I heard her say one time, "You know, old quilters never die. They just go to pieces." We buried her beside my father surrounded by beautiful flowers and the colors she loved. As the old spiritual says, "I'm going there to see my mother. She said she'd meet me when I come." Drops of grief could ne'er repay the debt of love I owe.

In the words of Robert Service in *The Wage Slave*, their long, long shift was finally over. Their faces were toil-furrowed, their hands calloused and, at times, broken, bent, and scarred. The sun had set low in the west. They had earned their rest.

POSTSCRIPT:
REDEEMING THE PAST

Remember the days of long ago; think about the
generations past.
Ask your father and he will inform you. Inquire of
your elders, and they will tell you.
—Deuteronomy 32:7 (NLT)

In the background of my growing-up years were shanty shacks along
the road and in the backwoods far out of sight. Shotgun houses were
bordered by cotton fields, clotheslines, and tractor tire flowerbeds.
There lived a people with their families, not only trying to survive
from day to day but also being careful not to be perceived as crossing
forbidden behavioral and attitudinal lines, which could be fatal. They
were almost invisible to white people living nearby. When work fell
behind, they often offered their labor. The obvious was sometimes
lost or at least misplaced in the hazy mist of the busy present.

After my Damascus Road experience, gradually, I began to
examine my own previous omissions over many years. I needed to
remove the thorn or at least attempt to redeem the past in some small
way. Perhaps it was because I needed to tell someone that once, 'twas

blind, but now I see. Maybe it was because I felt somehow I could cleanse my soul of some of the wretchedness of the past. Maybe it was because I realized that their memoirs were just as worthy to be told as mine. So I went back and found several African American families of my generation or older. They were Birbon Brooks, Lillie Pearl Bland and her daughter Lizzie Earle, and Pattie Lou Johnson Armstrong of Oakland and Mac Haywood, Johnnie Roland, and Lucille Hines of Coffeeville. Once I convinced them who I was and what my purpose was, they shared many unimaginable and incredible stories of survival, living off the land, service during World War II, lynchings, other forms of injustice, how the education of their children had improved, and how God had blessed their lives.

Rural life for them was quite similar to mine: raising their food, getting water from a well or spring, milking cows, killing hogs for meat, canning fruits and vegetables, making their clothes, picking cotton, chopping wood, raising chickens, poking clothes in a washpot, walking nearly every place they went, and going to town on Saturdays. Lucille Hines told about Buddy Fly, a white man who had a truck with a big bed, and on Saturdays, he would come by, and they piled into the back. Sometimes she rode to town on a wagon sitting on a board. "We socialized, and a dime bought some bologna and crackers, our lunch."

I noticed they mentioned those who were nice to them. Mrs. Hines said her father never let his children go onto the places owned by people who were mean. She complimented Creekmore Pipkin by stating, "You could work for him and get paid." She referred to Earl Burney as a nice man because during cotton-picking time, he would take a truckload of hands to the Delta to work all day. She said, "We got paid a dollar, which may not sound like much, but it was more than we had."

Mrs. Bland's story reflected how the system of peonage (perpetual indebtedness) worked in their lives. After the crops were in, there was a little money for clothes and shoes, but she said it "seemed like we were always in the hole." They were paid $15 for five months—March till August—and after that, they had to rely on garden stuff.

Mrs. Earle's life was not much different from her mother's—poor schools and not much opportunity for a better life. She described how they helped neighbors in need and how they buried the dead themselves. Her hope was strong in those days that because of social change and progress, things would be better for her children.

Mrs. Armstrong and Mrs. Bland referred to the Herron family in Oakland who had a good number of black people working on Mr. Aubry Herron's place and called him a nice man. "He was the one who lived in the big house. When Mr. Vernon Herron got his hands burned and couldn't use them, his work hands took care of him."

Adequate jobs in the county to support their families were scarce. Most worked on large farms for the white owner. Their personal and family treatment varied from farm to farm. Mrs. Johnson related how the white people would let them come up to their house and listen to the radio with them. "They liked to listen to the Grand Ole Opry and Amos and Andy. And sometimes we heard Joe Lewis boxing. The announcers would always tell him that he was a credit to his race." Mr. Brooks said that he would go anywhere there was work. "President Roosevelt got us some opportunities to work in the WPA. Mainly, I hauled gravel, cut limbs off roads, did some roofing, and filled up gas tanks." Others had to go north for jobs. (In 2018, Birbon Brooks passed through the valley toward the setting of the sun.) Mrs. Hines husband worked thirty-four years in steel mills after serving in the military and not finding work in his hometown.

The subject of getting an education in those early days caused a much more somber tone. For most, school was three to four months in a church building or in a one-room building with one teacher, wood heat, and an outhouse. The teacher was either the most educated person available or perhaps a graduate of Rust College or Mississippi Industrial College in Holly Springs. For others, attending one of these two colleges still made little difference in finding good jobs. Mrs. Bland and Mr. Haywood stated that they hoped that their children could get a better education than what they were given. In Oakland and Coffeeville in the early days, the black schools had few supplies and a dirt basketball court.

They related the stress and strain they had to put on the local systems to achieve equal educational opportunities. Mr. Haywood said he was determined that his children would have a better chance than he did and joined the Coffeeville Bi-Racial Committee for Civil Rights.

> Two of my daughters marched down the streets of Coffeeville and picketed in an effort to get some changes. They were arrested and tried in Oxford. I was there to support them, and the judge decided they had the right to picket. When the children would march down the streets carrying signs, the parents would walk along side of them to prevent them from getting hurt or roughed up. Some white people would hire black men to resist the marchers. One of them hit me with a tire tool after I stood between him and the children he was about to hit. At night we had to watch the house to prevent it from being burned down. We constantly lived in fear simply for trying to gain equal

rights in education. We didn't know whether we'd be killed, have our houses burned down, or be assaulted. You couldn't rely on the sheriff or police to do the right thing.

Finally, a judge in Greenville ruled that the public schools had to allow black students to attend. Haywood said that the school board countered by proposing two separate schools, one for the boys and one for the girls, but that was not approved. "I never knew what that was about."

Johnnie Roland also participated in the marches for a better education for their children.

Then Mr. Roland made this gut-wrenching observation: "You know I fought for my country both overseas and right here inside the United States."

Mac Haywood reflected on the present and the fact that seemingly, many young black children don't understand what their parents went through to achieve these rights. "Some are letting drugs take them down. But when I have aches and pain, I just say, 'Lord forgive me. I am really blessed.'" Life for Mac today is quite different as he described how he drank coffee every morning with some of the very white men that discouraged him from marching.

I was interested in how their children had done since the passage of civil rights legislation in the middle 1960s and enforcement of the *Brown v. Education* decision in 1954. This is when I saw a glint in the eyes and heard words filled with pride.

Mrs. Earle shared how one son earned his BS degree from Alcorn State and from there to Ole Miss for his master's and PhD. Today he teaches at Mississippi Valley State University at Itta Bena. Her other son served in Vietnam as an aircraft mechanic and now lives in Kansas City. "They have excelled in life. The opportunity for a good education has made all the difference."

Mac Haywood's countenance completely changed, looked me straight in the eye, and spoke with confidence and grit. His eldest daughter is an RN and teaches nursing in San Antonio. Another daughter is a pharmacist in Canton, Mississippi, and owns her own pharmacy. One daughter is a policeman in Jackson. Another son took a job with the government when he was discharged from the army and works where missiles are stored. This daughter said, "Lots of our family served in the military and in World War II."

Two factors were mentioned concerning their willingness to fight for their country in foreign wars. First, they did so under the illusion that this sacrifice would be recognized by a grateful nation upon their return from the battlefields. Second, they would surely be allowed more rights under the law. Most of the time, their names were not publicly noted. Upon returning, the Jim Crow laws were even more enforced by an entrenched resistance to change.

Johnnie Roland said, "When we came back home, things were actually worse. We were treated no better until the late 1960s and 1970s." Mr. Roland still had to pay money to vote for several years after the Voting Rights Act passed. All the witnesses referred to the refusal to allow them to vote and that some of the veterans had to go North for jobs.

What was so amazing to me was how they had refused to allow bitterness to overwhelm them. Mr. Roland spoke to me from the heart: "After all those years of resentment and hate, I learned how to love. I've been a preacher now for fifty-one years. Today I have a lot of love and respect from white people. Once I thought all white people had it good. Now I know that some of them had it harder than we did." In more recent years, Mr. Roland served as a city alderman for the town of Coffeeville. (In 2016, Mr. Roland passed on to a place where there are no more battles to fight and win.)

I knew I had to ask the question, but I hated to bring it up. "Besides what you experienced after the war, were there other injustices you heard about?"

Haywood said, "I cut and hauled pulpwood to the International Paper yard. I had to move the logs by hand to get them to the truck. The folks wouldn't measure it correctly, which meant I got less pay. By giving up material things, I just kept on hauling so my children could eat. I need a hernia operation today because of what we did for our children, but I'd do it over again if I had to." (Since this interview, Mac has passed on to the Promised Land, having left a legacy of making his part of the world more humane and just.)

Others remembered the Daniels case in Water Valley in which the sheriff beat the man to death and was acquitted. A black man went on a white man's place to see this woman who was also being seen by the white owner who shot him several times, and he died. A black soldier from Camp McCain was killed, and then the killer ran over him with his car. Again, they reported that nothing ever came of the case. At church one night, the sheriff and other men came up and called out a black man who knocked three of the white men down. Supposedly, the sheriff gave a gun to one of the men and told him to shoot the N—, which he did, and the man died. And the incident when the sheriff shot a black man on the backstreet of Coffeeville. There was Eddie Tidwell, who was shot in the stomach and killed while he sat in his car, leaving a wife and four children. "I hated to hear that he was killed for nothing." What bothered them the most in telling these stories was that they knew the futility and consequences of seeking a legal recourse for these injustices.

They may not have known the concept of *white privilege*, but they knew how it was demonstrated. They told about a married white man in town back in the 1940s who had a woman up on "the hill" and had several children by her. Supposedly, the man's wife knew about it, and her only demand was that she and the other woman could never be in town at the same time. Her husband gave the children money and made sure no one hurt them. Eventually, the children moved away to St. Louis.

What gave them hope and the will to carry on was an occasional light from somewhere. In Oakland, a white man named Ben Bailey had a lot of property and was willing to sell house lots to black people so they could have a decent place to live. Some white folks didn't like it, but he didn't seem to care what they thought. There were victories in federal courts, which gave the children an educational future. Eventually, factories and businesses couldn't discriminate in hiring. They obtained the legal right to vote in public elections.

Mrs. Earle said,

> We have come a long way, and the Lord has blessed my family. I always prayed that my children would grow up and take care of themselves, go to school, learn everything they could, and make something of themselves. We worked hard to get them better opportunities than what we had. Today they have their own jobs and places to live.

During these interviews, my emotions swung back and forth as I sought to identify with their long-suffering. The moment that made this endeavor worth everything was something that Mrs. Patty

Armstrong said when I asked her if her grandmother knew my grandmother Mom Bea Price:

> Oh, now my grandmother visited Miss Bea a lot. She
> was really a nice woman. She could go over to her
> house, and Miss Bea would cook something for her.
> And you know what? My grandmother and Miss Bea
> could sit down at the same table together.

Her statement about my Mom Bea made an enduring impression. When I grow weary from fighting through the gravel in my own life and in my culture, I think about Mom Bea and Mrs. Armstrong's grandmother sitting together at the same kitchen table. This memory inspires me to engage in a Southern gallantry that seeks the ideals of its good heart.

BIBLIOGRAPHY

Chapter 1: Licking Old Man Depression

Jonathan Alter. *The Defining Moment: FDR'S Hundred Days and the Triumph of Hope.* New York: Simon and Schuster, 2007.

Arthur M. Schlesinger, Jr. *The Coming of the New Deal: 1933–1935.* Paperback ed. New York: Houghton-Mifflin, 2003.

David Burner. *Herbert Hoover: A Public Life.* Norwalk, CT: Easton Press, 1996.

Howard Droker. *Hooverville.* Seattle Public Library, 1980.

John Steinbeck. *The Grapes of Wrath.* New York: Penguin, 2006.

Tom Brokaw. *The Greatest Generation.* New York: Random House, 1998.

The Network Medical Team. "Why Is Pneumonia Called 'The Old Man's Friend?'" Retrieved April 4, 2014, from www.netdoctor. co.uk.

Perry H. Merrill. *Roosevelt's Forest Army: A History of the Civilian Conservation Corps.* 1981. Published by Perry H. Merrill Dr.

"Looking Back." *Coffeeville Courier,* May 5, 2011.

Ethel L. Beers, "Not One Child to Spare," in E. B. Treat (editor). *Golden Thoughts of Mother, Home, and Heaven: Poetic and Prose*

Literature of All Ages and All Lands. New York: N. D. Thompson and Co.

Jim Garland. "I Don't Want Your Millions, Mister." Performed by Woody Guthrie and Pete Seeger. Retrieved April 4, 2014, from www.soundclick.com.

Michelle Mercer. *Will You Take Me as I Am*. New York: Free Press, 2009.

Chapter II: Birth and War

Gary B. Nash. *The Unknown American Revolution: The Unruly Birth of Democracy*. New York: Penquin Books, 2005.

Chapter III: Every Road Has A Bend

American History Through Folksong. Narrated and performed by Keith and Rusty McNeil. Riverside, California: WEM Records, 1989.

Erskine Caldwell. *Tobacco Road*. Athens, Georgia: University of Georgia Press, 1995.

Chapter IV: Family Ties

Kathleen M. Galvin, Carma L. Bylund, Bernard J. Brommel. *Family Communication: Cohesion and Change*. New York: Pearson, 2004.

Barbara Risantz Raymond. *The Baby Thief*. New York: Union Square Press, 2008.

W. E. Debnam. *Weep No More, My Lady*. Raleigh, North Carolina: The Graphic Press, 1950.

Ernest Matthew Mickler. *Sinkin Spells, Hot Flashes, Fits and Cravins*. Berkeley: Ten Speed Press, 1988.

Barbara Welter. "The Cult of True Womanhood." *American Quarterly*, vol. 18, pp. 151–174, 1966.

Betty Friedan. *The Feminine Mystique.* New York: Norton, Inc., 1963.

Linda Lear (1997). *Rachel Carson: Witness for Nature.* New York: Henry Hoyten.

Emily Stone. *Did Jew Know?* San Francisco: Chronicle Books, 2013.

"In Memory of my Grandfather." A poem by Juanita Sikes Canada.

Chapter V: High Living

John Dollard. *Caste and Class in a Southern Town.* New York: Doubleday Anchor Books, third edition, 1957.

George M. Moreland. *Yalobusha County History.* Yalobusha County Historical Society (August), 2012.

"A Short History of Coffeeville During the Civil War." *The Coffeeville Courier.* February 23, 2012.

Eunice Harrison Weaver. *Our Piece of Earth: The Story of Coffeeville and Adjacent Communities* (1833–1918).

Don Sides. *The Essential Guide to the Battle of Coffeeville.* Ha-bo-wa-si-an Books, 2015.

Deborah Sarah David and Robert Brannon. *The Forty-Nine Percent Majority: The Male Sex Role.* Addison-Wesley, 1976.

Seale Ballenger. *Hell's Belles: A Tribute to the Spitfires, Bad Seeds, and Steel Magnolias of the New and Old South.* Berkeley: Conari Press, 1997.

Vance Packard. *The Status Seekers.* New York: Pocket Books, 1961.

Elizabeth Grauerholz. "What's So Funny: A Serious Look at Women in Comic Strips." Paper presented at Mid-South Sociological Association, Jackson, Mississippi, 1978.

Aubrey Andelin. *Man of Steel and Velvet.* Santa Barbara: Pacific Press, 1994.

William Whyte. *The Organization Man.* New York: Simon and Schuster, 1956.

David Reisman, Nathan Glazer, Reuel Denny. *The Lonely Crowd: A Study of the Changing American Character.* New Haven: Yale University Press, 1950.

William Safire. *Lend Me Your Ears: Great Speeches in History.* New York: W. W. Norton and Co., p. 876, 1997. Retrieved on January 13, 2015, from http://laborsouth.blogspot.com/2011/09/ story-of-labor-town-in-deep-south-and.html

George Orwell. *Animal Farm.* New York: Harcourt, Brace and Company, 1946.

Sharon McKern. *Redneck Mothers: Good Ol' Girls and Other Southern Belles.* Viking, 1979.

Ingram Parmley. "Stalking the Good Ole Boy." Paper presented at the Mid-South Sociological Association, Memphis, Tennessee, 1979.

Martha W. Carter. "The Nice Girl": A Look at Behavioral and Social Responses in Southern Women." A paper presented at the Mid-South Sociological Association, Memphis, Tennessee, 1979.

Maxine Atkinson, Jacquiline Boles, Margaret Cassidy. "Ladies: South by Northwest." A paper presented at the Mid-South Sociological Association, Memphis, Tennessee, 1979.

Tillman Rodabough. "Southern Funerals: A Regional Ritual." A paper presented at the Mid-South Sociological Association, Memphis, Tennessee, 1979.

Julian B. Roebuck. "The Redneck: A Sensitizing Concept." A paper presented at the Mid-South Sociological Association, Memphis, Tennessee, 1979.

"The First Air Flight." Bob Bowman, TexasEscapes.com. Retrieved on January 10, 2015, from http://texasescapes.com/ AllThingsHistorical/ThefirstAirFlightBB902.htm

Chapter VI: Growing Pains

Timothy Tyson. *The Blood of Emmett Till*. New York: Simon and Schuster, 2017.

"The Ghosts of Emmett Till." Richard Rubin. *New York Times*, July 31, 2005.

John F. Kennedy. *Profiles in Courage*. New York: Harper and Brothers, 1956.

Lewis Cantor. *Dewey and Elvis*. University of Illinois Press, 2005.

Studs Turkel. *Race: How Blacks and Whites Think and Feel About the American Obsession*. New York: The New Press, 1992.

Alferdteen Harrison. *Black Exodus: The Great Migration from the American South*. Jackson: University of Mississippi Press, 1991.

Obituary for Josh Booker. *The Coffeeville Courier*. August 23, 2011.

Chapter VII: My Damascus Road

Robert Hamburger. *Our Portion of Hell: Fayette County, Tennessee: An Oral History of the Struggle for Civil Rights*. 1973.

"The Battle Between Ike and Faubus." Written in 1957 by an anonymous white Arkansan who identified himself only as "A Patriot."

Bill Bryson. *One Summer: America, 1927*. New York: Doubleday, 2013.

Randy Sparks. *Religion in Mississippi*. Jackson, Mississippi: University Press of Mississippi, Heritage of Mississippi Series, Vol. II, 2001.

Epilogue

Cleveland Amory. *The Proper Bostonians*. New York: Dutton, 1947.

"Do Not Stand by My Grave and Weep." A poem by Mary Elizabeth Frye, 1932.

Susan Glisson. "New Heroes of Civil Rights." Southern Living, September 13, 2013.

Charles Wilson Reagan. *Baptized in Blood: The Religion of the Lost Cause (1865–1920)*, Athens: University of Georgia Press, p. 101, 1980.

W. J. Cash. *The Mind of the South*. New York: Knopf, 1941.

John Allen Chalk. *Three American Revolutions*. New York: Carlton Press, 1970.

Charles Dunagin. "Late Duncan Gray Jr's 1962 Sermons Echo." HottyToddy.com. July 19, 2016.

Robert W. Service, "The Song of the Wage Slave."

Printed in the United States
By Bookmasters